The Book Of The Abbot Of Combermere. 1289 To 1529: Translated From The Original Ms. In The Possession Of Lord Combermere, Of Combermere Abbey, Cheshire

Combermere Abbey

THE ᴌRECORD SOCIETY

FOR THE

𝔓ublication of 𝔒riginal 𝔇ocuments

RELATING TO

LANCASHIRE AND CHESHIRE.

Publications

VOLUME XXXI.

1896.

Miscellanies,

RELATING TO

Lancashire and Cheshire.

VOLUME THE SECOND.

Containing :—

1. THE BOOK OF THE ABBOT OF COMBERMERE, 1289-1529.
2. THE EXCHEQUER LAY SUBSIDY ROLL FOR LANCA-SHIRE, 1332.

PRINTED FOR

THE RECORD SOCIETY.

1896.

WYMAN AND SONS, LIMITED,
PRINTERS,
GREAT QUEEN STREET, LINCOLN'S INN FIELDS, W.C.

The Book

OF THE

Abbot of Combermere.

The Book

OF THE

Abbot of Combermere.

1289 to 1529.

Translated from the Original MS. in the possession
of Lord Combermere, of Combermere Abbey,
Cheshire.

Edited

BY

JAMES HALL,

Author of "A History of Nantwich," "Civil War in Cheshire," &c.

PRINTED FOR

The Record Society,

1896.

WYMAN AND SONS, LIMITED,

PRINTERS,

GREAT QUEEN STREET, LINCOLN'S INN FIELDS, W.C.

Introduction.

"For all the temporal lands which men devout
By testament have given to the church
Would they strip from us; being valued thus."
—*Henry V. Act i. Scene* I.

HE original MS., written for the most part in contracted Latin, and in small court-hand, is a quarto volume (8 in. by 11 in.) of twenty-seven leaves of paper, very securely stitched together in a parchment cover. On the outside wrapper which forms the *recto* cover is written in large old English letters, "*Liber ab̄bis de Cumbermere No. 15*"; and on the back of the cover a capital L; both number and letter indicating that the MS. was only one of a number of MSS., which, with this exception, have been unfortunately lost or destroyed. A 17th century copy of this MS. is preserved among the Harleian Collection in the British Museum, Vol. 1,967, pp. 136-147; but as no other copies of records relating to Combermere Abbey are to be found in that volume, or, as far as is known, in any other volume of *Cheshire MSS.*, it seems most likely that the Combermere records disappeared or perished before the 17th century.

This MS. is a transcript of original documents. It contains very full abstracts of forty-two leases and indenture deeds, and eight complete rentals relating to lands, dwellings, salt-houses, and tithes in Nantwich, belonging to the Abbot and Convent of Combermere, and covering a period of nearly one hundred years prior to the dissolu-

B

tion of the Abbey. The earliest rental, however, belongs to the end of the 14th century ; and the first two deeds to the end of the 13th century.

A memorandum on the first page states when, by whom, and by whose authority and direction the documents were transcribed, in these words :—

> "Codex iste inceptus erat p̄ me Johannem massy suppriorem Anno Dñi millesimo quigentesimo vigesimo quarto ad instanciā et mandatū Reũ)di p̄ris in xp̄o xp̄oferi Whalley abbatis ac sacre theologie bacalaurii quocū temp̄e Wiłłm₃ Maisterson ballius feodi abbatis in Wico malbanc fuit."

The transcript, thus ordered to be made, probably for use of the prior, who was usually the responsible person in a capitular body for the management of the property of an abbey, commences on page 3 of the MS. with the following heading, which fully describes the contents of the volume.

iħc maria.

> "Registerium Ōniū et singularū r̄rarū et tenemēt̄ ad monasteriū de Cambirmere p̄tinent̄ in Wico malbano Jacent̄ et p̄ Indenturas ad terminū Diuersis hominibus Dimissarū. Vna cū Rentalibus p̄ balliuos iħm de Anno in Annū fact̄ vt inferius patebit intuentibus."

Immediately below, on the same page, are three deeds dated respectively 1296, 1289, and 1453 ; and the transcriber has, as a rule, copied the same number of deeds on each succeeding page, but quite regardless of chronological sequence. This want of chronological arrangement no doubt misled Dr. Ormerod, who, quoting the British Museum copy of the MS. as his authority, made out a list of Abbots from 1443 to 1525, with some inaccuracies that have appeared uncorrected in the second edition of the *History of Cheshire;* but the table of deeds given below will bring order out of apparent confusion and rectify those mistakes.

It is to be noted, too, that between the deed dated 1296 and the series of deeds belonging to the 15th and 16th centuries, the earliest of which is dated 1443, there is a gap of no less than 147 years. No explanation of this break in the series is given; but, it is reasonable to suppose that new leases would be granted from time to time as the old ones expired during that long interim, and that the original indentures, and, perhaps, transcripts of them, would be preserved in the Abbey.

The transcribed deeds occupy sixteen pages in the original MS.; and, after two blank leaves, follow twenty-six pages of rentals. Another rental, dated 1529, is commenced two pages farther on, but is abruptly left unfinished; and, with a single entry on the opposite page, giving the price of salt on May 11th, 1528, the MS. ends.

These fragmental entries of 1528 and 1529, together with the last complete rental dated 1526, were not written by the said scribe, John Massy; but probably by his successor in the scriptorium of the Abbey: for priors and sub-priors were generally appointed for a term of years and not permanently. John Massy, the sub-prior of 1524, obtained promotion at the hands of his brethren; and, after the death of the Rev. Father Christopher Whalley, B.D., he became Abbot. He was Abbot when the great Ecclesiastical Survey was made in 1534; and he it was, who at last surrendered the Abbey into the hands of the King on July 27th, 1539.

John Massy then retired on an annual pension of £50, which was regularly paid him until the year 1563. In the following year he died, and was buried "in the north ile" of Chester Cathedral in accordance with his will, which was proved in Feb., 1564-5. (See *Wills, Cheth. Soc. Publ.,* Vol. li., pp. 56-7.)

A third, and still later, handwriting, with different ink,

is found in marginal notes that give the names of some who put forth claims for the lands when the great disruption came. The principal scribe, however, was John Massy; and his writing, though very small, is the neatest and most legible of all.

Hugh Malbank, second baron of Wich Malbank, gave in 1133 a fourth part of the town of Nantwich, certain salt-houses there, and the rectorial rights of the church to the monks of Combermere. That property, constituting in after times the Abbot's Fee in Wich Malbank, lay chiefly on the north and east sides of the church. Frequent mention in the deeds of localities and street names in Nantwich, such as the *Beast Market* (the west end of Beam Street), *Ratonrowe*[1] (now Pepper Street), *Lothburne* (a watercourse that formerly ran from the churchyard to the river Weaver), *Monk's Lane*, *Tinker's Crofts*, *Beam Street*, and *Hospital Street*, clearly indicate the limits of the main portion of the Abbot's Fee; but, besides these lands, there were outlying properties in *Church Lane, Pillory Street, Mill Street*, and *High Town*, together with salt-houses near the *Town Bridge*, and in a locality once known as *Baywardsholt*, which cannot now be identified, though it appears to have been in the neighbourhood of *Snow Hill.*

For this Fee, manorial courts were regularly held; and an incidental allusion to the Abbot's Court occurs in the lease of lands to Richard Roope in 1466, the express words being "*sicut assignatur et deliberatur.*"

In the early deeds of 1289 and 1296 no surname occurs. Surnames, it will be remembered, were not hereditary among the upper classes before the 12th century, and not until the 14th and 15th centuries among the lower classes. Thus, in the later deeds, are mentioned Margery de Audlem, Thomas le baxter, William de Blackhurst, John de

---

[1] The Rev. C. W. Bardsley (*Chronicles of Ulverston*, 1885, pp. 15-16) says *Ratonrowe* is a street name commonly found in old towns in the north of England and in Scotland. It is also found at the villages of Freiston and Bennington in Lincolnshire, and at Bury St. Edmunds.

Brodfield, Peter de Castro, Richard de Chouall [Coole], David de Crouton, John de Egerton, John de Farlegh, David le glover, Richard de Godwynslegh, John de More, Benedict le shermon, John de Smallwode [near Sandbach], John de Stapeley, and Henry de Sutton.

In the same early deeds no money rent is specified. Probably actual services, or payments in kind, would be rendered ; and it would be the duty of the bailiff to see the work done, or the produce duly delivered at one of the granges of the Abbey, of which there were several in the neighbourhood.

Another curious fact is that *Robert le Monkesmon* held property in Nantwich in 1296 (page 15). Here is a difficulty not easy of explanation. Was this Robert one of the brethren of the Abbey? Or, had he been so long a tenant under the Abbey that he was commonly known in Nantwich as the Monks' man? Contemporary with Robert le Monkesmon occurs in another record (quoted in Morris's *Chester*, p. 100, *note*) *Thomas le Plumer*, a monk of Combermere Abbey, who was engaged in doing plumbing work at Chester Castle, and in other castles in North Wales, between the years 1299 and 1303.

Most of the later deeds commence, as was customary in legal documents of ancient times, with a religious preamble. Even the heading of the MS. is prefixed by IHC MARIA : and it is interesting to note how C for *conservator*, rather than S for *salvator*, is used in the monogram ; because during the Middle Ages Christ was regarded more as the preserver than the saviour of men, while the Blessed Virgin was reverenced as our lady of salvation.[1]

---

[1] In three neighbouring churches the same monogram is found in ancient work. At Nantwich, on one of the 15th century windows a IHC and M. At Acton, on the alabaster effigy of William Mainwaring, dated 1399, is the legend IHC NAZARENE R. (The Nazarene King, Jesus the preserver of men). The same motto is at Bartomley, on the effigy of Sir Robert Fulleshurst, who died in 13 Rich. II. (1389). Nantwich and Acton churches are dedicated to St. Mary. The Abbey of Combermere had a double dedication, St. Mary and St. Michael the archangel. The latter dedication was very common among Cistercian abbeys.

The usual formula of the preambles, which, unfortunately, are curtailed in the transcribed deeds, is "*Omnibus Christi fidelibus et cetera*"; but in deed No. 15, dated 1454, the words are "*Universis sancte matris ecclesiæ filiis et cetera*. Whether *universis* has here any special significa-tion, or, whether it is simply used, like *omnibus*, in a com-prehensive sense, is not very clear. By the same deed the Abbot lets to Thomas Bradford "*unam parloriam*"—a par-lour—a word explained in Halliwell's *Dictionary* as "a common room in religious houses." Another property situated between this "*parlour*" and the church is thus described in the Rental dated 1469 (with which *cf.* Rental 1445)—

"De Roberto Sonky capellano p tribus cotag̃
pp [prope] aulā in Cimitorio nup in tenura
Willi Shermañ senioris ... ... iiij^s."

Without pressing the phraseology of the deed and rental too far, it appears as if the words "*parloriam*" and "*aulam*" convey the idea of a common-hall and residences of priests in connection with the once collegiate church of Nantwich.

Another remarkable feature of the deeds is the varying length of the leases. During the abbacy of Roger it was customary to grant leases of 101 years; the practice of his successor was for 99 years; but Christopher Whalley, the last abbot but one, granted leases for much shorter terms.

It has been said "that the monastic houses, foreseeing the dissolution which threatened them, and for which there were very ominous precedents during the 15th century in the confiscation of alien priories, and the not infrequent suppression of individual religious houses on the plea of misconduct, began to grant long leases of forty years or more."[1] Although this may have been the practice of monasteries in some parts of England, yet it is noticeable that at Combermere, in the 16th century, there was a ten-dency rather to shorten than to lengthen the terms of leases.

[1] Rogers' *Six Centuries of Work and Wages*, 1886, p. 297.

The Abbot and Convent of a Monastery, being a corporate body, and continuing with each successive generation of monks, were able to give good security to their tenants ; and the feudal custom of claiming a substantial fine or heriot on the death of each tenant, doubtless paid the Monastery well and induced the Abbot to grant long leases. The increase or decrease in the length of the terms of the leases was probably regulated not so much by the impending dissolution, as by the changing usages of the times, consequent on the general prosperity of the nation ; and, as the 15th century was more prosperous in trade, and towns were wealthier than in any previous century, other landlords besides Abbots of Monasteries granted long leases to their tenants. It will be seen that at Combermere for many years previous to the dissolution of the Monastery, no property was leased for so long a term as 101 years ; and that fact alone is sufficient to prove that the unfinished and undated deed, which John Massy transcribed last, should really precede in order of time the deed dated 1443 ; the abbot *William*, who granted to Roger Prayers land for a term of 101 years, being *William Plymouth* who occurs as abbot between the years 1411 and 1435. (See Table of Deeds *postea*.)

Not the least interesting of the deeds and rentals in the original MS. are those written in English. They contain some curious words and expressions. In the mention of street names, for example, the definite article is invariably prefixed ; a usage that still obtains in the native folk-speech of the town. This peculiarity is shown in the original Latin, by the interpolation of the French article "le" ; and hence the frequent occurrence in the transcript of "*the* Beam Street," "*the* Hospital Street," &c.[1]

Of curious orthography in place names are "*street*," "*bersalt*," "*Lyllsyll*," and "*horepull*," being respectively, the contracted and phonetic forms of

---

[1] The native folk-speech of Nantwich also places stress on *street*, and not on the descriptive name.

street, Baywardsholt, Lilleshall, and Warpoole.   Of old
English words are "*curtilage*," for court-yard or inclosure;
"*syche*" and "*cistern*," for ditch or watercourse; "*mese*"
and "*mease*," for pasture—though "*messe*" is always used
for *messuagium*, or dwelling-house.   Of old trade names
are "*sherman*" and "*fryser*," for cloth-workers; and *waller*,
for salt-maker.   Of curious Christian names are *Gryffyny*,
Hankyn, *Janyn*, and *Peryn;* and of surnames it may be
noted that *David ap Res* in 1469 left a successor in 1485
who called himself William *Preece*.

The rentals, like the deeds, are transcribed in irregular
order, and one of them is wrongly dated; but the mistake
is the more easily accounted for as it occurs in a transcript
and not in an original document.   The heading of the
rental, which I have dated *circa* 1485, reads thus in the
MS.—

> "*Rentale Abbatis de Cambirmᵉe*
> *Renouat Anno Regis Ricardi tercii quarto.*"

But, as Richard III. was slain at Bosworth Field on
August 22, 1485, in the *third* year of his reign, it is most
likely that *tertio* (and not *quarto*) was written on the
original rent-roll.   Two other errors, due to accidental mistakes of the transcriber, are pointed out in notes to the
deeds numbered 21 and 38.

Again, the rentals appear to have been revised surveys
of the lands to which they relate.   In those of 1445 and
1465 it is expressly stated that they were made new
["*renovat*" and "*factus*" are the words used] at Michael-
mas; and, in the former of them, one property is described
as once worth 8 shillings, but that then the rent was fixed
at 3s. 6d.

Only two names of bailiffs occur—Robert Fulleshurst
in 1445 and William Maisterson in 1524 and 1526—both
of whom belonged to well-known local families.   Their
duties would be to collect rents from the tenantry, to have
oversight of the property, and to render a full account to
the Abbey every year.   It would seem that the rental
dated 1485 was a copy of one of the bailiffs' accounts; but

the sum stated to have been paid to the Abbey does not agree with the correct addition of the several items. It is remarkable, and quite inexplicable, that all the total amounts when given are incorrect. (See Table II. *postea*.)

The historical value and importance of this MS. will be understood, when it is remembered that very few facts indeed have been preserved in history that give special characteristics either of the internal or external administration of Combermere Abbey, although in pre-Reformation times the Abbot and Convent must have exerted considerable influence over both spiritual and temporal concerns in south Cheshire for more than 400 years.

The MS. particularizes what property belonged to the monks in Nantwich; it records values ranging from a cottage with an annual rent of one penny to the highly-rented lands and salt-houses. It not only gives the names of the tenantry, but of other persons holding adjacent lands; and many of those names will be familiar to those who are acquainted with the history of Nantwich. It is the sole authority for the list of abbots from 1443 to within a few years of the suppression of the Abbey. It illustrates the changing customs of the Convent in regard to the terms of years for which leases were granted; and it contains other matters of local and general interest that have been briefly commented on in this introduction.

In conclusion, the members of the Record Society should know that the late Mr. Earwaker had the following translation made in April, 1889, by a competent scholar, whose name is unknown to me; and that I have carefully compared it with the original MS., which was kindly lent to me by Lord Combermere for that purpose. I have also tabulated the principal facts contained in these records; and the two tables will, I trust, be useful to all readers of this volume.

JAMES HALL.

LINDUM HOUSE, NANTWICH,
    Michaelmas, 1895.

I. TABLE OF DEEDS CHRONOLOGICALLY ARRANGED.

No. of Deed.	Date.	Abbot.	Lessee.	Description of Property.	Situation.	Term of Years.	Rent. s.	d.	Remarks.
2	1289	Adam	William Fitz Samin	Land	Beme Street	40	—	—	Lease expired in 1329.
1	1296	Adam	Randle de Copynhale	Land	—	20	—	—	Lease expired in 1316.
42	Undated	William	Prayers, Roger	Land	Beme Street	101	—	—	Unfinished deed.
6	1443	Roger	Fletcher, William	Land	Beme Street	101	3	4	
14	1451	Roger	Willeson, Richard	Land	Hospell Street	99	3	4	
13	1452–3	Roger	Goldsmyth, Nicolas	Land	High Street	101	2	0	
3	1453	Roger	Prayers, Roger	Land	Beme Street	101	2	0	
5	1453	Roger	Dua, John	Land & buildings	Beme Street	101	3	6	
8	1453	Roger	Wright, David	Land & buildings	Hospital Street	101	8	0	
9	1453	Roger	Shaynton, Thomas	Land	Hospital Street	81	3	4	
10	1453	Roger	Dua, William	Land	Beme street	101	2	6	
4	1454	Roger	Asheton, Robert	Land	Hospell strete	101	3	0	
15	1454	Roger	Bradford, Thomas	Parlour & 4 houses	Ratonrowe	40	16	4	
21	1454	Roger	Churchehous, Thomas	Land	Beme strete	99	6	8	
12	1456	Roger	Spenser, Richard	Land	High St. towards Mill St.	101	2	0	
11	1458	Roger	Creswall, Thomas	Land	Hospital Street	101	1	0	
7	1461	Roger	Leeke, Robert	Land & buildings	Hospital Street	101	5	0	
23	1462	Roger	Leeche, John	Land	Beme Street	101	2	0	
27	1464	John	Aderton, Humphrey	Land	near Lothburne	99	8	0	
20	1466	John	Roope, Richard	Land	Hospell Street	99	3	4	
32	1466	John	Leche, John	Wyche house land	Baywardsholt	99	2	0	
25	1468	John	Leeche, John	Land	Beme strete	99	4	0	
17	1468–9 March 4.	Robert	Maisterson, John, junr.	Half a wyche-house	Baywardsholt	99	6	8	
22	1470	Robert	Churchehouse, John and Nicolas	Half a wyche-house	Baywardsholt	83	6	8	Date March 25th.
26	1470	Robert	Leeche, Richard	Meadow	Monkesyard	89	7	0	Date Nov. 30.
24	1470	Robert	Leeche, John	Two gardens	Monkesyard	96	4	0	Date Dec. 4.

No.	Date		Name	Property	Place			Notes
19	1470	Robert	Adderton, Humphrey	Land	near Monks orchard	96	1 8	Date March 21.
31	1474	Robert	Moore, Randle	Land	Hospell strete	91	3 4	
16	1482	Robert	Walthall, Alice	Land	Ratonrowe	99	6 0	Nov. 1.
28	1498	John	Sadler, Robert	Land	Beme strete	81	2 0	Dec. 8.
29	1499	John	Harroare, Robert	Wyche-house land	Baywardsholt	41	46 8	
34	1512	John	Poynton, (Sir) Thomas (priest)	Land	Between Monks lane & Monks orchard	71	4 0	
18	1515	John	Maisterson, George	Wyche-house land	Baywardsholt	99	6 8	
30	1516	John	Crue, Rondle	One meadow	near Lothburne			
				One garden	near Monks lane			
				One cottage	Hospell Street			
				One garden	East side of Chancel nr Hospell Streete	63	42 4	
				Seven gardens	Between Hospell St. & Churchyard			
				One house	at Hospital St. end			
35	1519	Christopher	Harroware, William	One garden	N. of Churchyard	59	13 4	Deed in English.
36	1519	Christopher	Blyth, John (shoomaker)	Mese [pasture] & stable	Between Hospital St. & High town	61	16 4	Deed in English.
37	1519-20	Christopher	Sadler, Margaret	Tithes	In Wich Malbank / In Baddington, Allstaston [Austerson] and Hack [Green]	31 / —	45 4 / 20 0	Deed dated Feb. 11.
38	1520	Christopher	Sparke, Henry / Guddeare, John	Wychehouse of 12 leads	—	59	2 0 / 13 4	for seven years. / for remainder of the term.
33	1521-2 Jan. 16	Christopher	Wright, Roger	Wyche-house	Between R. Weaver & Baywardsholt	61 / —	13 4 / 20 0	for 5 years / for rest of term } Deed in English. / for gardens
40	1521	Christopher	Smyth, John (sherman)	Two gardens	near Monks lane		5 0	
42	1521 March 4.	Christopher	Clayton, William (gentleman)	Messuage	near Lothburne	59	3 4	
		Christopher	Ormeshaae, Richard (clerk, Vicar of Acton)	Tithes	Parish of Acton	31	60 0	Clayton during his life to retain 26s 8d.
11		Christopher	Harware, Nicholas (clerk)	Land	Between Monks lane & Monks orchard	71	5 0	The same property as in Deed No. 15.

II. TABLE OF RENTALS CHRONOLOGICALLY ARRANGED.

No. of Rental.	Date.	No. of Tenancies.	Total Amount as recorded.			Total Amount Correct addition.			Remarks.
			£	s.	d.	£	s.	d.	
1	1385	33	13	18	6	14	17	2	
2	1445	50	14	11	0	14	12	0	Including chief-rent of 10s. per ann. from Horepoole [Warpoole.]
5	1465	48	not given			12	16	1	Ditto (In English.)
4	1469	50	13	6	8	13	16	1	Ditto..
3	1479	54	not given			15	1	3	Ditto.
6	1485	46	10	1	6	11	2	9	Ditto. (In English.)
7	1487	44	13	18	7	12	8	9	Ditto. (In English.)
8	1526	47	14	10	8¼	14	11	8¼	This latter sum assumes the sixth item from the end to be twenty pence. (In English.)

The Ecclesiastical Taxation of Pope Nicholas IV. (*c.* 1291) gives the following (translated) :—

" Also Combermere Abbey has rents in Wych Mauban, per ann. £5 0^s 0^d."

The Valor Ecclesiasticus, 26 Hen. VIII. [1534] gives as " Income of the Abbey in temporals "—

" Rents and Profits in Wich Malbank, £14 14^s 5^d."

The total rents from Nantwich for the last year of the Abbey's existence, 1539, was £15 17s. 6d., Thomas Wright being then bailiff (*History of Nantwich,* p. 279).

THE BOOK

OF THE

ABBOT OF COMBERMERE.

---

15 Henry biii. [1524].

THIS MANUSCRIPT [CODEX ISTE] WAS WRITTEN BY ME, JOHN MASSY, SUB-PRIOR, IN THE YEAR OF OUR LORD ONE THOUSAND FIVE HUNDRED AND TWENTY-FOUR, AT THE INSTANCE AND BIDDING OF THE REVEREND FATHER IN CHRIST CHRISTOPHER WHALLEY, ABBOT AND BACHELOR OF DIVINITY, AT WHICH TIME WILLIAM MAISTERSON WAS BAILIFF OF THE ABBOT'S FEE IN WICH MALBANK. [NANTWICH.]

ißc maria.

A Register of all and several the lands and tenements appertaining to the Monastery of Cambirmere, situated in Wich Malbanke, and let by indentures for a term to divers persons, together with the Rentals drawn up by the Bailiffs in the same place from year to year, as will be plain to all lookers below.

[Randle de Copynhale, 1296.]

1 This is the covenant made between brother ADAM, abbot of Combirmere, and the convent of the same place on the one part and Randle de Copynhale on the other part : namely, that the aforesaid abbot and convent have delivered and let to the aforesaid Randle one place of ground for a curtilage in the vill of Wich Malbanke, that one, to wit, which Adam, son of Luke, formerly held of the same in the same, and it lies in breadth between the curtilage which William Samin then held on the one side and the curtilage which Robert le Munkesmon then held on the other side, and in length between their garden and the Beme strete. To have and to hold until the end and term of twenty years. Given at the aforesaid monastery in the year of our Lord one thousand two hundred and ninety-six.

[William Fil Samin, 1289.]

2. This is the covenant made between Brother ADAM, lord abbot of Combermere, and the convent of the same place of the one part and William Fil Samin of the other part : namely, that the said abbot and convent have delivered to the said William all that land with its appurtenances which he held before from the same in the vill of Wich Malbanke in the Bemestrete, adjoining the land which aforetime was Hugh Wimonde's and adjoining the garden which Peter de Castro held in the same vill. To hold and to have from the feast of Easter in the year of grace one thousand two hundred and eighty-nine unto a term of forty years next following.

Roger Prapers [1453].

3. To all Christ's faithful people, &c. ROGER, abbot of the monastery of Combermere, and the convent of the same place greeting. Know ye that we have delivered and let to Roger Praers one void place of land with its appurtenances situated in Wich Malbanke, in the Bemestrete, in length between the High Street and a certain meadow of ours called the Munkes orchard, and in breadth between our land late in the holding of William Daa on the one side and the land of the abbot and convent of the monastery of St. Werburgh of Chester and the land of Thomas Brayn on the one side. To have and to hold from the day of the making of these presents until the end of a hundred and one years next following. Rendering therefore annually two shillings of silver at the four terms of the year. Given in our chapter-house in the year of our Lord one thousand four hundred and fifty-three.

Robert Asheton [1454].

4. To all Christ's faithful people, &c. ROGER, abbot, &c., greeting. Know ye that we have granted to Robert

Asheton one void place of land with its appurtenances in Wich Malbanke, situated in Hospital Street (*vico Hospitali*): namely, in length between the High Street and the land sometime belonging to William Fouleshurst, and in breadth between the land of the aforesaid William de Fouleshurst and the land of William Cuttegore, lately in the holding of Adam de Wettnall. To have and to hold from the day of the making of these presents until the end of a hundred, and one years next following. Rendering therefore annually three shillings of silver at the four terms of the year. Given in our chapter-house on the Sabbath day next after the feast of the Invention of the Holy Cross [3 May] in the year of our Lord one thousand four undred and fifty-four.

John Daa [1453].

5. To all Christ's faithful people, &c. ROGER, abbot, &c., greeting. Know ye that we have granted to John Daa one void place of land with its appurtenances situated in Wich Malbanke, in the Bemestrete, and in length between the High Street and a certain meadow of ours called the Munkes orchard, and in breadth between our land late in the holding of William Flechere on the one side and our land late in the holding of Richard Walis on the other side. To have and to hold from the day of the making of these presents to the end of a term of a hundred and one years next following. Rendering therefore annually three shillings and sixpence at the four terms of the year. Given in the chapter-house of Combermere on the Tuesday next after the feast of the Annunciation of the Blessed Virgin Mary [25 March] in the year of our Lord one thousand four hundred and fifty-three.

William Flecher [1443].

6. To all Christ's faithful people, &c. ROGER, abbot, &c., greeting. Know ye that we have granted to William

C

Flecher one void place of land with its appurtenances in Wich Malbanke, situated in the Beme Street, in length between the High Street and a certain meadow of ours called the Munkes orchard, and in breadth between our land late in the holding of William Daa on the one side and our land late in the holding of John Daa on the other side. To have and to hold from the day of the making of these presents until the end of a term of a hundred and one years next following. Rendering therefore annually three shillings and fourpence of silver at the four terms of the year. Given in our chapter-house of Combermere on the Monday after the feast of St. Edward the King [18 March] in the year of our Lord one thousand four hundred and forty-three.

Robert Leeke [1461].

7. To all Christ's faithful people, &c. ROGER, abbot, &c. Know ye that we have granted and let to Robert Leeke one void place of land with buildings and all other its appurtenances situated in Wich Malbanke, in length between the High Street, called the Hospital Street (*inter alia strata vocat le Hospitle streete*), and our land late in the holding of Adam Wettnall, and in breadth between the land of Thomas Maisterson which he holds of us on the one side and the land of Thomas Creswall and the said Thomas Maisterson which they hold of us on the other side. To have and to hold from the day of the making of these presents until the end of a term of a hundred and one years next following. Rendering therefore annually five shillings of silver at the four terms of the year. Given in our chapter-house of Cumbyrmere on the feast of the Annunciation of the Blessed Mary [25 March] in the year of our Lord one thousand four hundred and sixty-one.

Dabyd Wright [1453].

8. To all Christ's faithful people, &c. ROGER, abbot, &c., greeting. Know ye that we have granted and let to David

le Wright one place of land with buildings and other its appurtenances situated in Wich Malbanke, in Hospital Street [*in vico hospitali*], in length between the high street and our land in the holding of John, son of John Wettenall, and Thomas Lee, and in breadth between our land in the holding of Thomas Wyrvyn on the one side and our land sometime in the holding of Richard Maisterson on the other side. To have and to hold from the day of the making of these presents until the end of a term of a hundred and one years next following. Rendering therefore annually eight shillings of silver at the four terms of the year. Given in our chapter-house in the year of our Lord one thousand four hundred and fifty-three on the Monday next after the feast of the Annunciation [25 March].

Thomas Shaynton [1453].

9. Know all men present and future that we, ROGER, abbot, &c., have granted and let to farm unto Thomas Scheynton and his assigns one place of land with the buildings built thereupon situated in Wich Malbanke, in the Hospital Street, between the high street at one end of the said place of land, which extends in length as far as the land formerly in the holding of Richard Alvaa, and in breadth between the land of Richard de Rope on the one side and the land now in the holding of Nicholas Hewster, for a term of years : namely, from the feast of the Purification of the Blessed Mary [2 Feb.] in the year of our Lord one thousand four hundred and fifty-three, to have and to hold until the term and end of eighty-one years next following. Rendering therefore annually three shillings and fourpence of silver at the four terms of the year. Given at Combermere aforesaid on the fourth day of April in the year of our Lord aforesaid.

William Baa [1453].

10. To all Christ's faithful people, &c. ROGER, abbot, &c. Know ye that we have granted and let to farm to

William Daa one void place of land with its appurtenances situated in Wich Malbank, in the Bemestreet,
between the high street and a certain meadow of ours
called the Munkes orchard, and in breadth between our
land late in the holding of William Flecher on the one
side and our land late in the holding of Roger Praers
on the other side. To have and to hold from the day
of the making of these presents until the end of a term
of a hundred and one years next following. Rendering therefore annually two shillings and sixpence of silver
at the four terms of the year. Given in our chapter-
house on the Thursday next after the feast of the
Annunciation of the Blessed Mary [25 March] in the
year of our Lord one thousand four hundred and fifty-
three.

Thomas Cresswall [1458].

11. To all Christ's faithful people, &c. ROGER, abbot,
&c. Know ye that we have granted and let to Thomas
Cresswell, of Wich Malbanke, one void place of land with
its appurtenances in the Wich aforesaid, lying in Hospital
Street [in vico hospitali]: namely, in length between the
high street and the land of Thomas Maisterson which he
holds of us, and in breadth between the land of the aforesaid Thomas Maisterson, which he likewise holds of us, on
the one side and the land of William Leeke which he
holds of us on the other side. To have and to hold the
aforesaid void place of land with all its appurtenances from
the day of the making of these presents until the end of a
term of a hundred and one years next following. Rendering therefore annually twelve pence of silver at the four
terms of the year. Given in our chapter-house of Cumbirmere on the Sabbath day in the feast of the Annunciation
of the Blessed Mary [25 March] in the year of our Lord
one thousand four hundred and fifty-eight.

Richard Spenser [1456].

12. To all Christ's faithful people, &c. ROGER, abbot, &c. Know ye that we have granted and let to Richard Spenser a void place of land with its appurtenances situated in Wich Malbanke, in length between the King's high street (*inter altā stratā regiā*) which leads towards the Mylne street and the land of William Geykyn, and in breadth between our land late in the holding of John Stanyhurst on the one side and the land of Robert Burwardesley on the other side. To have and to hold from the day of the making of these presents until the end of a term of a hundred and one years next following. Rendering therefore annually two shillings of silver at the four terms of the year. Given in our chapter-house of Combirmere aforesaid on the Thursday in the feast of the Annunciation of the Blessed Virgin Mary [25 March] in the thirty-fourth year of the reign of King Henry the sixth since the conquest of England [1456].

Nicholas Goldsmyth [1453].

13. To all Christ's faithful people, &c. ROGER, abbot, &c. Know ye that we have granted and let to farm unto Nicholas Goldsmyth a void place of land with its appurtenances situated in Wich Malbanke, in the Bemestreet, in length between the high street and a certain meadow of ours called the Munkes orchard, and in breadth between our land late in the holding of John Kyngesley on the one side and our land in the holding of John Shermon, friezer, on the other side. To have and to hold from the day of the making of these presents until the end of a term of a hundred and one years next following. Rendering therefore annually to us, &c., two shillings of silver at the four terms of the year. Given in our chapter-house of Cumbirmere aforesaid on the Monday next after the feast of St. Chad, Bishop [2 March], in the thirty-first year of the reign

of King Henry the sixth since the conquest of England [1453].

Richard Willeson, Draper [1452].

14. This indenture, made between ROGER, abbot, &c., of the one part and Richard Willeson, of Wybumbury, Draper, of the other part, witnesseth that the aforesaid abbot and convent have granted and let to farm unto the aforesaid Richard, &c., one place of land with all its appurtenances situated in Wich Malbanke, in the street called Hospell street, in length between the said street and the land which was lately John Aleyn's, and in breadth between Lotheburn on the east side and the land of Robert Fouleshurst on the west side. To have and to hold the whole of the aforesaid place, with all its appurtenances, &c., from the day of the making of these presents until the end of a term of ninety-nine years next following. Rendering therefore annually to us, &c., three shillings and four pence at the four terms of the year. Given in our chapter-house of Cambirmere aforesaid on the day after the Nativity of Saint John the Baptist [24 June] in the thirtieth year of the reign of King Henry the Sixth [1452].

Thomas Bradford [1454].

15. To all the sons of holy mother church, &c. ROGER, abbot, &c. Know ye that we have granted and let to farm unto Thomas Bradford, of Wich Malbanke, a parlour (*unam parloriam*) situated in that same place at the north end of a certain street called Ratonrowe, which extends from the graveyard of the church as far as to the Beast Market (*ad forum animalium*) of the same town, with the four houses attached to it and all other easements now belonging to them. To have and to hold from the day of the making of these presents until the term and end of forty years next following. Rendering therefore annually to us, &c., sixteen shillings and four pence of silver at the

four terms of the year, &c. Given at Combermere aforesaid on the feast of the Assumption of the Blessed Virgin Mary [15 August] in the year of our Lord one thousand four hundred and fifty-four.

Alice Walltball [1482].

16. This present indenture witnesseth that we, ROBERT, abbot, &c., have granted and set to farm unto Alice Walthail, of Wich Malbanke, formerly wife of Thomas Walthail, a place of land[1] situated at the end of a certain street called Ratonrow, which extends in length from the Beast Market, called the Beme street, as far as the land of John Egerton of Egerton, and in breadth between the street of the Ratonrow and our land, as it is called, now in the holding of the said John Egerton. To have and to hold, &c., from the day of the making of these presents until the end and term of ninety-nine years next following. Rendering therefore annually to us, &c., six shillings of silver. And the aforesaid Alice, her heirs and assigns, shall build on the place of land new and good houses which they shall keep up, &c. Given at our monastery aforesaid on the vigil of All Saints [1 Nov.] in the twenty-second year of the reign of King Edward the fourth since the conquest of England [1482].

John Maisterson the Younger [1468].

17. To all Christ's faithful people, &c. ROBERT, abbot, &c. Know ye that we have granted and let to farm unto John Maisterson the younger, of Wych Malbanke, one half wych-house of six leads[2] (*unam dimidiam salinam sex*

---

[1] "This is called the Frehold of Gylbert Walthall." [In the margin by a later hand.] A pedigree of this family, commencing with *Thomas Walthall* and *Alice* his wife, and showing Gilbert Walthall to be heir, is given in the *Visitation of Cheshire*, 1580, p. 236 (*Harl. Soc. Publ.*).

[2] "Note that George Maisterson doth clayme thys as hys freeholde." [In margin by later hand.]

plumborum) situated in the aforesaid Wych adjoining the high road which is called Bayartesholt, of which said wych-house the other moiety belongs to the aforesaid monastery of Cumbirmere, now in the holding of Richard Eskebrenner. To have and to hold the aforesaid half wych-house of six leads with all its appurtenances unto the aforesaid John Maisterson and his assigns from the day of the making of these presents until the end of a term of ninety-nine years next following thereafter. Rendering therefore annually to us, &c., six shillings and eight pence of silver at the four terms of the year. Given in the aforesaid monastery on the fourth day of the month of March in the year of our Lord one thousand four hundred and sixty-eight.

George Maisterson [1515].

18. To all Christ's faithful people, &c. JOHN, abbot, &c. Know ye that we have granted and let to farm unto George Maisterson and his assigns one place of land of half a wych-house of six leads situated in Wych Malbanke, adjoining the high road which is called Bayartesholt, of which said wych-house the other moiety belongs to the monastery of Cumbirmere, now in the holding of Thomas Sheynton. To have and to hold the aforesaid wych-house of six leads, and from the day of the making of these presents until the end of a term of ninety-nine years next following thereafter. Rendering therefore annually to us, &c., six shillings and eight pence of silver at the four terms of the year, and the aforesaid George and his assigns shall build a new house on the aforesaid place at their own costs. Given in the monastery aforesaid on the 27th day of the month of April in the year of our Lord one thousand five hundred and fifteen.

Humfrey Adderton (*alias* Athurton) [1470].

19. To all Christ's faithful people, &c. We brother ROBERT, abbot, &c. Know ye that we have granted and

let to farm unto Humfrey Athurton, of Wich Malbanke, a place of land,[1] built upon, and situated in the aforesaid town between our garden, then in the holding of the aforesaid Humfrey, on the east side and Lothburn, and between the garden aforesaid on the north side and Monkes-yarde. To have and to hold from the day of the making of these presents until the end of a term of ninety-six years next following thereafter. Rendering therefore annually to us, &c., twenty pence at the four terms of the year. Given in our chapter-house of Combermere aforesaid in the year of our Lord one thousand four hundred and seventy, on the day of Saint Benedict, abbot [21 March].

Richard Roope [1466].

20. To all Christ's faithful people, &c. JOHN, abbot, &c. Know ye that we have granted and let to farm unto Richard Roope all that place of land[2] of ours with its appurtenances situated in Wich Malbanke between the King's high street, called the Hospital Street, on the south side, and the land which Adam Wettenhall and Richard Dyckkes hold of us on the north side, and between the land formerly belonging to Philip Egerton, of Egerton, and the high way which leads from the Wych aforesaid towards Willaston on the east side and the land which Richard Eign lately held of John, son of John Wettenhall, on the west side, as it is assigned and deliberated [*sicut assignatur et deliberatur*] on the day of the making of these presents. To have and to hold, &c., from the day of the making of these presents until the end of a term of ninety-nine years next following. Rendering therefore annually to us, &c., three shillings and four pence of silver at the four terms of the year. Given at Comber-

---

[1] "Note that Adderton doth clayme thys for hys ffreholde." [In margin by later hand.]

[2] "Note that Laurance Roup dothe consayll y*." [In margin in later hand.]

mere aforesaid on the Sabbath day next before the feast of
the Ascension of our Lord, in the sixth year of the reign of
King Edward the Fourth since the conquest of England
[1466].

Thomas Churchehous [1454].

21. To all Christ's faithful people, &c.   ROGER, abbot,
&c.   Know ye that we have granted and let to farm unto
Thomas Chirchehouses a void place of land[1] lately in the
holding of William Smalwode, situated in the Beme Street
in the town of Wich Malbanke, in length between the
Bemestrete on the one side and the land of the aforesaid
abbot and convent on the other side, and in breadth between the land sometime belonging to John Filleson and
lately to William Praers on the east side and the land of
the aforesaid abbot and convent on the west side.

We have also granted and delivered to the aforesaid
Thomas Chirchehouses a moiety of a wych-house of six
leads with its appurtenances situated in the Wych aforesaid
in Baywardesholt, without leads : to wit, in length between
the road which leads to the wych-house, once William
Pulle's, lately in holding of Thomas Dawson, at the one
end and the road which leads to the wych-house of the
lord of Wrenbury, nearer to the aforesaid wych-house,
once William Pulle's, with all its conveniences and easements, &c.   To have and to hold, &c., until the end of a
term of ninety-nine years.   Rendering therefore annually
to us, &c., six shillings and eight pence at the four terms of
the year.   Given in the monastery aforesaid on the Monday next before the feast of the Nativity of our Lord
[25 December] in the year of our Lord one thousand [four
hundred[2]] and fifty-four.

---

[1] "This is called the frehold of Gylbert Wayethall."   [In margin in later
hand.]

[2] Omitted by mistake in the original.

John Churchhouse and Nicolas his Brother [1470].

22. To all Christ's faithful people, &c. ROBERT, abbot, &c. Know ye that we have granted and let to farm unto John Chirchehousez and Nicolas his brother one place of land lately[1] in the holding of Thomas Chirchehouses, their father, situated in the Bemestreete in the town of Wych Malbanke, in length between the Bemestreete on the one side and the land of the aforesaid abbot and convent on the other side, and in breadth between the land lately William Praers' on the east side and the land of the aforesaid abbot and convent on the west side. We have also granted and delivered to the aforesaid John and Nicolas his brother one moiety of a wych-house of six leads, with its appurtenances, situated in the place of the Wych aforesaid, called Baywardesholt : to wit, in length between the road which leads to the wych-house lately in the holding of Thomas Dawson at the one end and the road which leads to the wych-house of the lord of Wrenbury, nearer to the aforesaid wych-house, once William Pull's, with all its appurtenances. To have and to hold from the day of the making of these presents until the end of a term of eighty-three years next following. Rendering therefore annually to us, &c., six shillings and eight pence at the four terms of the year. Given in our chapter-house of Cumbermere aforesaid on the day of the Annunciation of the Blessed Mary [25 March] in the year of our Lord one thousand four hundred and seventy.

John Leeche [1462].

23. To all Christ's faithful people, &c. ROGER, &c. Know ye that we have granted and let to farm

---

[1] "This is called the frehold of [torn in the original] his wyffe." [In margin in later hand.]

John, son of David Leche, of Wych Malbanke, one void place of ground with its appurtenances situated in Wych Malbanke, in length between a certain street called the Bemestrete and a certain meadow of ours called the Monkes orchard, and in breadth between the land which Thomas Chirchehouse holds of us on the one side and the land which Nicholas Goldsmyth likewise holds of us on the other side.   To have and to hold, &c., from the day of the making of these presents until the end of a term of a hundred and one years next following.   Rendering therefore annually to us, &c., two shillings of silver at the four terms of the year.   Given at Cumbermere on the Thursday next after the feast of the purification of the Blessed Mary [2 February] in the first year of the reign of King Edward, the fourth since the conquest of England [1462].

John Leeche [1470].

24. This Indenture, &c.   We, ROBERT, abbot, &c., have granted and let to farm to John Leeche, son of David Leeche, of Wych Malbanke, two gardens situated in the aforesaid town within a certain close of ours called the Munkesyorde, the one of which is marked out by these boundaries : to wit, on the east side from our garden, then in the holding of Thomas Wright, as far as our garden opposite to it, then in the holding of Humphrey Atherton, and on the south side from Monke's lone as far as our meadow opposite to it, then in the holding of Randle Maynwaring ; but the other lies in length on the east side from our garden, then in the holding of Randle Maynwaring, as far as our meadow opposite to it, then in the holding of the aforesaid Randle, and in breath on the south side from our garden, then in the holding of the wife of Ralph Layeyter, and our meadow opposite to it, then in the holding of Richard Leeche, son of the aforesaid John Leeche.   To have and to hold, &c., from the day of the making of these presents until the end of a term of ninety-six years next following.   Rendering therefore annually

to us, &c., four shillings of silver at the four terms of the
year. Given at our monastery aforesaid in our chapter-
house, on the day of St. Benedict, about the December in
the year of our Lord one thousand four hundred and ...

John Leeche 1468.

25. To all Christ's faithful people ...
&c. Know ye that we have granted ...
John Leche, son of David Leche, one ...
its appurtenances in Wych Malbank ...
Bemestrete: to wit, between the King ...
a certain meadow of ours called the M...
in breadth between our land late ...
Nicholas Goldsmyth on the one side ...
road [careitalem viam] leading from ...
far as our said meadow on the other ...
hold, &c., from the day of the ma...
the end of a term of ninety... ...
Rendering therefore annual...
at the four terms of the year. ...
of Combermere aforesaid or ...
of the Blessed Mary ...
reign of King Edward the ...

Richard Leche, son of Joh...

26. This Indenture ...
granted and set to farm ...
Leche, of Wych Malban...
attached to a situation ...
tain close of our ...
Nicolas Maisterson ...
close aforesaid ...
our lands now ...
Nicolas Goldsmyth ...
the holding of ...
to hold, &c. ...

until the end of a term of eighty-nine years next following. Rendering therefore annually to us, &c., seven shillings
of silver at the four terms of the year, &c. Given in our
chapter-house of Cambermere aforesaid on the vigil of St.
Andrew the Apostle [30 Nov.] in the year of our Lord one
thousand four hundred and seventy.

Humfrey Aderton [1464].

27. To all Christ's faithful people, &c. JOHN, abbot,
&c. Know ye that we have granted and let to farm unto
Humfrey Aderton all that our place of land, with the buildings and all other its appurtenances, situated in Wych Malbanke, between our land, lately in the holding of Richard
Spenser on the east side and a certain cistern [*cisterna*]
called Lothburne on the west side, and between the land
that was once Edmund Wordehull's and a certain road
leading towards the Monkes lone on the south side and a
certain meadow of ours called the Monkesyordes, lately in
the holding of Randle Maynwaring, esquire, on the north
side. To have and to hold, &c., from the day of the making of these presents until the end of a term of ninety-nine
years next following. Rendering therefore annually to us,
&c., eight shillings of silver at the four terms of the year.
Given in our chapter-house the eleventh day of the month
of March in the year of our Lord one thousand four
hundred and sixty-four.

Robert Sadler [1498].

28. To all Christ's faithful people, &c. JOHN, abbot,
&c. Know ye that we have granted and let to farm unto
Robert Sadler of Wych Malbanke and to Laurence Sadler
his son one place of land with buildings situated in Wych
Malbanke aforesaid in the Bemestrete, in length between
the high street and a certain meadow of ours called the
Monkes-orchard, and in breadth between our land lately in
the holding of John Kyngesley on the one side and our land

formerly in the holding of John Sherman, lying on the other side. To have and to hold the same from the day of the making of these presents until the end of a term of eighty-one years next following. Rendering therefore annually to us for two shillings of silver at the four terms of the year. Given in our chapter-house of [Combermere] aforesaid on the Monday after the feast of the [Assumption] of the Blessed Mary [the date] in the year of our Lord one thousand four hundred and ninety-eight.

Robert Harrison 1499.

By. This indenture made between [J. R. abbot &c.] and Robert Harrison of Wych Malbank of the other part, witnesseth that the aforesaid abbot &c. have granted and let to farm unto the aforesaid Robert one place of land with buildings for one value wych-house of twelve leads free from all [therein &c. &c.], situated in the aforesaid wych in Bagvardestich in breadth between the wych-house lately in the holding of Hugh Egerton on the east side and the wych-house of Philip Egerton or Egerton on the west side. To have and to hold the same from the day of the making of these presents until the end of a term of forty-one years next following. Rendering therefore annually to us for forty-six shillings and eight pence at the four terms of the year. Given in our chapter-house in the year of our Lord one thousand four hundred and ninety-nine, and in the fifteenth year of the reign of King Henry the seventh.

Randle Crue 1516.

To all Christ's faithful people &c. [J. R. abbot] &c. Know ye that we have granted and let to farm unto Randle Crue of Wych Malbank tanner [barmaker], one meadow situated in the Wych aforesaid in length between the cistern [interven] called Lordmun and our meadow in the holding of Richard Leche and in breadth between our land in the holding of Thomas Partriche on the north side and our land in the holding of Roger Wright on the south side ; and one garden in the holding of John Rutter, situated in breadth between our land in the holding of Roger Wright on the one side and our land in the holding of John Goldsmyth on the other side, and in length between a lane called Monks lone on the one side and our land in the holding of Ranulph Leche on the other side ; and one house or cottage with buildings and the garden adjacent in the holding of George Hassall situated in the Hospell strete, in length between the said street on the one side and our land in the holding of John Ashton on the other side ; and one meadow situated at the east side of the chancel, in length between the graveyard on the one side and the land of John Leche on the other side, in breadth between the lane called monkslone on the one side and our garden formerly in the holding of Adam Wetten-hall on the other side ; and seven gardens adjacent to the aforesaid meadow in breadth on the one side, and they extend towards Hospell strete on the other side to our land in the holding of George Hassall and our land in the holding of Henry Sparke and our land in the holding of John Ashton, and in length between the graveyard and the aforesaid land of John Leche ; and one house built in the holding of Benedict Dokynton and two cottages with the granary [*horreo*] and the void place lying altogether [*insimul jacentes*], in length between the graveyard on the one side and the said street called Hospell Strete on the other side, and in breadth between the road leading from the said graveyard to Hospell Strete on the one side and the cistern called Lotheburne on the other side. And one garden situated at the end of Hospell Strete towards the east, in length between Tynker's Croftes on the one side and our land in the holding of Laurence Roope on the other side, and in breadth between the land of Philip Egerton on the one side and the land of Randle Mayn-waring on the other side. To have and to hold, &c., from the day of the making of these presents until the end of a term of sixty-three years next following. Rendering therefore annually to us, &c., forty-two shillings and four pence at the four terms of the year. Given in our chapter-house of Cambermere aforesaid on the feast of St. George the Martyr [23 April] in the year of our Lord one thousand five hundred and sixteen, and in the eighth year of the reign of King Henry the eighth.

Randle Moore [1474].

31. To all Christ's faithful people, &c. ROBERT, abbot of the monastery, &c. Know ye that we have granted and let to farm unto Randle More, of Wych Malbanke, one place of land with the buildings and garden adjacent and their appurtenances situated in the Wych aforesaid in Hospital Street [*in vico hospitali*] : to wit, in length between the High Street on the south side and the land of John Leeche, senior, which he holds of us on the north side, and in breadth between the land of Thomas Byckley, carpenter, on the east side and the land of Robert Fouleshurst, knight, late in the holding of the aforesaid Randle, on the west side. To have and to hold, &c., from the day of the making of these presents until the end of a term of ninety-one years next following. Rendering therefore annually to us, &c., three shillings and four pence of lawful silver at the four terms of the year. Given in our chapter-house on the twenty-fourth day of March in the fourteenth year of the reign of King Edward the Fourth since the conquest [1474].

John Leche [1466].

32. To all Christ's faithful people, &c. JOHN, abbot, &c. Know ye that we have granted and set to farm unto John, son of David Leeche, of Wych Malbanke, one void place of land[1] of one wych-house of six leads without leads

---

[1] " This is called the freholde of John Leche." [In margin in later hand.]

D

situated in the Wych aforesaid : to wit, in length between
the high street called Baywardesholt on the east side and
the water of Wever on the west side, and in breadth between
the land of Hugh Egerton, esquire, lately in the holding of
Thomas Barfford, on the north side and the land of the
abbot of Lylsyll [Lilleshall], late in the holding of William
Prayers, on the south side.   To have and to hold, &c.,
from the day of the making of these presents until the end
of a term of ninety-nine years next following.   Rendering
therefore annually to us, &c., two shillings of silver at the
four terms of the year.   Given in our chapter-house of
Cumbermere on the aforesaid day, being the Thursday
next after the feast of St. Michael the archangel [29 Sept.]
in the sixth year of the reign of King Edward the fourth
since the conquest of England [1466].

Roger Wright [1520].

33. This Indenture[1] made the xvi[th] day of Januarye in
the xi yeare of the reigne of King Henrye the viii[th] [1520]
betweene X̄POFER [Christopher] Abbott of the Monasterie
of Cumbremere, etc., and Roger Wright of the Wiche Malbanke draper on the other partie, witnesseth that the said
Abbott, etc., have graunted and to ferme dymysed to the
said Roger one Wyche hows of vi leades without leads
lying and sett in the Wyche forsaid bytwix the water of
Wever on the west partie and Baywardeshold on the Est
partie and a wiche hows of William Jennason on the north
partie and the wiche hows of Thomas Partriche on the
sowth partie late in the holdyng of Rondulph Leche. Also
the forsaid abbott and cōvent have graunted to the said
Roger two gardens lying in the wiche forsaid betwene the
gardens now in the holdyng of John Rutter on the Este
partie and the Commyn Syche [common ditch] on the
west partie and a medow in the holdyng of Gylbert Wal-

---

[1] The original is in English.

thall on the north partie and the Monkes lone on the south partie.   To have and to hold the forsaid Wiche hous of vi leades and gardens with theyr appurtenauncez from the feast of Pentecost next to come after the date of thiez presentez unto the ende of the terme of lxi yeares next folowyng.   Paying y'fore [therefore] yerely to the forsaid abbott and cōvent for the said wiche hous duryng the space of v years of the terme forsaid xiijs. ivd. of lawfull money of Yngland at iiij usuall feasts by evyn porcions : and after the v yearis to pay to the said abbott and co[n]vent duryng the said term xxs. and for the gardens vs. duryng the said terme, etc.   Yeven the day and yeare above saidez [*i.e.* saideth].

[Sir] Thomas Poynton, Priest [1512].

34. This indenture,[1] made between JOHN, abbot, &c., and Thomas Poynton, clerk, witnesseth that the aforesaid abbot and convent have granted and set to farm unto the aforesaid Thomas all that place of land situated in Wych Malbanke, between the land of the said Abbot in the holding of Randle Leeche on the east side and the land of Robert Fowleshurst which he holds of us on the west side, and the lane called Monkes lane on the south side and a meadow called Monkes orchard in the holding of Margaret,[2] Relict of Roger Maynwaring, on the north side. To have and to hold, &c., from the day of the making of these presents until the end of a term of seventy-one years next following. Rendering therefore annually to us, &c., four shillings of silver at the four terms of the year.   Given in our chapter-house in the fourth year of the reign of King

---

[1] "The bounds of this indent'e be wrong, y'fore looke at this sygne ● and ye shall fynd the truthe." The sign is found in the margin opposite deed No. 41, dated 1525. (See p. 40.)

[2] Roger Mainwaring, escheator of Cheshire, died 5 October, 1510. His wife's name is wrongly printed Mary in the pedigree in my *History of Nantwich*, p. 457. The name *Margaret* is correct, and occurs in a MS. pedigree book at Dorfold Hall, and in the *Harl. MSS.*, Vol. 1,535, pp. 347-8.

Henry the Eighth on the feast of St. Michael the Archangel [29 Sept. 1512].

William Harroware [Harwar, 1519].

35. This indenture[1] made betwix X̃pofer [Christopher]
abbott of Cumbremere and the cōvent of the same place on
the one partie and William Harroware [Harwar] of the
Wyche Malbanke marc̃ [merchant] on the oder partie
Witneshith that the said Abbott etc. have demysed and set
to ferme unto the said William a mease [pasture] place in
the Wiche forsaid.   Joynyng to the church yorde upon the
northe syde and the land of Hugh Egerton the which he
holdyth of us upon the est partye and our lande to the
streete upon the west syde, and the land of Adam Wettenhall now in the holdyng of William Harroware upon the
sowth partye.   To have and to hold etc. from the feast of
the nativitie of our Lord unto the ende and terme of lix
yeares next folowyng.   Gyvyng yearly y^{er}of etc. xiijs. iiijd.
of lawfull money of England at iiij tymes of the yeare.
Yeven at Cumbremere the xxiij day of Decembre the yeare
of our Lord a thowsand fyve hundert and xix.

John Blyth [1519].

36. This indenture[1] maide betwix X̃pofer abbott of
Combermere etc. and John Blythe of the Wyche Malbanke shoomaker etc. berith wittness that the said abbott
etc. have dymysed and set to ferme unto the said John a
mese[2] place in the Wyche Malbanke lying to the Kynge's
hye streete upon the west partie and the land of the forsaid
abbott and co[n]vent upon the est partie and the hye strete
called Hospell strete upon the sowthe partie and the lande
of the heris of Robert Wybu[n]burye upon the north partie.

---

[1] The original is in English.
[2] Mese is an old word for *pasture*.

Also the forsaid abbott and co[n]vent have dymysed unto
the said John a certeyn grounde with a stable therupon
standyng; joynyng to the grounde of [Sir] John Savage
Knyght and Edward ffouleshurst esquyer upon the north
partie and the land of the forsaid abbott and co[n]vent
upon the south p[ar]tie and the land of Thomas Maisterson upon the est partie and the land of the forsaid Thomas
upon the west partie. To have and to hold etc. from the
feast of the Nativitie of our Lord unto the end and terme
of lxi yeres next folowyng etc. Yeldyng yearly etc. xvjs.
iiijd. sterlyng at iiij tymes of the yere. Yeven at Combermere in our chapiture hows the xxiij day of decembre the
yere of our Lord a M¹ fyve hundert and xix. [1519].

Margarett Sadeler [1519-20].

37. This indenture, made, &c., between CHRISTOPHER,
abbot, &c., and Margaret Sadeler, of Wych Malbanke, for-
merely wife of Robert Sadeler, witnesseth that the aforesaid abbot and convent have granted and let to farm unto
the aforesaid Margaret the following tithes: to wit, the
tithes of sheaves [*decimas garbarum*] of Wych Malbanke;
also the tithes of lambs and of wool of the parish of Wych
Malbanke aforesaid; the tithes of flax and hemp [*canopis*]
from divers streets in the Wych aforesaid, called thus:
namely, the pyllery streete, Hospell streete, and Barkers
strete; further, the tithes of sheaves of Badyngton, Allstaston, and Hacke. To have and to hold the aforesaid tithes
to the aforesaid Margaret from the day of the making of
these presents until the end of a term of thirty-one years
next following. Rendering therefore annually to us, &c.
for the tithes of sheaves of Wych Malbanke, forty shillings
for the tithes of lambs and of wool of the parish of the
Wych aforesaid, three shillings and four pence; for the tithes
of flax and hemp of the aforesaid streets, two shillings;
for the tithes of Badyngton, Allstaston, and Hacke, seven
shillings of good and lawful money of England, to be

at the feast of St. John the Baptist.   Given in our monastery of Cumbirmere on the eleventh day of the month of February in the year of our Lord one thousand five hundred and nineteen [1519–20].

Henry Sparke and John Guddeare [1520].

38. This indenture, made between CHRISTOPHER, abbot, &c., and Henry Sparke and John Guddeare, witnesseth that the aforesaid abbot and convent have granted and let to farm unto the same Henry and John a wych-house of twelve leads free from toll [*liberam de tolneto*] situated in Wyci Malbanke, in length between the high road leading to the land of the abbot of Lylleshull and a wych-house of twelve leads of Richard Churchehous, which he holds of [Sir] Jo! Savage, Knight ; and in breadth between a wych-house twelve leads of Richard Walthall, which he holds of : prior of Wenlocke[1] on the one side and a void place land for six leads of the aforesaid abbot of Lylleshull the other side.   To have and to hold, &c., from the da the making of these presents unto the end of a term of : nine years next following.   Rendering therefore ann to us, &c., for the space of seven years immediately f ing two shillings of lawful money.   Then rendering same abbot and convent, &c., during the term of t maining twenty[2] [*sic*] years thirteen shillings a. pence at the feasts of Pentecost and Michael the are Given in our monastery aforesaid in the year of o one thousand five hundred and twenty.

---

[1] Hugh Malbank, the Norman baron, gave a salt-house of Nantwich, free from tolls and customs, to the then newly foun Wenlock. (*Harl. MS.* 2,115, f. 168; also in *Add. MSS. Br*. f. 94).

[2] The original runs: " Per terminum annorum reliquo.. decim solidos et quatuor denarios." Possibly it means " for remaining 52, not 20, years thirteen shillings and fourpence

RENTALS OF WYCH MALBANKE.

[1385.]

𝕿𝖍𝖊 𝕽𝖊𝖓𝖙𝖆𝖑 𝖔𝖋 𝖙𝖍𝖊 𝕱𝖊𝖊 𝖔𝖋 𝖙𝖍𝖊 𝖆𝖇𝖇𝖔𝖙 𝖔𝖋 𝕮𝖆𝖒𝖇𝖊𝖗𝖒𝖊𝖗𝖊 𝖎𝖓 𝖂𝖞𝖈𝖍 𝕸𝖆𝖑𝖇𝖆𝖓𝖐𝖊 𝖎𝖓 𝖙𝖍𝖊 𝖞𝖊𝖆𝖗 𝖔𝖋 𝖔𝖚𝖗 𝕷𝖔𝖗𝖉 𝖔𝖓𝖊 𝖙𝖍𝖔𝖚𝖘𝖆𝖓𝖉 𝖙𝖍𝖗𝖊𝖊 𝖍𝖚𝖓𝖉𝖗𝖊𝖉 𝖆𝖓𝖉 𝖊𝖎𝖌𝖍𝖙𝖞-𝖋𝖎𝖛𝖊.

Hospell Streete.

William de ffouleshurst holds three cottages with the curtilages adjacent and pays yearly ... ... ijs.

Richard de Godwynsleghe holds three cottages with the curtilages adjacent and pays yearly ... ... iijs.

Nicholas Marcer, chaplain, holds a messuage which was William Cuttegore's and pays yearly ... ... ijs.

Thomas le Maisterson holds a messuage with the curtilages adjacent and pays yearly ... ... ijs.   vd.

John Hopekynson holds a messuage with the curtilages adjacent and pays yearly ... ... ijs.

William ffouleshurst holds a messuage with the curtilages adjacent and pays yearly ... ... ijs.

John Peecocke, chaplain, holds a messuage with curtilages adjacent and pays yearly ... ... xjs.   viijd.

Thomas Redhoode holds a messuage
with two curtilages and pays
yearly   ...   . xviijs.

William de ffouleshurst holds a garden,
which once was John de Moore's,
situated in length between the
graveyard of Wych Malbanke and
the land of Matilda Collfox, and
pays yearly ...   .   vjs.

William de Prayers holds a garden,
which once was Henry Barber's,
adjoining the graveyard of the said
Wych and pays yearly   ...   .   xs.

Roger Hulleson holds a curtilage and
pays yearly ...   .   xijd.

The High Street [Alta via].

Geoffrey [*Galfridus*] Redhode holds a
messuage and four shops [*quattuor
shoppas*] with the curtilages adjacent
and pays yearly   ...   . xxvjs. viijd.

Henry Crumpe holds a messuage and
pays yearly ...   .   xld.

David le Glovere holds a messuage with
its appurtenances and pays yearly   ... xxvjs. viijd.

William de Blackhurst, the younger,
holds a messuage and pays yearly   ...   ixd.

William Saywart holds a messuage and
pays yearly ...   . xxijs.

John de ffarlegh holds a bakehouse near
Churchelane and pays yearly   ...   ... xixs.

Henry de Sutton holds a place of a
curtilage adjoining the graveyard
and pays yearly   ...   .   ijs.

Nicholas Collfox holds two messuages
and pays yearly   ...   .   xxviijs.

Roger Legh holds a place adjoining the Lotheburne and other cottages with the curtilages adjacent and pays yearly ... ... xijs.

Thomas Marcer holds a messuage with curtilages adjacent and pays yearly ... iiijs.

Richard de Chouall holds a messuage with curtilages adjacent and pays yearly ... ... iiijs.

The same Richard holds one place of land with all the orchard [*pomario*] which John Brodefield held and pays yearly ... ... xs.

David de Crouton holds a curtilage in the Bemestrete and pays yearly ... ... iijs.

John de Stapelegh holds three curtilages and pays yearly ... ... ixs.

William de Wettenhall holds a granary with curtilages and pays yearl y ... ... ijs.

Peryn French holds a curtilage and pays yearly ... ... iiijs.

John Janny holds a messuage and pays yearly ... ... ixs.

The heirs of Ralph fitz Robert hold a messuage and pay yearly ... ... xijd.

Matilda de ffouleshurst holds a house with courtyard [*aulam*] and pays yearly ... ... xiijs. iiijd.

The same Matilda holds an entire wych-house and pays yearly ... ... vjs. viijd.

Richard Spenser holds an entire wych-house and pays yearly ... ... xiiijs.

John de Smallwode holds an entire wych-house ... ... xvjs. viijd.

Sum total ... ... xiijli. xviijs. vjd.

[1445.]

The Rental of divers lands and tenements of the Abbot of Cumbermere in Wych Malbanke which were in the holding of Robert ffouleshurst; made on the Monday next before the feast of Saint Michael the archangel in the twenty-fourth year of the reign of Henry the Sixth: namely

Randle Maynwaring, junior, and his fellows, the feoffees of John Kingesley deceased, for a certain parcel of land[1] in the Bemestrete adjoining the Mykule barne-place, at the end [ex parte] of the street towards the Wallfield: paid at the four usual feasts	xviijd.	
From Nicholas Goldsmyth for a void place of land, formerly built upon, with a garden sometime in the holding of the said John Kingesley ...	ijs.	
From Benedict the Shermon for a certain meadow called the Monkes yordes lately in the holding of the said John Kyngesley: paid at the usual feasts ... ...xxiijs.	iiijd.	
From Edmund Wordehull for three cottages in the Bemestreet	iijs.	
From William Smalwode for two void places of land for two cottages with gardens in the Bemestrete	iijs.	viijd.
From Thomas Wettenhall for two void		

---

[1] "This is called the freholde of Rañ Maynwaring." [In margin in later hand.]

places of land for two cottages, with gardens, in the Bemestrete, formerly built upon, and in the holding of William Jackkeson, and he pays yearly ... ... ijs.

From John Daa for two void places of land for two cottages, with gardens, in the Bemestrete, formerly built upon, and in the holding of William Barton and Thomas le Baxster, and they used to pay yearly viijs., now let for ... ... iijs. vjd.

From William fflecher for a void place of land for one cottage, formerly built upon, and in the holding of Margery de Aldelem, with a garden, who used to pay yearly vjs., now let to the same William for ... ... iijs.

From William Daa for a void place of land for one cottage, once built upon, with a garden lately in the holding of John Stapeley ... ... ijs. vjd.

From Roger Praers for a garden in the Bemestrete ... ... ijs.

From John Maisterson for a place of land late in the holding of Richard Wright, carpenter ... ... xijd.

From the same John for a wych-house of six leads in the holding of John Mercer, waller ... ... iijs. ivd.

From William Dunne for a place of land in the Bemestrete ... ... ijs. vjd.

From Randle Maynwaring the elder for certain lands, formerly John Janny's, namely, for those lands on which the same John had his dwelling-house and he pays yearly... ... ... vs.

From the same Randle for other lands,

formerly the said John ... ...
upon, with the cottage adjacent to
the aforesaid land ... ... i.s.

From William Sherwin the elder for
three cottages near the ... in the
graveyard *prop. ... in cimitorio* ... ... i.s.

From Robert Sonky chaplain for a
garden, formerly in the holding of
William Glassey and John ...
adjoining the graveyard ... ... iij.s.

From Thomas Lee for a garden near the
church ... ... xijd.

From John Wettenhall for a croft near
the church and for a garden lately
in the holdyng of Janyn Cutteler ... ... iijs. ivd.

From Ralph Egerton for a garden adjoining the graveyard and the Lothburn, formerly in the holding of
John Tervyn ... ... ijs.

From John Daa for his house in which
he now lives ... ... viijs.

From Nicholas Dokynton for the house
in which he lives himself ... ... xxs.

From Thomas Boller for the house in
which he now lives himself ... ... xxvs.

From Cecily Plynton for the house in
which she used lately to live ... ... iijs. ivd.

From Robert Fouleshurst for a house in
the holding of William Jenkyn ... ... vs.

From Nicholas Hewster for a house at
the end of Churchelone towards
Hospel strete, lately in the holding
of his mother ... ... xvjd.

From the same Nicholas for a house

---

¹ Probably Guild Hall, afterwards the Grammar School. (See *History of Nantwich.*)

formerly in the holding of Richard Dokynton	... vjs.	
From Richard Eskbrenner for a house in the holding of John Hudd ...	... iiijs.	iiijd.
From Davyde Wright for a house in the holding of John Haller	... vjs.	
From the same David for a cottage formerly in the holding of William fysher	... viijs.	
From Richard Maisterson for two cottages in the Hospell Strete ...	... ijs.	ijd.
From Robert Alva for lands once Robert ffysher's	... iijs.	ivd.
From William Leeke for a house in the holding of Christiana Johneson ...	...	d.
From Randle Maynwaring the younger and his fellows, the feoffees of the aforesaid John Kingesley, for three cottages in the Hospell strete lately in the holding of John Kingesley and he pays yearly...	... viijs.	
From the same Randle and his fellows for two places for two cottages adjoining the house of William Leeke in the holding of Christiana Johnesone and he pays yearly	... iiijs.	
From Matilda Parker for a parcel of land lately in the holding of John Kingesley	... iijs.	
From John Wettenhall for a cottage in the holding of Richard Eygn ...	... iiijs.	
From the same John for a house now in the holding of Matilda Parker ...	... ijs.	
From the same John for a house in the holding of John Fysher and for other parcels adjoining the said house ...	... xxijs.	
From the same John for certain parcels in the holding of John Hill		xd.

From the line Ross for the lots
Hoore Pile

Sum total

_ Dekay is a word.
is an old French word.

[**1479.**]

The Rental of the Abbot of Cambermere made anew in the nineteenth year of the reign of King Edward the fourth since the conquest.

From Richard Roope for three cottages in the Bemestrete	iijs.	
From the heirs of Thomas Churchehows for a place of land with a garden adjacent in the same street	iijs.	iiijd.
From the heirs of Nicholas Goldsmyth for a place of land with a garden adjacent in the same street	ijs.	
From John Leeche the elder for a place of land with a garden adjacent in the same street	ijs.	
From the same John for a place of land formerly in the holding of Richard Wallys, with a garden adjacent in the same street	iiijs.	
From the same John for two gardens within the close called Monkes-yordes	iiijs.	
From Randulph Leeche for certain parcels with gardens adjacent formerly in the holding of John Daa in the same street	vs.	
From Randle Maynwaring for a certain place of land adjoining the Mykule barne-place at that end of the street towards Wallfield[1]	xviijd.	

---

[1] A very ancient barn stood there until the early part of the 19th century.

From the same Randle for a certain
    meadow called Monkesyordes ... ...   **xx**s.
Likewise from the heirs of Robert Saer
    for a place of land with a garden in
    the same street   ...   .   ijs.   vjd.
From William Praers for a place of land
    with a garden in the same street ...   ...   ijs.
From Dame Agnes Brooke for certain
    parcels of land, formerly in the
    holding of John Janny, in the same
    street   ...   .   viijs.   iiijd.
From Thomas Wallthall for a place of
    land in Ratonrowe in the same
    street   ...   .   vjs.
From Thomas Shaynton for a cottage
    in the holding of William Brooke
    in the same street ...   .   ijs.   vjd.
From Nicholas Maisterson for two cot-
    tages, formerly in the holding of
    John Maisterson, in the same street   ...   xijd.
From Humfrey Aderton for a place
    of land, situated between Munkes-
    yordes and Lotheburne ...   .   viijs.
From the same Humfrey for a parcel
    of land, formerly in the holding of
    Edmund Wordehull, situated near
    the graveyard   ...   .   xxd.
From Randle Maynwaring for a mill[1]   ...   iijs.   iiijd.

High Street [Alta strata].

From Thomas Massy for a tenement in
    the aforesaid street ...   .   xxd.
From Henry Stooke for a tenement near
    Churchestele formerly in the holding
    of Nicholas Dokynton   ...   .   viijs.   viijd.

---

[1] "This called the freholde of Rañ Maynwaring." [In margin in later hand.]

E 2

From Roger Bradburn for a tenement
in the same street...   ...   .   vs.

From Hugh Egerton for a tenement
near the graveyard in the same
street   ...   .   ijs.

From the heirs of John Farleghe for a
bakehouse near Churchelane   ...   ...   xixs.

From the heirs of Richard Choueall for
divers parcels of land with all the
orchard which John de Brodfield
held ...   .   xiiijs.

From Adam Wettenhall for a tenement
lately in the holding of John Hyllis
in the same street ..   ..   ixd.

From Richard Blythe for a tenement
lately in the holding of Thomas
Boller   ...   .   xvjs.

From the heirs of Richard Willson,
draper, for a tenement in which
Thomas Chestre used to dwell ...   ...   iijs.   iiijd.

The Hospell Strete.

From Adam Wettenhall for a tenement
lately in the holding of John Fysher
and for other parcels adjoining the
same tenement in the same street   ...   xxijs.

From the same Adam for a croft above
the chancel of the church [*supra
cancellam ecclesiæ*] and for a certain
garden in the holding of Robert
Alva   ...   .   vijs.

From Robert ffouleshurst, knight, for a
tenement in the holding of John
Bottell   ...   .   vs.

From William Brynere for a tenement
at the end of Churchelane towards
the Hospell Strete in the holding of
John Smyth, sherman   ...   .   vjs.

From the same William for another
house   ...   .   xvjd.

From Thomas Shaynton for a tenement
in the same street ...   .   iijs.   iiijd.

From Randle More for a tenement now
in the holding of Davyd Wright in
the same street   ...   .   iijs.   iiijd.

From the same Randle for a tenement
in the holding of David Wright in
the same street   ...   .   viijs.

From Richard Maisterson for two cot-
tages[1]   ...   .   ijs.   vd.

From Thomas Creswall for a cottage ...   ...   xijd.

From Robert Leeyke of Congulton for
a tenement ...   .   vs.

From Randle Maynwaring for three cottages lately in the holding of John
Kingesley ...   .   viijs.

From the same Randle for two other
cottages adjoining the house of
John Leeke, late in the holding of
John Kyngesley, in the same street   ...   iiijs.

From the wife of Robert Ashton for a
tenement   ...   .   iijs.

From Richard Roope for a tenement ...   ...   iijs.   iiijd.

From Richard Dykes for a garden   ...   ...   ijs.   iijd.

From John Leeche the elder for a
garden near the graveyard above
the chancel of the church [*supra
cancellam ecclesiæ*] ...   .   xijd.

The Pyllery Strete.

From John Leche the elder for a tenement...   ...   .   ijs.

---

[1] " This is called the frehold of Thomas Maisterson." [In margin in
later hand.]

From Thomas Chester, sherman, for a
    tenement   ...   .   vjs.
From Joan Leche, widow, for a cottage   ...   vjs.

From the Wych-houses [de salinis].

From John Wettenhall for a wych-house
    of xij. leads adjoining the bridge of
    Wych Malbanke   ...   .   vjs.   viijd.
From John Frodsam for an entire wych-
    house of twelve leads   ...   .   ijs.
From John Wybunbury for an entire
    wych-house of twelve leads ·   ...·   ...   xxs.
From John Churchhous for a wych-
    house of six leads ...   .   iijs.   iiijd.
From John Leche the elder for a wych-
    house of six leads ...   .   ijs.
From Richard Roope for a wych-house
    of six leads ...   .   vjs.   viijd.
From the free Rent of Horepull   ...   ...   xs.
    Concerning this rent look at the end
    of the book at this sign ✳.[1]

[1469.]

𝕿𝖍𝖊 𝕽𝖊𝖓𝖙𝖆𝖑 𝖔𝖋 𝖙𝖍𝖊 𝕬𝖇𝖇𝖔𝖙 𝖔𝖋 𝕮𝖆𝖒𝖇𝖊𝖗𝖒𝖊𝖗𝖊 𝖋𝖗𝖔𝖒 𝖑𝖆𝖓𝖉𝖘 𝖎𝖓 𝖂𝖎𝖈𝖍 𝕸𝖆𝖑𝖇𝖆𝖓𝖐𝖊, 𝖒𝖆𝖉𝖊 𝖆𝖓𝖊𝖜 𝖎𝖓 𝖙𝖍𝖊 𝖞𝖊𝖆𝖗 𝖔𝖋 𝖔𝖚𝖗 𝕷𝖔𝖗𝖉 𝖔𝖓𝖊 𝖙𝖍𝖔𝖚𝖘𝖆𝖓𝖉 𝖋𝖔𝖚𝖗 𝖍𝖚𝖓𝖉𝖗𝖊𝖉 𝖆𝖓𝖉 𝖘𝖎𝖝𝖙𝖞-𝖓𝖎𝖓𝖊.

From Richard Roope for three cottages
    in the Bemestrete   ...   .   iijs.
From Thomas Churchhows for one place
    of land with the garden adjacent ...   ...   iijs.   iiijd.

---

[1] No such mark is to be found at the end of the MS. But " *Horepull*,"
or *Warpoole*, is a manor in Poole township a few miles from Nantwich. (See
Ormerod, Vol. iii., p. 351, new edition.)

From Nicholas Goldsmyth for one void
place of land ... ... iijs.
From Edmund Wordhull for three cottages in the Bemestrete ... ... iijs.
From William Smalewode for two void
places of land for two cottages with
gardens in the Bemestrete, formerly
built upon and in the holding of
William Jackson, and he pays
yearly ... ... ijs.
From Thomas son of Henry Wettenhall
for two void places of land for two
cottages with gardens in the Bemestreet ... ... ijs.
From a certain void place of land lately
in the holding of Richard Walleys ... xijd.
From John Daa for two void places of
land with gardens in the Bemestrete ... iijs. vjd.
From the same John for another void
place of land lately William
Fysher's ... ... iijs.
From Catherine wife of William Daa for
a void place of land in the Bemestrete ... ... ijs. vjd.
From William Prayers for a void place
of land in the Bemestrete ... ... ijs.
From John Maisterson the elder for a
place of land lately in the holding
of Richard Wright ... ... xijd.
From the same John for a wych-house
of six leads now in the holding of
Thomas Parys ... ... iijs. iiijd.
From Richard Eskbrennere for a void
place of land in the Bemestrete now
in the holding of John Sworeton ... ... ijs. vjd.
From Sir John Maynwaring Knight for
certain parcels of land lately John
Janny's, namely, those upon which

the said John Janny had his own
dwelling-house in which he lived ...   ...   vs.

From the same John for other lands of
the said John Janny, lately built
upon, with a cottage adjacent to the
aforesaid messuage ...   .   iiijs.

From Robert Sonky, chaplain, for three
cottages near the hall in the graveyard [*prope aulam in cimitorio*]
lately in the holding of William
Sherman the elder ...   .,   iiijs.

From the same Robert for a garden,
lately in the holding of William
Glasby and John Colefox, adjoining
the graveyard   ...   .   iiijs.

From Thomas Lee for a garden near the
church   ...   .   xijd.

From Adam Wettenhall for a croft near
the church and for a certain garden
in the holding of Janyn Cutteler ...   ...   iijs.

From Hugh Egerton for a certain garden
near the graveyard and the Lotheburne, lately in the holding of Gruf-
fyny Tervyn   ...   .   ijs.

From John Wrixham for a tenement in
which he dwells   ...   .   viijs.

From Nicholas Dokynton for a tenement
in which he dwells himself   ...   ...   xxs.

From Thomas Boller for a tenement in
which he dwells himself   ...   .   xxvs.

From Richard Willeson, draper, for a
tenement in which Thomas Chestre
dwells   ...   .   iijs.

From Robert Fouleshurst for a tenement in the holding of William
Jeynkyn   ...   .   vs.

From Nicholas Heuster for a tenement
at the end of Churchelone towards

Hospell Strete, now in the holding of the mother of the said Nicholas ...		xvjd.
From the same Nicholas for a tenement now in the holding of Ralph Cutteler	vjs.	
From Richard Eskebrenner for a tenement in the holding of Robert Roper	iijs.	
From Davyd Wright for a tenement now in the holding of David ap Res	vjs.	
From the same David Wright for a cottage lately in the holding of William Fysher	viijs.	
From Thomas Maisterson for two cottages in the Hospell strete	ijs.	vd.
From the heirs of Robert Alva for lands lately Robert Fyssher's	iijs.	iiijd.
From William Leeke for a tenement lately in the holding of William Cawdray		jd.
From Randle Maynwaring the younger and his fellows, the feoffees of John de Kyngesley, for three cottages in the Hospell strete	viijs.	
From the same for two places of land for two cottages adjoining the house of William Leeke	xiiijs.	
From Matilda Parker for a parcel of land lately in the holding of John Kyngesley	iijs.	
From Adam Wettenhall for a cottage in the holding of Richard Eign	iiijs.	
From the same Adam for a tenement now in the holding of Matilda Parker	ijs.	
From the same Adam for certain parcels now in the holding of John Fyssher		

and for other parcels adjoining the
said tenement   ...   . **xxijs.**

From the same Adam for certain parcels
now in the holding of John Hille ...   ...   **ixd.**

From Joan Leeche for the tenement in
which she now dwells herself   ...   ...   **vijs.**

From Nicholas Tasker for a tenement
lately in the holding of William
Cooton   ...   .   **vijs.**

From Richard Spenser for a parcel of
land in the holding of Robert Bur-
wardesley   ...   .   **ijs.**

From Reginald Moñ [*sic*] for a tenement
in which he now dwells   ...   .   **xxd.**

From Richard Wybunbury for a wych-
house of six leads ...   .   **xxs.**

From Thomas Churchehous for a wych-
house of six leads ...   .   **iijs.**   **iiijd.**

From John ffrodsam for a wych-house of
twelve leads ...   .   **xxs.**

From the heirs of Robert Alva for a
void place of land for twelve leads
situated at the bridge-end near the
wych-house of Saint Mary   ...   ...   **ijs.**

From the free rent of Hoore pulle   ...   ...   **xs.**

Sum total   ...   ...   **xiijli. vjs. iiijd.**

1465.

The Rental of the Abbot of Combermere made anew on the feast of saint Michael the Archangel in the year of our Lord one thousand cccclxv,[1] 5 Edward iv.

Rondull Reede for a gardeyn ...	js.	
The heyris of Thomas Churchenous or a place of grounde with a garden	js.	iiijd.
The wiffe of John Broke	js.	
The heyris of Nicolas Goldsmythe for a place of ground with a garden ...	js.	
Margrett Sadler for a garden place ...	js.	
John Leeche the elder for a place of land with a garden	js.	
Ysabell Layceyter for a garden ...		xijd.
The above said John Leeche for ij gardens within the Monkes yordes ...	js.	
The same John for a meddow in the Monkes yordes	vjs.	iiijd.
Richard Leeche for a meddow in the Monkes yordes	vijs.	
The forsaid John Leche for a parcell of land sumtyme in the holdyng of Hugh Egerton		ixd.
The said John Leeche for a garden anends ye hygh chaunsell ende		xijd.
Roger Maynwaring		ixd.
John Wright, draper, for a garden in the Monkes yordes	iijs.	
The forsaid John Leeche for a wychehows of vj leedes	ijs.	
Rauff Leche for dyvers parcels of		

---

[1] The original heading is in Latin ; what follows is in English.

ground that sumtyme Jenkyn Daa held ... ... vs.	vs.	
The heyris of Robart Sawer for a place of land with a garden in the Beme-strete ... ... ijs.	ijs.	vjd.
The heyris of William Prayers for a place of land with a garden ... ... ijs.	ijs.	
The heyris of Dame Agnes Broke for dyvers parcells that sumtyme John Janny hilde ... ... viijs.	viijs.	iiijd.
Thomas Walthall for a place of land in Ratonrowe ... ... vjs.	vjs.	
Humfrey Aderton for a place of land betwene the monkes yordes and Lotheburne ... ... vjs.	vjs.	
The same Humfrey for a parcell of land sumtyme Edmond Wordhull hild besyde the church yord		xxd.
Hankyn Maynwaring for the hors mylne ... ... iijs.	iijs.	iiijd.
The heyris of Thomas Massy for a tene-ment in the hye town		xxd.
Roger Bradburne for a tenement by the church stele laate in the holdyng of Henry Stooke ... ... vijs.	vijs.	
The said Roger for a tenement by the churche syde ... ... vs.	vs.	
John Wybunbury for the Swan in the highe town		ixd.
Richard Blith for a tenement ... ... xvjs.	xvjs.	
John Wettenhall for a tenement laate in the holdyng of John ffysher and for other parcels in the same strete called Hospell strete ... ... xxijs.	xxijs.	
The said John Wettenhall for a tene-ment that Thomas Gyllowe holdes ... ijs.	ijs.	
The said John for a croft anends the hye chancell ... ... vijs.	vijs.	

Thomas Shaynton for a tenement	iijs.	iiijd.
Rondull More for a tenement late in the		
holdyng of Davyd Wright	iijs.	
The said Rondull for a tenement late in		
the holdyng of the said Davyd	viijs.	iiijd.
Thomas Maisterson for ij cotages	ijs.	ijd.
Thomas Willey for a cotage		xijd.
Robart Leyke of Congultone for a cot-		
age	vs.	
John Asheton for a cotage	iijs.	
The heyre of Richard Roope for a tene-		
ment	iijs.	iiijd.
Esabell Glovere for a mese place	vs.	
William Wright for a tenement late in		
the holdyng of Thomas Twysse	vjs.	
John Wettenhall for a which hous of		
xij leeds	vjs.	viijd.
Thomas Frodsam for a wych-hous of		
vj leeds	ijs.	
John Wibunburie for a wyche hous of		
xij leeds	xlvjs.	viijd.
Thomas Shaynton for a cotage...	ijs.	vjd.
Laurence ffrodsam ffor a wiche hows	vjs.	viijd.
Thomas Maisterson for a cotage		xijd.
The cheefe Rent of Hoore pull	xs.	

[*circa* 1485.[1]]

𝕿𝖍𝖊 𝕽𝖊𝖓𝖙𝖆𝖑 𝖔𝖋 𝖙𝖍𝖊 𝕬𝖇𝖇𝖔𝖙 𝖔𝖋 𝕮𝖆𝖒𝖇𝖎𝖗𝖒𝖊𝖗𝖊 𝖒𝖆𝖉𝖊 𝖆𝖓𝖊𝖜 𝖎𝖓 𝖙𝖍𝖊 𝖋𝖔𝖚𝖗𝖙𝖍 𝖞𝖊𝖆𝖗 𝖔𝖋 𝖙𝖍𝖊 𝖗𝖊𝖎𝖌𝖓 𝖔𝖋 𝕶𝖎𝖓𝖌 𝕽𝖎𝖈𝖍𝖆𝖗𝖉 𝖙𝖍𝖊 𝖙𝖍𝖎𝖗𝖉.

The heyris of Thomas Churchehous for		
a place of land with a garden	iijs.	iiijd.
The heyris of Nicolas Goldsmythe for		
a place of land with a garden	ijs.	

---

[1] See remarks on this date in the Introduction, page 8. The original
Rental is in English except the heading, which is in Latin.

John Leche the Elder for a place of land
with a garden   .   ...   ijs.

The same John for a place of ground
sumtyme in the holdyng of Richard
Walys with a garden   ...   .   iiijs.

The same John for ij gardens in the
Monkes yordes   ...   .   iiijs.

The same John for a hows in the Pyllere
streete   ...   .   ijs.

The same John for a parcell of ground
sumtyme in the holdyng of Hugh
Egerton ·   ...   .   xviijd.

The same John for a garden anends the
hye chaunsell   ...   .   xijd.

The same John for a wychehows of xij
leades   ...   .   ijs.

Rauffe Leche for dyvers parcels of
land with three gardens sumtyme
Jeynkyn Daa   ...   .   vs.

The heyris of Robart Sare for a place
of land with a garden in thc Beme-
strete   ...   .   ijs.   vjd.

The heyris of William Prece for a place
of land with a garden   ...   .   ijs.

The hcyris of Dame Agnes Brooke for
dyvers parcels of land sumtyme in
the holdyng of John Janny   ...   ...   viijs.   iiijd.

Thomas Wallthall for a place of land in
Ratonrowe ...   .   vjs.

Thomas Shaynton for a cotage in the
holdyng of Broke ...   .   ijs.   vjd.

Thomas Maisterson for ij cotages sumtyme in the holdyng of John Mais-
terson   ...   .   xijd.

Humfrey Atherton for a place of land
lying betwix · monkesyordes and
Lotheburne ...   .   vjs.

The same Humfrey for a parcell of land

yᵗ sumtyme Edmonde Wordehull held be the syde of the churche yorde		xxd.
Hankyn Maynwaring for the hors mylne ...	iijs.	iiijd.
The heyris of Thomas Massy for a tenement in the hye towne		xxd.
Roger Bradburne for a tenement by the churche stele late in the holdyng of Henry Stooke	vijs.	
The same Roger for a tenement by the churchyorde syde	vs.	
John Wybunbury for the swan¹ in the hye towne		ixd.
Richard Blythe for a tenement...	xvjs.	
The heyris of Richard Willson for a tenement	iijs.	iiijd.
Adam Wettenhall for a tenement late in the holdyng of John Fysher	xxijs.	
The same Adam for a tenement yᵗ Thomas Gyllow holdyth	ijs.	
Item the same Adam for a crofte anends yᵉ hye chauncell	vijs.	
William Brynner for a tenement in the ende of the Churche lane	vjs.	
Thomas Shaynton for a tenement	iijs.	iiijd.
Rondulph More for a tenement late in the holdyng of Davyd Wright	iijs.	
The same Rondulph for a tenement late in the holdyng of the same Davyd ...	viijs.	iiijd.
Thomas Maisterson for ij cotages	ijs.	ijd.
Thomas Wylley for a cotage		xijd.
Robert Leeke of Congulton for a cotage ...	vs.	
John Asheton for a cotage	iijs.	

¹ The Swan Inn was destroyed in the great fire at Nantwich in 1583; and at that time the owner was a John Wybunbury. (See *History of Nantwich*, p. 105.)

The heyris of Richard Roope for a tenement	iijs.	iiijd.
John Wright, sharman, for a garden	ijs.	
William Wright for a tenement	vjs.	
Thomas Twysse for a tenement	vjs.	
John Wettenhall for a wyche hows of xij leads	vjs.	viijd.
Thomas Frodsam for a wyche hows of xij leads	ijs.	
John Wybunbury for a wyche hows of xij leads	xxs.	
Nicolas Churchehows for a wiche hows of vj leads	iijs.	iiijd.
The heyris of Richard Roope for a wyche-hows of vj leads	vjs.	viijd.
The free rent of Hore pull	xs.	

Payde at my accompt ... ... xli. xviijd.

[1487.]

The Rental[1] of the Abbot of Cambirmere made anew in the second year of the reign of King Henry the Seventh since the conquest of England.

Richard Roope for iij cotages in the Bemestrete	iijs.	
The heyris of Thomas Churchehous for a place of ground with a garden	iijs.	iiijd.
The heyris of Nicolas Goldsmythe for a place of land with a garden	ijs.	
John Leeche the Elder for dyvers parcels of ground	xxiijs.	xd.

---

[1] The original Rental is in English except the heading, which is in Latin.

Raufe Leche for dyvers parcels with
    three gardens sumtyme in the hold-
    yng of Jenkyn Daa   ...   .   vs.

Thomas Wright, draaper for a garden in
    the Monkes yordes...   ...   .   iijs.

Richard Leeche for a parcell of grounde
    in the same Monkes yordes   ...   ...   vijs.

The heyris of Robart Saare for a place
    of grounde with a garden ...   .   ijs.   vjd.

William Preyers for a place of land
    with a garden   ...   .   ijs.

Dame Agnes Brooke for dyvers parcells
    of land sumtyme in the holdyng of
    John Janny ...   .   viijs.   iiijd.

Thomas Wallthoos for a place of land in
    Ratonrowe ...   .   vs.

Thomas Shaynton for a cotage in the
    holdyng of William Broke   ...   ...   ijs.   vjd.

Nicolas Maisterson for ij cotages sum-
    tyme John Maisterson   ...   .   xijd.

Humfrey Atherton for a place of lande
    lying betwene the monkes yordes
    and Lothburne   ...   .   vjs.

The said Humfrey for a parcell of land
    sumtyme in the holdyng of Ed-
    monde Wordehull ...   .   xxd.

Hankyn Maynwaring for the hors
    mylne   ...   .   iijs.   iiijd.

The Hye Strete.

Thomas Massy for a tenement in the
    holdyng of Robt. Harrore   ...   ...   xxd.

Henry Stooke for a tenement besyde the
    churchestele late in the holdyng of
    Nicolas Dokynton ...   .   vijs.

Roger Bradburne for a tenement   ...   ...   vs.

Adam Wettenhall for a tenement late in
    the holdyng of John Hill ...   .   ixd.

F

Richard Blythe for a tenement late in the holdyng of Thomas Boller	... xvjs.	
The heyris of Richard Willson, draaper, for a tenement the which Thomas Chestre dwellys in	... iijs.	ıvd.

The Hospell Strete.

Adam Wettenhall for a tenement late in the holdyng of John Fysher and other parcels in the same strete ...	... xxijs.	
The same Adam Wettenhall for a tenement yᵗ Ruddocke holdith	ijs.	
The same Adam for a crofte agaynest the chauncell ende ... '... ...	... vijs.	
Robart Fouleshurst, Knyght, for a tenement yᵗ John Bottell held	vs.	
William Brenner for a tenement in the end of the church lane	vijs.	viijd.
Thomas Shaynton for a tenement	iijs.	iiijd.
Rondulph Moore for a tenement laate of Davyd Wright	iijs.	
The same Rondulph for a tenement late of the said Davyd ... .: ...	viijs.	iiijd.
Nicolas Maisterson for ij cotages	ijs.	ijd.
Thomas Willey for a cotage ... '		xijd.
Robert Leeke of Congulton for a tenement	vs.	
The wif[e] of Robert Asheton for a tenement	iijs.	
William Wright, carpenter	vjs.	
Richard Roope for a tenement	iijs.	iiijd.
Richard Deykes for a garden	ijs.	
Thomas Chester, sherman for a tenement in the Pyllorye strete	vjs.	

Wich-houses.

John Wettenhall for a wiche hous of xij leadys at yᵉ brige end	vjs.	viijd.

John Frodsam for a wyche hous of xij

    leadys ... ...   **ijs.**

John Wybunbury for a wiche hous of xij

    leadys ... ...   **xxs.**

John Churchhous for a wiche hous of vj

    leadys ... ...   **iijs.**   **iiijd.**

Richard Roope for a wiche hous of vj.

    leedys ... ...   **vjs.**   **viijd.**

The ffree Rent of Hoore pull ... ...   **xs.**

    Sum total ... ...   **xiijli. xviijs. vijd.**

    [THE FOLLOWING RENTAL IS IN ANOTHER HAND.]

[1526.]

𝕿𝖍𝖊 𝕽𝖊𝖓𝖙𝖆𝖑 𝖔𝖋 𝖙𝖍𝖊 𝕬𝖇𝖇𝖔𝖙 𝖔𝖋 𝕮𝖔𝖒𝖇𝖊𝖗𝖒𝖆𝖗𝖊 𝖒𝖆𝖉𝖊 𝖎𝖓 𝖙𝖍𝖊 𝖗𝖛𝖎𝖎ᵗᵇ 𝖞𝖊𝖆𝖗 𝖔𝖋 𝕳𝖊𝖓𝖗𝖞 𝖙𝖍𝖊 𝖊𝖎𝖌𝖍𝖙𝖍 𝖇𝖞 𝖂𝖎𝖑𝖑𝖎𝖆𝖒 𝕸𝖆𝖎𝖘𝖙𝖊𝖗𝖘𝖔𝖓 𝖇𝖆𝖞𝖑𝖊𝖞 𝖙𝖍𝖊𝖗.[1]

Gylbert Walthow as yt aperethe by in-

    denture ... ... **xlijs.**   **iiijd.**

Idem Gylbert for a messe in Rattenrowe ... **vjs.**

Idem Gylbert for vj leds in make wᵗ

    Elsabethe Walker ... ... **iijs.**   **iiijd.**

Idem Gylbert for grounde that Rauffe

    Leche helde ... ... **xjs.**   **ixd.**

Rodger Harwar for xij leds in bersalt[2] ... **xlvjs.**   **viijd.**

Idem Rodger for a tenement that he

    dwylles in of the v heyres of

    Robert Masse [Massy] ... · ... ... **xxd.**

---

[1] This heading in the original is partly in Latin, and partly in English. What follows is in English.

[2] *Bersalt* is the bailiff's phonetic spelling of the local pronunciation of *hayardsholt*.

Gorge Maisterson for vj leds in bersalt
    in make w^t Thomas Schenton that
    he holdes of us ... ... vjs. viijd.
Laurance Rope for a xij lede at the
    brege end ... ... xiijs. iiijd.
Idem Laurance for dyvers parcels of
    gronde in the Ospell strete .. ... iijs. iiijd.
Rodger Wryght for vj leds in bersalt ... ... xxs.
Idem Rodger for ij gardenes ... ... vs.
Idem for a garden late in the holdyng
    of Thomas Partryche in the Beme-
    stret ... ... xijd.
Idem Rodger for a garden that John
    Rutter holdes ... ... ijs.
Henry Sparke and John Goder for a
    wyche howse ... ... ijs. & vs.
Thomas Harware for a tenement lat[e]
    John Blythes and a stabull in the
    ospell stret ... ... xvjs. iiijd.
Elsabethe Walker for a vj led and a
    cottage[1] ... ... iijs. iiijd.
Merget Leche for a medo ... ... vijs.
Merget Sadeler for certain gardenes ... ... vjs.
Merget Sadeler for a messe ... ... ijs.
Rodger Broke for a messe ... ... iiijs.
Idem Rodger for a garden ... ... iiijs.
Hughe Poote for a garden late John
    Scherentons ... ... xxd.
Sir Nycholas Harwar for gardenes ... ... iiijs.
Idem Sir Nycholas for the stabull ... ... ijs.
Item the horse mele [horse mill] ... ... iijs. iiijd.
The heyres of John Wedenbyre for the
    Swan ... ... ixd.

---

[1] This wych-house and cottage were granted by the King in 1541, after the dissolution of Combermere Abbey, to Richard Ince. (*Harl. MSS. Brit. Mus.*, 2,077, f. 39.)

Thomas Schanton for a mese[1] in the Bemstret	ijs.	vjd.
Idem Thomas for a messe[1] in the Hospell stret	iijs.	iiijd.
Willyam More for certain parceles of gronde	vs.	
Thomas Maisterson for ij cottages in the Ospelstret	ijs.	ijd.
Thomas Welley for a cottage		xijd.
Rauffe Stockton for a cottage	iijs.	
John Woode for a messe late Willyam Lewes	iiijs.	
Rychard Browne for a messe	vs.	
Thomas Maist'son for a Cottage in the beaymstret		xijd.
John Smyght, scharman, for a messe	iijs.	iiijd.
Rychard Arosmyght	vjs.	
Willyam Harwar for a messe at the churche stell	xiijs.	iiijd.
Idem Willyam for a garden be hende [sic] hys howse		ixd.
Henre Sparke for a messe that he dwyles in	vs.	
Elen Symkoc for a lettell medo pele [parcel?]		xx[2]
Robert Molton	iijs.	iiijd.
Rondull Manwaryng	iijs.	iiijd.
The heyres of Hught [sic] Molton nowe in the holdyng of Thomas Gybbenes ...		xxiijd.
Robert Molton		xijd.
Hughe ffolkenor [?]		vd. ob.

Sum total ... ... xiiijli. xs. viijd. ob.

---

[1] *Mese* means *pasture field;* but *messe* means *messuage*, or dwelling-house.
[2] It is not stated whether shillings or pence.

[On a further page are these entries in the second hand.]

Rentall ano bicesimo ꜧ. octabi [1529].

Rc. of Willyam Harwar ... ... xiiijs. jd.
Rc. of Henre Hassall ... ... iijs. iijd.

[On the opposite page this entry in the first hand.]

An° H. viij° xix° [1528].

Item delyvert to Laurance Jonson the
    xj day of Maye año r̃. r̃. H. viij^to
    xix^to ij baroos[1] of salt ... ... xvjd.

---

[1] *Barroos* = barrows, which were conical wicker baskets, each containing 6 pecks of salt. The price of one barrow of salt in 1674 was 16 pence (Ray's *Collection of Words*), being double the price of salt in 1528.

Index of Surnames.

ADAM, Abbot of Combermere, 15, 16.
Aderton. *See* Atherton.
Aldelem [Audlem], Margery de, 46.
Aleyn, John, 22.
Alva, Richard, 19, 57.
——, Robert, 48, 49, 52, 58.
Ap Res, Davyd, 57.
Arosmyght, Richard, 69.
Asheton, John, 32 *bis*, 61, 63.
——, Robert, 16, 17, 53, 66.
Atherton, *or* Athurton, Humfrey, 24, 25, 28, 30, 51, 60 *bis*, 62, 65.

BARBER, Henry, 43.
Barfford, Thomas, 34.
Barton, William, 46.
Baxter, Thomas le, 46.
Blackhurst, William de, 43.
Blythe, John (*shoemaker*), 36, 39, 68.
——, Richard, 52, 60, 63, 66.
Boller, Thomas, 47, 52, 56, 66.
Bottell, John, 52, 66.
Bradburne, Roger, 52, 60, 63, 65.
Bradford, Thomas, 22.
Brayn, Thomas, 16, 41, 49.
Brenner, *als.* Brynner, William, 66.
Brodfield, John de, 44, 52.
Brooke, *als.* Broke, Dame Agnes, 51, 60, 62, 65.
——, John, wife of, 59.
——, Rodger, 68.
——, Thomas, 41.
——, William, 51.
Browne, Richard, 69.
Brynere, *als.* Brynner, William, 52, 53, 63, 66.
Burwardesley, Robert, 21, 49, 58.
Byckley, Thomas (*carpenter*), 33.

CASTRO, Peter de, 16.
Cawdray, William, 57.
Chester, Abbot of, 41.
Chester, Thomas (*sherman*), 52, 54, 56, 66 *bis*.
Chouall [Coole], Richard de, 44, 52.
Christopher, Abbot. *See* Whalley, 13, 34, 36 *bis*, 37, 38, 39 *bis*, 40.
Churchehouse, *als.* Chirchehouses, John, 27, 29, 54, 67.
——, Nicolas, 27, 64.
——, Richard, 38, 58.
——, Thomas, 26, 27, 28, 49, 50, 54, 59, 61, 64.
Clayton, William, *gentleman*, 39.
Collfox, *als.* Colefox, John, 47, 56.
——, Matilda, 43.
——, Nicholas, 43.
Cooton, William, 58.
Copynhale, Randle de, 15.
Creswall, Thomas, 18, 20, 53.
Crouton, David de, 44.
Crue [Crewe], Rondle (*tanner*), 31.
Crumpe, Henry, 43.
Cuttegore, William, 17, 42.
Cutteler, Janyn, 47.
——, Ralph, 57.

DAA, Jenkyn, 60, 62, 65.
——, John, 17, 18, 46, 47, 55.
——, William, 16, 18, 19, 20, 41, 46.
——, Catherine, wife of William, 55.
Dawson, Thomas, 26, 27.
Deykes. *See* Dykes.
Dokynton, Benedict, 32.
——, Nicholas, 47, 51, 56, 65.
——, Richard, 48.

The
Exchequer
Lay Subsidy Roll

OF

Robert de Shireburn

AND

John de Radcliffe,

TAXERS AND COLLECTORS

IN THE

County of Lancaster.

A.D. 1332.

EDITED BY

J. PAUL RYLANDS, F.S.A

LONDON:

WYMAN & SONS, LIMITED.

1896

WYMAN AND SONS, LIMITED,

PRINTERS,

GREAT QUEEN STREET, LINCOLN'S INN FIELDS, W.C.

Introduction.

T HE following pages contain a transcript of the Subsidy Roll for Lancashire, made by Robert de Shireburn and John de Radcliffe, the chief Taxers and Collectors of the subsidy of a fifteenth in the County and a tenth in the Boroughs of the goods of all persons who were liable to be so taxed, granted to King Edward III. in his Parliament holden at Westminster on the morrow of the Nativity of our Lady in the 6th year of his reign, and in the year of our Lord 1332.

The money to be raised by this taxation was intended chiefly for the purpose of enabling the King to prosecute his attempt to bring Scotland under feudal subjection to England. In this attempt he was aided by Edward Balliol, who had been crowned King of Scotland at Scone on the 27th September, 1332, and had purported to subject the crown of Scotland to that of England.

The expedition, which was made by King Edward, met the Scots, when they invaded England, at Halidon near Berwick in the month of July, 1333 ; Douglas, the Regent of Scotland, was slain in the engagement which then took place, and David II., the young King of Scots, shortly afterwards fled to France. In October Balliol was received as king by a parliament held at Perth, and in the following year he ceded the whole of the south of Scotland to the English, thereby offending his supporters, and so making it necessary for him to seek safety in flight. He subsequently invaded Scotland, in company with Edward, but in the end their enterprise failed.

Cotton's *Abridgment of the Records*,[1] at page 13, gives the following account of the grant to the King of this subsidy :—

" *Anno Sexto Edwardi Tertii.*

" The Parliament holden at Westminster the morrow after the Nativity of our Lady, in the Sixth year of King E. 3.

" The Bishop of *Winchester* Chancellor of *England* declareth, That the Parliament was called touching French affairs, and the Kings expedition thither for repressing his Enemies.

" At this day were proclaimed the Articles contained in the last Parliament, 1. 2. 3.

" The parliament was adjourned until Thursday following ; at what time considering the news from the North, they doubted the *Scots* arrival : Wherefore, the *Bishops by themselves*, the *Lords by themselves*, and the *Knights by themselves*, advised the King to stay his journey into Ireland, and to send thither a new supply of men and money ; to stay within the Realm, and with an armed power to go towards the North, there to lie ready for the *Scot*.

" Towards which exploit, *They granted to the King one Disme, and one Fifteen, to be levied of the Laity, so as the King will live of his own without grieving of his subjects with outragious prizes, or such like.* Whereupon the *King revoked the new Commissions for rearing of Tallages ; and promiseth from henceforth to remise the same according to the old rate.*"

On the Patent Roll of 7 Edw. III., preserved in the Public Record Office there is a record of the exact instructions by which the taxers were to be guided in levying this tax. It is in Law or Norman French, and is here printed in extenso, with a translation.

Patent Roll.

(7 EDW. III., P. 2., M. 9.)

Ceo est la forme quele les asseours & taxours du quinesyme gᵃunte a nr̃e Seignᵣ le Roi a son plement tenuz a Westmonster lendemein de la Natiuite nr̃e Dame lan de son regne sisme p Countes Barouns Francshomes & les

---

[1] An exact Abridgment of the Records in the Tower of London: From the Reign of King Edward the Second, unto King Richard the Third, of all Parliaments holden In each King's Reign, &c. Collected By Sir Robert Cotton Knight and Baronet. Revised, &c., By William Prynne, Esquire, Late Bencher of Lincoln's Inne. London. Printed for William Leake & John Leake at the Crown in Fleetstreet between the two Temple Gates. 1679. *folio.*

cōmunaltez des toutz les Countes du roialme 't ensement du disme gᵃunte a nr̄e
dit seignʳ le Roi illoeqz en totes les Cites Burgħs & les auncienes demeignes le
Roi du mesme le Roialme de touz lour biens q̄ eux auoient le iour de seint
Michel lan sus dit deiuent garder 't mesme les quinessime & disme asoer taxer
cuiller & leuer Cest assaū q̄ les Chiefs taxours saunz delai facent venir deuant
eux de chescune Cite Burgħ & autre ville du Countee deinz Fraunchise & de hors
des plus loiaux hōmes & mieutz vanez de meisme les lieux a tiele nombre dont
les chiefs Taxours puissent suffiseaument eslire quatre ou sis de chescune ville
ou plus si mester soit a lour discrecion ꝑ les queux la dite taxacion & ces q̄ a
ceo apent afaire mieutz pʳra estre faite & acomplie. Et qᵃnt ils aūont tielx
eslieutz adonq̄s les facent iurer sur seintes Ewangeles cest asaū ceux de chescune
ville ꝑ eux q̄ ceux issi iurez loialment & pleinement enquerront queux biens
chescun de meismes les villes auoit le iour de seint Michel auant dit en meson
& de hors ou q ils fuissent saunz nul desporter sʳ greue forfaitʳe. 't touz ceux
biens ou q ils soient deuenutz depuis en cea ꝑ vente ou en autre manere loialment taxeront solonc lour veroie value sauue les choses desoutz forprises en
ceste forme 't les frount enbreuer & mettre en roule endente tut pleinement
le plus en haste q ils pʳront & liūer as chiefs taxours lune ꝑtie desoutz lour seals
't reprendre deūs eux lautre ꝑtie desoutz les sealx des chiefs Taxours. et qᵃnt
les chiefs Taxours aūont resceu en tiele maūe les endentures de ceux q̄ ſont
iuretz a taxer en Cites Burghs & autres villes meismes les chiefs Taxours lail-
ment & peniblement examinent celes endentures. et si eux entendent qil eit
ascune defaute eux tantost laddressent issi qi rien ne soit concelee ne pʳ doun
ne pʳ regard de ꝑsone mieux taxe q̄ reson demande. et voet le Roi q̄ les chiefs
Taxours aillont de hundred en hundred & de ville en ville la ou mester ſerra a
suruer & enquere q̄ les soutz Taxours en les meismes villes eient pleinement
taxe & a eux ꝑsente les biens de chescun. 't sils troessent rien concelee mein-
tenant laddressent & facent assaū al Tresorer & as Barouns de lescheqer les
nouns de ceux q̄ issint aūont trespassez & la maūe de lour mesprise. Et la
taxacion des biens de soutz Taxours des villes soit faite ꝑ les chiefs Taxours
& ꝑ autres ꝑ des hōmes q̄ eux elirent a ceo faire issi q̄ les biens de ceux soient
taxez bien & loialment en mesme la maūe q̄ des autres. Lataxacion des biens
as chiefs Taxours & de lour Clerks soit reserue as Tresorer & Barons de
lescheqer. Et les chiefs Taxours si tost come ils aūont resceu ꝑsentement
de soutz Taxours facent leuer les quinesyme 't disme al oeps le Roi saunz
delai & saunz desport faire a nuli en la forme q̄ en ioint lour est ꝑ cōmis-
sion. Et facent faire deux roules de la dite Taxacion acordantz en touz
pointz & retiegnent lun deūs eux pʳ leuer la Taxacion & lautre eient al
Escheqer a lendemeyn de la cluse de Pask ꝑchein auenir a quel iour ils
frount lour pᵢmer paie. Et fait assaū q̄ en ceste taxacion des biens de la cōalte
de tous les Counteez ſront forspris armure mounture Joeux & robes as Chiualers
& as gentys hōmes & a lour femmes & lour vessele dor & dargent 't darrein.
Et en Cites & en Burghs soient forpris une robe pʳ la hōme & vne autre pʳ la
femme & vn lit pʳ ambedeux vn anel & vn Fermail dor ou dargent & vne
Ceynte de seye qil vsent touz les iours & auxint vn hanap dargent ou de
mazre dont ils beiuent. Et les biens des Meseaux la ou ils sont goūnez ꝑ
Souerein Meseal ne soient taxez ne prisez. Et sils soient meseaux goūnez ꝑ
Mestre sein soient lours biens taxez come des autres. Et fait a remembrer

q̄ des Biens des gentz des Countees hors de Cites Burghs & demeignes le Roi qen tut ne passent la value de dys soldz ne soit rien demande ne leue. Ne des Biens des gentz de Cites Burghs ne demeignes le Roi q̄ ne passent la value de sys soldz en tut ne soit rien demande ne leue.

·TRANSLATION.

This is the form which the Assessors and Taxers of the Fifteenth granted to our Lord the King in his Parliament holden at Westminster on the morrow of the Nativity of our Lady in the sixth year of his Reign[1] by the Earls Barons Freemen and the Commons of all the Counties of the Realm also of the Tenth granted to our said Lord the King at that time in all the Cities Boroughs and ancient Demesnes of the King of the same Realm of all their goods which they had on the day of St. Michael in the year aforesaid must keep and the same Fifteenth and Tenth must assess tax collect and levy   That is to say that the chief Taxers without delay cause to come before them out of every City Borough and other Vill[2] of the County within the Franchise and without some of the most loyal and best esteemed men of the same places to such number as the chief taxers may think sufficient to elect four or six out of each Vill or more if the business require it at their discretion by whom the said Taxation and whatever belongs thereto may be best made and accomplished   And when they have elected such that then they cause them to swear upon the Holy Evangelists that is to say those of each Vill that those so to be sworn without shewing favour and under a grave penalty shall loyally and fully enquire what goods each of the same Vills had on the day of St. Michael aforesaid in the house or out of it wherever they were   And all such goods wherever they be which shall have since come until now either by sale or in any other manner they do loyally tax according to their true value except those things hereafter in this form excepted   And do them reduce into writing and fully put them into an indented roll and with all the haste they can deliver to the chief Taxers the one part thereof under their seals and retain in their own hands the other part under the seals of the chief Taxers and when the chief Taxers shall in this manner have received the indentures of those who have been sworn to tax in the Cities Boroughs and other Vills the same chief Taxers are loyally and carefully to examine the same indentures   And if they find there is in them any fault that they forthwith correct it so that nothing be concealed either by favour or respect of person but all be taxed as reason demands   And the King willeth that the chief Taxers should go from Hundred to Hundred and from Vill to Vill where their business shall be to make sure and enquire whether the sub Taxers of the same Vills have fully taxed and presented the goods of everyone and if they find anything concealed that they forthwith take notice of it and make known to the Treasurer and to the Barons of the Exchequer the names of those who have so transgressed and the nature of their offence   And let the Taxation of the goods of the sub Taxers of the Vills be made by the chief Taxers and for others by the men whom they shall choose to make it so that

---

[1] The Nativity B.V.M. 6th Edward III. was 8 September, 1332.

[2] The word *Vill* has been translated as *Vill* throughout, because it evidently has a wider meaning than is conveyed by the word *town*.

their goods be fully and loyally taxed in the same manner as those of the others
Let the taxation of the goods of the chief Taxers and of their Clerks be reserved
for the Treasurer and Barons of the Exchequer And let the chief Taxers as
soon as they have received the presentments of the sub Taxers cause the Fifteenth and Tenth to be levied to the use of the King without delay and without
any favour shewn to anyone in the form which is annexed to this Commission
and let them make two rolls of the said Taxation agreeing one with the other
in all points and let them retain one in their own hands whereby to levy the
Taxation and the other let them have in the Exchequer on the morrow of the
close of Pasch next coming on which day they will make their first payment
And be it known that in this Taxation of the goods of the Commons of all the
Counties the armour riding-horses jewels and robes of the Knights and Gen-
tlemen and of their wives and also their vessels of gold silver and brass are to
be excepted And in Cities and Boroughs one dress[1] for the man and another
for his wife and one bed for them both one ring and a chain of gold or silver
and a girdle of silk for every day use and also a silver hanap[2] or a mazer to
drink from let these be excepted And let not the goods of Lepers wherever
they are governed by a Superior Leper be taxed or valued. And if the lepers
be governed by their own master[3] let their goods be taxed as others are And
be it remembered that of the goods of the persons of the Counties outside the
Cities Boroughs and the King's Demesnes which are not in the whole of the
value of ten shillings nothing is to be demanded or levied nor of the goods of
the persons of Cities Boroughs or the King's demesnes which are not above
the value of six shillings in the whole is anything to be demanded or levied.

It appears from the above entry on the Patent Roll that
the names of all lay persons of full age (except lepers
residing in a lazar-house) who were possessed of goods in
the towns to the value of six shillings, and in the counties
to the value of ten shillings, beyond those articles specially
excepted, would appear in the rolls prepared by the taxers.
We therefore have, in effect, in the Subsidy Roll, a Direc-
tory of the Lancashire men of substance 560 years ago; and
when we consider the scope and completeness of this
record and the knowledge of the social status of the
persons named in it which may, to some extent, be gathered
from the amounts respectively paid by them upon a
valuation of their goods and chattels, we find such information as will make ample amends for the fact that
individuals only, and not either descents of families or

---

[1] The word *Robe* here clearly must mean dress.
[2] *Hanap*, a goblet.
[3] This probably means those lepers who were at large.

events in local history, form the subject matter of this important document.

It must not, however, be forgotten that in the year 1332, Lancashire was much more densely populated than a casual perusal of the Subsidy Roll might lead us to suppose, and that a very large proportion of the people were not possessed of sufficient goods to bring them within the scope of this taxation.

Some idea of the small proportion of those who were taxable in 1332 may be gathered from the document printed in *Appendix B*, which is a list of the inhabitants of Ormskirk, Scarisbrick with Hurlton, Bickerstaffe, Burscough with Marton, Westhead with Lathom, and Skelmersdale, who had promised to contribute to the stipend of the priest of the altar of our Lady at Ormskirk, in the year 1366. The original of this document, a vellum roll of three membranes measuring from two and a half to three inches in width by four feet ten inches in length, is among the Scarisbrick muniments in the possession of the Count DE CASTÉJÀ. It has been lent by the Rev. EDWARD POWELL, of Lydiate, and has been transcribed by Mr. W. F. IRVINE and Mr. W. E. GREGSON for publication in this volume.

The Ormskirk List is thirty-four years later than the Subsidy Roll. During that time the "First and Great Pestilence" of 1349 and the "Second Great Pestilence" of 1361 had carried off a very large number of the people, so large that it has been estimated nearly half the inhabitants perished in these two plagues. If, after two such terrible visitations, the inhabitants about Ormskirk were so much more numerous than those named in the Subsidy Roll, we may fairly assume that in 1332 a very small proportion of the Lancashire people were taxed, and that the large majority of them were mere tillers of the soil.

The subject of the value of money in 1332 as compared with to-day is a question too large to enter upon here; but the figures before us suggest that the difference in the value of household goods is greater than is generally supposed. In looking at the amounts recorded in the roll as having been paid, however, it must be remembered that most articles of intrinsic value were excluded from taxation, and that houses in those days contained comparatively little furniture.

Our ancestors in the fourteenth century, unlike their descendants of to-day, preferred ostentation to luxury; they loved splendour, but were content to live in what to us would be discomfort. Their garments were often rich and magnificent in material and colour, not unfrequently sumptuously embroidered and sometimes even adorned with gold and precious stones; their long golden chains, their jewels, and their beautifully ornamented weapons and armour, doubtless made a brave show; and these and their vessels of silver and gold must have represented a very large part of their personal property.

But their houses contained, besides the great hall, only a few small, dark rooms, with doors and windows which admitted draughts, only partially excluded, in some cases, by curtains. The floor was strewn with rushes or straw in place of carpets; the long table of plain boards in the great hall was laid upon trestles and was removed when the meal was finished; and benches or seats of wood and stone, with here and there a wooden stool, took the place of chairs, though occasional cushions were reserved for persons of consideration. In the whole house there were but two or three beds, the servants sleeping for the most part on the floor of the great hall. The walls of the house, to a modern eye, would seem bare and cold, for in those early days tapestry was not in general use in the houses of the gentry, and, besides the oak panelling and great screen, which were, it is true, sometimes handsomely carved, the only decorative objects would be the antlers of the deer, weapons and implements of the chase, lighted up here and there by the bright colours and gilding of escutcheons of arms.

The agricultural labourer's hut, at the date of the Subsidy Roll, in point of personal comfort, would probably be comparable only to a modern cow-house, his whole worldly possessions, as a rule, being a plain table, one or two stools or a bench, a box-bed laid with dried bracken, an ark or chest of oak, a very few indispensable household utensils of the simplest kind, the clothes he stood in, and his long sharp knife.

The curious spelling of the names of a few of the townships mentioned in the Subsidy Roll rendered their identity somewhat obscure until after some little investigation ; but all were ultimately identified, and the modern spelling has been inserted in italic type under each place name in the margin. For the purpose of comparison the names of the Lancashire townships in the Exchequer Lay Subsidy Roll of 1 Edw. III., A.D. 1327, are given in *Appendix A.* Parts of this Roll are so much faded that the greatest difficulty was experienced in making them out, and other parts are torn away, so that the names of some places are wanting.

It will be observed that the names of some important parishes, such as Eccles, Ormskirk, Rochdale, Leigh, Cartmel, and Winwick, do not appear in the Roll of the year 1332, but that the townships in such parishes are, for the most part, included in it. The absence of the names of these parishes is apparently accounted for by the fact that their churches, and also the land appertaining to them, upon which there would very probably be goods of not inconsiderable value, were the possessions of various abbeys and priories. and, therefore, such goods would not be included in a lay subsidy.

Although the chief taxers are not described as knights in the Subsidy Roll, there is little doubt that they are to be identified with two knights of considerable influence and importance in their day.

Sir Robert Shireburn, who was knighted on the 3rd March 19 Edward I. [1291], was M.P. for Lancashire in 9 Edward III. [1335], and Seneschal of Blackburnshire and Clitheroe. He married Alice, daughter and co-heiress of John Blackburn, of Wiswall, by Margaret Holland his wife,

and was the father of Sir John Shireburn, who fought at
Crecy under the banner of his kinsman, Thomas Lord
Holland. Sir John Shireburn was M.P. for Lancashire
in 1346, afterwards M.P. for the City of York, and died in
29 Edward III. [1355].[1]

Sir John Radcliffe, of Ordsall, was the youngest son of
Richard Radcliffe of the Tower, and married Joan, eldest
daughter of Sir Robert Holland. He fought at Caen,
Crecy, and Calais in 1347, being then a knight; sat as
M.P. for Lancashire in 14 Edward III. [1340]; and died
in 32 Edward III. [1358].[2]

The fifteenth, it will be seen, realised the sum of
£287 13s. 8d., and the tenth £11 3s. 8d., making together
a total sum for Lancashire of £298 17s. 4d., and the two
chief taxers paid 20s. each.

The original vellum Subsidy Roll, which is now preserved in the Public Record Office (Exchequer Lay
Subsidy $\frac{130}{6}$, 6 Edward III.), consists of nineteen membranes with writing on both sides; and, though slightly
injured in some parts, it is written in a clear hand and is
not difficult to read.

The scribe had a curious habit of sometimes writing his
final *e* with a downward flourish, so as to make it resemble
the sign ℮, which is generally read as *es*. This occurs in
such names as Kynge, Hogge, Bullinge, Martinscrofte,
Derlinge, Balrigge, Eskrige, &c., and in these and the like
cases the ordinary *e* has been used in printing the names.

He also wrote, as was common at the time, his *c* and *t*,
and his *n* and *u*, so exactly alike that in some names it is
impossible to say which is intended. For example, we
have Bonker, Barñ, Grayne, Angrum, Bondessoule, Gynes,
&c., which may be intended for Bowker, Barun, Grayve,
Boudessoule, Gyves, &c.

Again, owing to the fact that the letter *i* is not always
dotted, or rather stroked, there is occasional difficulty in

---

[1] "Stonyhurst College," by the Rev. John Gerard, S.J., 1894.
[2] Information of Mr. R. D. Radcliffe, M.A., F.S.A.

deciding whether, when accompanied by the letter *n*, it should be read *in* or *ni*, and a similar difficulty is experienced where the letters *i* and *m*, or *m* and *n*, come together, especially as the scribe used five strokes instead of six for such a name as Emma, which he wrote Emna.

It will be observed that the sign ꞌ) is used irregularly ; Roger is written both as Roğ) and Roğ ; frequently, also, the letter ğ is so flourished that it might pass for g), as in the township of Melling, which could not be intended to read Mellinger.

The reason for using the marks of abbreviation in many cases is not clear, but they have been scrupulously followed throughout the Roll, with the intention of reproducing the original as nearly as it is possible to do so in type, and brackets have in all cases been used where editorial additions are made.

In the Index of Places the modern spelling has been followed, a course which could not be adopted in the Index of Names owing to uncertainty as to the exact modern equivalent of some of the names in the Roll.

After correction, the printed sheets have, in every instance, been finally compared with the original Roll by Miss EMMA M. WALFORD, who also made the transcript, and to whom the Editor is indebted for the careful and accurate manner in which she has done her portion of the work. He also desires to record his indebtedness to Mr. SALISBURY, of the Public Record Office, for valuable assistance whenever difficulties occurred.

Heather Lea, Claughton, Cheshire.
    1st Feb., 1896.

Contents.

Exchequer Lay Subsidy Roll,
Lancashire,
A.D. 1332.

Lancastr̃.

Rotulus indentatus Roƀti de Shirburñ ⁊ Johis de
Radecliue. tax̃ ⁊ Collc̃oȝ. xv^e. ⁊ x^e. đno Regi a
laicis concess in Com̃. Lanc̃. tam de burgis. qᵃm
de aliis villis. in Eodm Com̃. de anno. r̄r̄. Edward.
Ƿcii. a conquestu sexto.

Wapeñ de Derbishire.

[HUNDRED OF WEST DERBY.]

Wygan
[*Wigan*]

Burg̃ tax ad	...	...	...	[illegible]
D J.	..	...	...	
„ Ric̃ ff	...	...		
„ Roᵍo de	...	...	v. ᵴ.	
„ Almerico de	...	...	v. ᵴ.	
„ Jońne fił Hugõis . . . . ałł	...	vj. ᵴ.		
„ Roƀto del Hey . . .	...	...	iiij. ᵴ.	
„ Wilłmo Botteler	...	...	ij. ᵴ. viij. đ.	

B

Ð Joħne fit Hugõis ... ... iiij. ß.
„ Riĉo le Lister ... ... iiij. ß.
„ Henr̃ de ffulshaghe ... ... iiij. ß.
„ Simone Payn ... ... iij. s. iiij. đ.
„ Wilťo le Lyster... ... ... iij. s. iiij. đ.
„ Wilťmo fit Walťi ... ... xvj. đ.
„ Wilťmo de Chastreshire ... v. ß.

Smᵃ. lx. s. pᵬ.

[Lyuer]pull
[*Liverpool*]
[Ð] . . . . Cholh[ale] ... ... v. ß.
„ Edwardo le Marchaunt ... xviij. đ.
„ . . . . . fit Simoñ ... ... iijß. xj. đ.
„ . . . . . le Yate ... ... iij. ß.
„ [Wil]lo fit Riĉi ... ... iij. ß.
„ Hugõe de Cholhale ... ... v. ß.
„ Wilťo de Aynesdale ... ... iiij. ß.
„ Wilťo de Grenolf ... ... iij. ß.
„ Joħne le Lyster ... ... xij. đ.
„ Riĉo fit Wilťi ... ... xij. đ.
„ Joħne Whitside ... ... xij. đ.
„ Matho fit Riĉi ... ... xij. đ.
„ Riĉo Tewe ... ... xij. đ.
„ Joħe de la More ... ... ij. ß.
„ Riĉo de Waltoñ ... ... ij. ß.
„ Adam Cťico ... ... xij. đ.
„ Adam fit Wilťi ... ... v. s. j. đ.
„ Adam Baroun ... ... xij. đ.
„ Wilťmo ffox ... ... xviij. đ.

Smᵃ. xlvij. ß. pᵬ.

Crosseby Magna
[*Great Crosby*]
Ð Riĉo ffillesone ... ... iiij. ß.
„ Roƀto le White ... ... ij. ß.

Ð Alañ fił Roği	...	...	...	iij. s.
„ Wilło fił Roği	...	...	...	iiij. s.
„ Joħe Saumoñ	...	...	...	iij. s.
„ Roǧ fił Ade	...	...	...	iij. s.

Smᵃ. xx. s. pɓ.

Knouselegh
[Knowsley]

Ð Rico de Rome	...	...	...	iij. s. iiij. đ.
„ Roɓto de Wirhale	...	...	ij. s.
„ Adam le Sire	...	...	iij. s.
„ Wilło de Wyndhulł	...	...	xvj. đ.
„ Rico ffabro	...	...	xvj. đ.
„ Adam de Moselegħ	...	...	xvj. đ.
,, Joħne del Ryddegate	...	...	iij. s.
„ Rico de Moseleghe	...	...	ij. s. viij. đ.
„ Rico de Stokelegħ	...	...	ij. s. viij. đ.
„ Rico fił Pymne	...	...	ij. s.
„ Rico de Snellestoñ	...	...	iiij. s. viij. đ.
„ Joħe de Stokkelegħ	...	...	iij. s.
„ Joħe ffox	...	...	ij. s.
„ Rico le Riche	...	...	iiij. s. iiij. đ.
,, Roɓto Pye	...	...	...	iiij. s. iiij. đ.

Smᵃ. xl. s. pɓ.

Haghe
[Haigh]

Ð Henr̃ de Sotheworth	...	...	ij. s. iiij. đ.
„ Wilło de Grimesford	...	...	xij. đ.
„ Gilɓto fił Ric̃i	...	...	xvj. đ.
„ Henr̃ de Haselhurst	...	...	xvj. đ.
„ Adam le Walker	...	...	ij. s.

Smᵃ. viij. s. pɓ.

Hyndeley
[Hindley]

Ð Gilɓto de Kulchith	...	...	iij. s.
„ Huǧ le Jeu	...	...	...	iiij. s.

Ð Wilƚo de Harpersone ...   ... iiij. ઠ.
„ Adam de Kulchith ... ... ij. ઠ.
„ Hugõe de Thurskar ... ... xij. đ.
„ Riĉo fiƚ Joħis ... ... xvij. đ. qᵃ.

Smᵃ. xv. ઠ. v. đ. qᵃ. ƥƀ.

Euerton
[*Everton*]

Ð Wilƚo le Reue ... ... ij. ઠ.
„ Roĝo fiƚ Wilƚi ... ... ij. ઠ. iiij. đ.
„ Joħe fiƚ Wilƚi le Reue ... ... ij. ઠ. iiij. đ.
„ Roƀto fiƚ Wilƚi le Reue ... ij. ઠ. iiij. đ.
„ Riĉo fiƚ Stepħi ... ... ij. ઠ. iiij. đ.
„ Wilƚo del Wodeland ... ... ij. ઠ.

Smᵃ. xiij. ઠ. iiij. đ. ƥƀ.

Kulchith
[*Culcheth*]

Ð Gilƀto de Kulchith ... ... ij. ઠ.
„ Adam de Holecroft ... ... ij. ઠ.
„ Roƀto de Riselegħ ... ... xij. đ.
„ Egidio de Penketh ... ... xij. đ.
„ Adam de Kynkenhale ... vj. ઠ.
„ Joħe fiƚ Hugõis ... ... iiij. ઠ.
„ Wilƚmo de Aspeshalgħ ... iiij. ઠ. vj. đ.
„ Huĝ del Hurst ... ... xij. đ.
„ Riĉo fiƚ Stepħi ... ... xij. đ.
„ Joħne Carpentař ... ... viij. đ. oƀ.
„ Joħe de Middeltoñ ... ... xv. đ. oƀ.

Smᵃ. xxiiij. ઠ. vj. đ. ƥƀ.

Allerton
[*Allerton*]

Roƀto [Hole in document.] Grelley ... ij. ઠ.
Ð Wilƚo le Haiward ... ... xviij. đ.

D Wilto fit Henr̃ ...   . xij. đ.
„ Robto de Outstayninge   ... ij. s. ij. đ.

Smᵃ. vj. ꝝ. viij. đ. pꝗ.

Skelmersdale
[*Skelmersdale*]

D Robto Mollesone ...   ... iiij. ꝝ.
„ Adam fflatherhale ...   ... iiij. ꝝ.
„ Alañ de Marehalgħ ...   ... ij. ꝝ.
„ Adam Sporoun ...   ... ij. ꝝ.
„ Joħne Wilkemogħ ...   ... ij. ꝝ.
„ Henr̃ le Swon ...   ... ij. ꝝ.
„ Adam del Scoler ...   ... ij. ꝝ.
„ Ric̃o le Hunte ...   ... ij. ꝝ.
„ Joħe de Horskar ...   ... ij. ꝝ.
„ Joħe le Hunte ...   ... iij. ꝝ.
„ Robto de Wodefall ...   ... iiij. ꝝ.
„ Ric̃o Maggesone ...   ... ij. ꝝ.

Smᵃ. xxxj. ꝝ. pꝗ.

Skaresbrek cū Hurleton
[*Scarisbrick with Hurlton*]

D Gilbto de Skaresbrek ...   ... vij. ꝝ. viij. đ.
„ Robto de Hurletoñ ...   ... iiij. ꝝ.
„ Joħe de Gosefordsik ...   ... iiij. ꝝ.
„ Adam de Shoreacres ...   ... iij. ꝝ.
„ Simoñ del Shagħ ...   ... iij. ꝝ.
„ Walto del Shaghe ...   ... iiij. ꝝ.
„ Alano fit Simoñ ...   ... v. ꝝ.
„ Gilbto de Aspenwalt ...   ... iij. ꝝ.
„ Joħe de Whattoñ ...   ... v. ꝝ.
„ Joħe fit Robi ...   ... v. ꝝ.
„ Alex̃ de Marclan ...   ... vj. ꝝ. viij. đ.
„ Henr̃ fit Ade ...   ... v. ꝝ.
„ Robto de Wythinsnape ...   ... vj. ꝝ.
„ Joħe Massone ...   ... vij. ꝝ.

Smᵃ. lxix. ꝝ. pꝗ.

Ins in Makerfeld
[*Ince in Makerfield*]

Đ Ricõ de Ins	...	...	...	iij. ꝩ.
„ Ricõ fił Henr̃ de Ins	...		...	xij. đ.
„ Wiłło de Mikelfen	...		...	xij. đ.
„ Adam de Thurskar	...		...	xij. đ.
„ Joħe fił Henr̃ de Childres			...	xij. đ.
„ Thom̃ de Childres	...		...	xij. đ.

Sm̃ᵃ. viij. ꝩ. pᵬ.

Burtonwode
[*Burtonwood*]

Đ Henr̃ le Parker	...	...	...	iij. ꝩ. v. đ. oᵬ. qᵃ.
„ Adam de Sotheworthe		...		iij. ꝩ.
„ Wiłło Muskełł	...	...	...	iij. ꝩ. viij. đ.
„ Ricõ fił Hugõis		...	...	xij. đ.
„ Roᵬto fił Ricĩ	...	...	...	ij. ꝩ.
„ Roᵬto fił Rađ	...	...	...	xij. đ.
„ Ricõ del Reues		..	...	xij. đ.
„ Wiłło fił Roᵬi	...	...	...	x. đ. qᵃ.

Sm̃ᵃ. xvj. ꝩ. pᵬ.

Croynton
[*Cronton*]

Đ Joħe Cłico	...	...	...	vj. ꝩ. viij. đ.
„ Joħe Cutfox	...	...	...	vj. ꝩ.
„ Ricõ del Lawe	...	...	...	iiij. ꝩ.
„ Adam del Snape	...		...	ij. ꝩ. iiij. đ.
„ Ricõ fił Patricii		..	...	ij. ꝩ.
„ Roḡo de Raynhułł		...	...	ij. ꝩ.
„ Joħe del Grene		...	...	ij. ꝩ.

Sm̃ᵃ. xxv. ꝩ. pᵬ.

Huytoñ cū Roby
[*Huyton with Roby*]

Đ Joħe del fford	...	...	...	v. ꝩ. j. đ.

D ... ...

„ Adam ... ...

„ ... ...

„ ... ...

„ ... ...

„ ... ...

„ ... ...

„ ... ...

Torbo[...]
[*Tori[...]*]

D E[...] ... ...

„ Henr ... ...

„ ... ...

„ Henr ... ...

„ Roger ... ...

„ Ela ... ...

„ Robtu ... ...

„ Willo ... ...

„ Adam ... ...

Aghtoï
[*Angizton*]

D Ric̄ le Waley[...] ... ... v. x. d.

„ Henr̄ de Litherlond ... ... vii. s. i. d.

„ Henr̄ de Bikerstatt ... ... viij. s. x. d.

„ Willo fr̄ Henr̄ ... ... viij. s. x. d.

„ Johe de Swynyard ... ... iiij. s. x. d.

„ Gilbto de Broidfeid ... ... iiij. s.

„ Willmo Shakeshaft ... ... xx. d.

„ Will de Haie ... ... xix. d. ob.

„ Henr̄ fil Madoci ... ... v. s.

Sm̄a. l. s. p̄b.

Dalton
[*Dalton*]

Đ Riĉo de Asshhurst	...	...	v. ȿ.
„ Huḡ del Scoles...	...	...	ij. ȿ.
„ Joħe le Harper ...	...	...	xij. đ.
„ Joħe Hichsone ...	...	...	ix. đ.
„ Alañ fit Roƀi	...	...	xij. đ.
„ Thoñ Smult	...	...	xij. đ.
„ Adam de Asshhurst	...	...	xij. đ.
„ Riĉo fit Henȓ	...	...	xviij. đ.
„ Riĉo fit Wilłi	...	...	ij. ȿ.
„ Alañ fit Roḡi	...	...	ix. đ.

Sm^a. xvj. ȿ. pƀ.

Ins Blundeł
[*Ince Blundell*]

Đ Wiłt Blundeł	...	...	iij. ȿ.
„ Jorđo de Morhouses	...	...	iij. ȿ. iiij. đ.
„ Roƀto Ballardsone	...	...	iij. ȿ. viij. đ.
„ Riĉo fit Eleñ	...	...	ij. ȿ. vj. đ.
„ Riĉo Blaunchard	...	...	ij. ȿ. vj. đ.
„ Roƀto fflook	...	...	iij. ȿ.
„ Riĉo le Bole	...	...	ij. ȿ.

Sm^a. xx. ȿ. pƀ.

Wolueton Magna
[*Great Woolton*]

Đ Roƀto del Eues	...	...	ij. ȿ. ix. đ.
„ Riĉo de Boulde	...	..	ix. đ.
„ Joħe fit Ade	...	...	xij. đ.
„ Joħe Gillesone ...	...	...	xij. đ.
„ Riĉo fit Galfȓ	...	...	ix. đ.
„ Wiłto le Wodeward	...	...	xj. đ.
„ Roḡo de Laghoke	...	...	xij. đ.
„ Wiłtmo Hullesone	...	...	xij. đ.
„ Wiłto fit Ade	...	...	xj. đ.
„ Adam fit Joħis ...	...	...	xxiij. đ.

Sm^a. xij. ȿ. pƀ.

Derby
[*West Derby*]

Ɖ Roƀto de Derby ... ... iij. ꝭ. iiij. đ.
„ Wilŧo del Hetħ ... ... iij. ꝭ. iiij. đ.
„ Henr̃ fiŧ Rađi ... ... iiij. ꝭ. viij. đ.
„ Riĉo del Accres ... ... iiij. ꝭ. viij. đ.
„ Huᵹ̃ le Reue ... ... iiij. ꝭ.
„ Riĉo de Longelegħ ... ... iiij. ꝭ.
„ Wilŧo Rose¡ ... ... v. ꝭ. viij. đ.
„ Wilŧo del Rydyng ... ... iiij. ꝭ. viij. đ.
„ Joħe le Deye ... ... iiij. ꝭ. iiij. đ.
„ Riĉo del Hetħ ... ... iiij. ꝭ.
„ Hugõe fiŧ Ađ ... ... iiij. ꝭ.

Smᵃ. xlvj. ꝭ. viij. đ. pƀ.

Speek
[*Speke*]

Ɖ Joħe le Norrays ... ... vj. ꝭ. iiij. đ.
„ Wilŧo del Brokes .. ... iij. ꝭ. iiij. đ.
„ Riĉo de Laghok ... ... iiij. ꝭ.
„ Wilŧo fiŧ Gilƀti ... ... ij. ꝭ. viij. đ.
„ Wilŧo fiŧ Thoñ ... ... iiij. ꝭ.
„ Roᵹ̃ fiŧ Alcok ... ... iij. ꝭ.
„ Wilŧmo fiŧ Simoñ ... ... ij. ꝭ. viij. đ.
„ Adam del Bonk ... ... ij. ꝭ.
„ Alañ de Moselegħ ... ... ij. ꝭ. viij. đ.
„ Henr̃ fiŧ Hancoke ... ... xvj. đ.
„ Joħe fiŧ Roƀti ... ... ij. ꝭ.

Smᵃ. xxxiiij. ꝭ. pƀ.

Wolueton ꝑua
[*Little Woolton*]

Ɖ Joħe fiŧ Elcok ... ... ij. ꝭ. iiij. đ. qᵃ.
„ Wilŧo fiŧ Benedc̃i ... ... xviij. đ.
„ Adam fiŧ Joħ ... ... ij. ꝭ.
„ Henr̃ fiŧ Roƀti ... ... xix. đ.
„ Riĉo Ormesone ... ... xxij. đ. oƀ.
„ Riĉo fiŧ Elie ... ... xiij. đ. qᵃ.
„ Riĉo fiŧ Hugõis ... ... xix. đ.

Smᵃ. xij. ꝭ. pƀ.

Asteleghe
[*Astley*]

Ð Hugōe de Morlegh	...	...	iij. s. viij. đ.
„ Henr̄ Valentin ...	...	...	ij. ꝼ. v. đ.
„ Wilto de Astelegh	...	...	iij. ꝼ. iij. đ.
„ Henr̄ del Birches	...	...	ij. ꝼ. iiij. đ.
„ Thom̄ Gilibrond	...	...	xvj. đ.
„ Ric̄o de Claydelegh	...	. .	xij. đ.
„ Adam Scot	...	...	...	xij. đ.

Sm\ᵃ. xv. ꝼ. pꝺ.

Tildeslegh
[*Tildesley*]

Ð Hugōe de Tildesley	...	...	v. ꝼ. iiij. đ.
„ Henr̄ de Shakerlegh	...	...	iiij. ꝼ. viij. đ. qᵃ.
„ Adam de Tildeslegh	...	...	ij. ꝼ. iiij. đ.
„ Henr̄ de Tildeslegh	...	...	ij. ꝼ. viij. đ.
„ Henr̄ de Chaidok	...	...	xij. đ.
„ Thom̄ fit Wilti ...	...	...	xij. đ.
„ Thom̄ Hopkrone	...	...	xij. đ.
„ Adam de Chaidok	...	...	xij. đ.

Sm\ᵃ. xix. ꝼ. qᵃ. pꝺ

Athertoñ
[*Atherton*]

Ð Henr̄ de Athertoñ	...	...	iij. ꝼ.
„ Wilto Pree	...	...	...	ij. ꝼ.
„ Johe de Turtoñ...	...	...	ij. ꝼ.
„ Alex̄ le Nayler ...	...	...	ij. ꝼ.
„ Roḡ del Lache ...	...	...	ij. ꝼ. viij. đ.
„ Wilto Chapmon	...	...	ij. ꝼ. iiij. đ.
„ Roḡo fit Nutric̄...	...	...	ij. ꝼ.
„ Ric̄o de Ingelwode	...	...	xvj. đ.
„ Wilto fit Alañ ...	...	...	ij. ꝼ. iiij. đ.
„ Johe Carpen̄ ...	...	...	iij. ꝼ.
„ Henr̄ del Mosse	...	...	ij. ꝼ.
„ Thom̄ de Gortoñ	...	...	ij. ꝼ.

Sm\ᵃ. xxvj. ꝼ. viij. đ. pꝺ.

Quistan
[*Whiston*]

Ð Roƀto Trauers ...	...	...	vj. ꝝ.
„ Nicħo Cappłano	...	...	iiij. ꝝ.
„ Roƀto de Bradelegħ	...	...	ij. ꝝ.
„ Adam fił Ranulpħ	...	...	ij. ꝝ.
„ Roƀto fił Joħis ...	...	...	ij. ꝝ.

Smᵃ. xvj. ꝝ. pƀ.

Sotheworth cū Crofte
[*Southworth with Croft*]

Ð Riĉo fił Dogge ...	...	...	xij. đ.
„ Wilło de Haidok	...	...	xij. đ.
„ Henr̃ de Wheteley	...	...	iiij. ꝝ.
„ Roḡo de Ryhale	...	...	ij. ꝝ.
„ Adam de Haydok	...	...	xviij. đ.

Smᵃ. ix. ꝝ. vj. đ. pƀ.

Neutoñ
[*Newton-le-Willows*]

Ð Adam de Okeshagħ	...	...	iij. ꝝ. iiij. đ.
„ Henr̃ de Ecclistoñ	...	...	ij. ꝝ. viij. đ.
„ Jacobo Ꝛuiente ...	...	...	iiij. ꝝ.
„ Roƀto fił Joħis ...	...	...	iij. ꝝ.
„ Wilło del Held...	...	...	ij. ꝝ. viij. đ.
„ Wilło fił Wilłi ...	...	...	iiij. ꝝ.
„ Roƀto Kutte	...	...	x. đ.
„ Joħe de Kyngesley	...	...	ij. ꝝ.
„ Henr̃ de Sotheworth	...	...	iiij. ꝝ. ij. đ.
„ Joħe fił Wilłi ...	...	...	ix. đ.

Smᵃ. xxvij. ꝝ. v. đ. pƀ.

Rixtoñ
[*Rixton*]

Ð Alan de Rixtoñ	...	...	ij. ꝝ.
„ Roƀto de Mostoñ	...	...	ij. ꝝ.
„ Wilło de Rixtoñ	...	...	ij. viij. đ. [*sic*]
„ Alañ del Shaghe	...	...	iiij. ꝝ.

Ð Wilło de Vrmestoñ ... · ... xx. đ.
 „ Johe de Barwe ... ... ij. ꝰ.
 „ Thoñ de Martinescrofte ... ij. ꝰ.
 „ Roǧo Banastr̃ ... ... ij. ꝰ. viij. đ.
 „ Johe le Swon ... ... ij. ꝰ.

Smᵃ. xxj. ꝰ.

Wolstoñ
[*Woolston*]

Ð Riĉo de Wolstoñ ... ... ij. ꝰ. vj. đ.
 „ Riĉo de Martinescroft ... ... xx. đ.
 „ Johne de Hepay ... ... xx. đ.
 „ Robto fił Wilłi ... ... ij. ꝰ.
 „ Henr̃ le Wolfe ... ... xvj. đ.
 „ Wilło de Medewalle ... ... x. đ.
 „ Wilłmo del Wode ... ... ij. ꝰ. viij. đ. ob.
 „ Robto de Martinescroft ... ij. ꝰ. viij. đ. ob.
 „ Henr̃ fił Thoñ ... ... ij. ꝰ. viij. đ. ob.
 „ Robto de Emnes ... ... ij. ꝰ. x. đ. ob.

Smᵃ. xxj. ꝰ. pb.

Lautoñ cū Kenyan
[*Lowton with Kenyon*]

Ð Wilło de Lautoñ ... ... ij. ꝰ.
 „ Adam de Swynlegh ... ... xij. đ.
 „ Henr̃ de Wodehouses ... ... ij. ꝰ.
 „ Adam fił Riĉi ... ... iiij. ꝰ.
 „ Hugōe de Lautoñ ... ... ij. ꝰ.
 „ Wilło fił Rađi ... ... ij. ꝰ.
 „ Adam le Gardenner ... ... iij. ꝰ. vj. đ.

Smᵃ. xvj. ꝰ. vj. đ. pb.

Mideltoñ cū Erbury
[*Middleton with Arbury*]

Ð Wilło fił Johis ... ... xvj. đ.
 „ Riĉo le Reue ... ... xx. đ.

D Hug̃ fil Gille ...	...	...	xij. đ.
„ Gilbto Lucassone	...	...	ix. đ.
„ Robto le Piper̃ ...	...	...	xv. đ.
„ Johe de Holand	...	...	xij. đ.

Smª. vij. s. pƀ.

Adburghªm
[*Abram*]

D Ric̃o de Aldburgªm	...	...	iij. s.
„ Wilto Gilibrond	...	...	iij. s.
„ Wilto de Asshtoñ	...	...	ij. s.
„ Rog̃o del Wode	...	...	ij. s.
„ Johe del Wychñ	...	...	ij. s. qª.

Smª. xij. s. qª. pƀ.

Haydok
[*Haydock*]

D Gilbto de Haidok	...	...	iiij. s.
„ Wilto Peese ...	...	...	xviij. đ.
„ Wilto Grenefissh	...	...	xij. đ.
„ Robto de Goldburñ	...	...	xij. đ.
„ Ric̃o del Lone ...	...	...	xiiij. đ.
„ Wilto Hardy ...	...	...	xij. đ.
„ Robto de Adburgham ...		...	xij. đ.

Smª. x. s. viij. đ. pƀ.

Glasebroke
[*Glasebrook*]

D Robto de Mostoñ	...	...	ij. s.
„ Henr̃ fil Betok ...	...	...	ij. s.
„ Gilbto del Shaghe	...	...	ij. s.
„ Rog̃o Banastr̃ ...	...	...	xij. đ.

Smª. vij. s. pƀ.

Dittoñ
[*Ditton*]

D Johe de Dittoñ ...	...	...	iiij. s.
„ Johe de Dychefeld	...	...	iij. s. vj. đ. oƀ.

Ð Thoᷘ fiᴛ Stephi	... ...	iij. ꙅ. j. ꝺ. qᵃ.
„ Joħe fiᴛ Joħis fiᴛ Henᷧ ...	...	iij. ꙅ. ij. ꝺ. oꝺ.
„ Henᷧ Trauers ...	...	ij. ꙅ. viij. ꝺ.
„ Adam Tinᷔttore	... ...	iiij. ꙅ. iiij. ꝺ.
„ Joħe del Merssħ	... ...	vij. ꙅ. ix. ꝺ.
„ Joħe Astebrok ...	...	iiij. ꙅ. v. ꝺ.
„ Roꝛto le Tarper	...	iiij. ꙅ. xj. ꝺ. oꝺ. qᵃ.

Smᵃ. xxxviij. ꙅ. pꝺ.

Boulde
[Bold]

Ð Riᴄo de Boulde	... ...	vij. ꙅ. ix. ꝺ.
„ Riᴄo de Aluandelegħ ...	...	viij. ꙅ.
„ Wilᴛo del Heie ...	...	ix. ꙅ.
„ Wilᴛo de Dalhom	...	ix. ꙅ.
„ Roꝫo Gernet ...	...	ix. ꙅ.
„ Henᷧ de Erneshed	...	v. ꙅ. vj. ꝺ.
„ Riᴄo fiᴛ Matħi ...	...	v. ꙅ. vj. ꝺ.
„ Joħe de Holebrok	...	iij. ꙅ.
„ Joħe fiᴛ Dandy ...	...	iij. ꙅ.

Smᵃ. lix. ꙅ. ix. ꝺ. pꝺ.

Dounholand
[Down Holland]

Ð Riᴄo de Holand	... ...	vj. ꙅ. viij. ꝺ.
„ Henᷧ de Holand	...	vj. ꙅ. viij. ꝺ.
„ Alicia vᷧ Ade de la More	...	vj. ꙅ. viij. ꝺ.
„ Thoᷘ Dollan ...	... ...	ij. ꙅ.
„ Joħe fiᴛ Henᷧ ...	...	ij. ꙅ.
„ Roꝫo fiᴛ Riᴄi de Bartoꝝ	...	ij. ꙅ.
„ Adam fiᴛ Anabille	...	iij. ꙅ.

Smᵃ. xxix. ꙅ. pꝺ.

Northmeles
[North Meols]

Ð Wilᴛo de Coudray	... ...	vj. ꙅ. viij. ꝺ.
„ Wilᴛo fiᴛ Wilᴛi ...	...	ij. ꙅ.

Đ Riĉo de Swartbrek ... ... ij. ꝫ.

„ Roḡo fił Thoɱ ... ... xvj. đ.

„ Roƀto de Heskeytħ ... ... xiiij. đ.

„ Adam fił Wilłi ... ... iij. ꝫ.

„ Wilło fił Wilłi fił Całłi ... xviij. đ.

„ Adam fił Roƀti ... ... xij. đ.

„ Wilł fił Hugōis ... ... xvj. đ.

Smᵃ. **xx. ꝫ. pƀ.**

Gerstan
[*Garston*]

Đ Roƀto de Blakeburn ... ... iij. ꝫ.

„ Roƀto fił Ade ... ... iij. ꝫ.

„ Hugōe fił Joħis ... ... ij. ꝫ.

„ Joħe fił Ade ... ... xxij. đ.

„ Joħe fił Thoɱ ... ... xij. đ.

„ Wilło fił Joħis ... ... xiiij. đ.

„ Roḡ fił Ade ... ... ij. ꝫ.

„ Joħe fił Ade ... ... iiij. ꝫ.

Smᵃ. **xviij. ꝫ. pƀ.**

Bykarstatħ
[*Bickerstaff*]

Đ Riĉo de Stotfoldshagħ ... iiij. ꝫ. ij. đ.

„ Roƀto fił Simoñ ... ... iij. ꝫ. v. đ. oƀ. qᵃ.

„ Joħe Cłico ... ... iiij. ꝫ.

„ Alañ de Barwe... ... ... iiij. ꝫ. ij. đ.

„ Wilło fił Wilłi ... ... v. ꝫ.

„ Wilło del Hyles ... ... xvj. đ. oƀ.

„ Wilło de Rayneford ... ... iij. ꝫ. vj. đ.

„ Roƀto fił Nicħi ... ... xx. đ. oƀ. qᵃ.

„ Roḡo fił Riĉi ... ... xix. đ.

Smᵃ. **xxix. ꝫ. pƀ.**

Suttoñ
[*Sutton*]

Đ Riĉo de Holand ... ... vj. ꝫ. viij. đ

„ Roƀto le Norrais ... ... iiij. ꝫ.

D Johe de Sherdelegh ... ... ij. s. iiij. d.
„ Henr de Eltonheued ... ... iiij. s. viij. d.
„ Henr Raweknaue ... iiij. s. iiij. d.
„ Wilto de Neuton ... ... iiij. s.
„ Robto de Wodefalt ... ... ij. s.
„ Rico de Thorniheued ... ... ij. s.
„ Johe de Wiresdale ... ... iiij. s.

Smᵃ. xxxiiij. s. pb.

Weringtoñ
[*Warrington*]

D Wilto Lembe ... ... vj. s. viij. d.
„ Henr de Merlond ... ... xij. s.
„ Robto le Sotheren ... ... xij. s.
„ Wilto del fford ... ... iiij. s. ij. d.
„ Robto de Vptoñ ... ... iiij. s. ij. d.
„ Henr de Glasebroke ... ... iiij. s. ij. d.
„ Johe le Herdmon ... ... iiij. s. ij. d.

Smᵃ. xlvij. s. viij. d. pb.

Raynehult
[*Rainhill*]

D Rogo fit Robti ... ... iiij. s.
„ Wilto fit Henr del Lee ... iiij. s. viij. d.
„ Robto de Raynehult ... ... iiij. s.
„ Rogo le Cariour ... ... ij. s.
„ Rogo Trauers ... ... iiij. s. iiij. d.
„ Johe Paa ... ... v. s.

Smᵃ. xxv. s. pb.

Goldeburñ
[*Golborne*]

D Thoñ del Dene ... ... iiij. s.
„ Simoñ del Mosse ... ... ij. s.
„ Elia Dikesone ... ... ij. s.
„ Wilto fit Cecilie ... ... ij. s.
„ Wilto fit Radi ... ... ij. s.

Smᵃ. xiij. s. pb.

Childewalle
[*Childwall*]

D̶ Edm̄o de Childewalle	...	...	xvj. đ. ob̄.
„ Wil͡to Croket	...	...	ix. đ. ob̄.
„ Joħe de ffourneis	...	...	xiij. đ.
„ Ric̄o del Dale	...	...	xvj. đ. ob̄.
„ Adam del ffernes	...	...	ix. đ.
„ Joħe fit Ric̄i	...	...	iiij. s̄. vij. đ. ob̄.

Sm^a. x. s̄. pb̄.

Appelton̄
[*Appleton with Widnes*]

D̶ Ric̄o de Denton̄	...	...	vj. s̄.
„ Ric̄o fit Rađi	...	...	vj. s̄.
„ Ric̄o de la More	...	...	iiij. s̄.
„ Ric̄o le Kynge	...	...	v. s̄. iiij. đ.
„ Joħe fit Rađi	...	...	iiij. s̄.
„ Ric̄o fit Pħi	...	...	iiij. s̄.
„ Wil͡to del Merssħ	...	...	iiij. s̄.
„ Wil͡to de Haurdyn	...	...	iiij. s̄.
„ Henr̄ de Denton̄	...	...	iiij. s̄.
„ Wil͡to del Hetħ	...	...	iiij. s̄. viij. đ.

Sm^a. xvj. s̄. pb̄.

Lytherlonđ
[*Litherland*]

D̶ Jordan̄ de Lynacr̄	...	...	ij. s̄.
„ Ric̄o fit Marger̄	...	...	iiij. s̄.
„ Rob̄to le Roter	...	...	ij. s̄.
„ Ric̄o le Demand	...	...	ij. s̄.
„ Ric̄o fit Alan̄	...	...	ij. s̄.
„ Roḡo del fford	...	...	ij. s̄.
„ Wil͡to ffox	...	...	ij. s̄.

Sm^a. xv. s̄. pb̄.

Holand
[*Up Holland*]

D̶ Wil͡to de Orel͡t	...	...	ij. s̄. iiij. đ.
„ Alan̄ le Waynwright	...	...	ij. s̄.

Đ Adam Waltheu	...	...	ij. s.
„ Wilto fabr	...	...	xx. đ.
„ Rico del yate	...	...	xx. đ.
„ Robto de ffrekilton	...	...	ij. s. iiij. đ.
„ Henr fit Thom	...	...	iiij. s.
„ Thom del Legh	...	...	iiij. s.
„ Ran fit Benedci	...	...	iiij. s.

Sm^a. xxiiij. s. pb.

Asshton
[Ashton in Makerfield]

Đ Galfr de Werburghton ...	...	iiij. s.
„ Agn relicta Henr de Athirton	vj. s.
„ Hug fit Henr de Haidok	...	iiij. s.
„ Wilto de Haidok	...	...	iiij. s.
„ Rogo de Westehult	...	...	iij. s.
„ Thom Ryngotherose	...	iiij. s.
„ Robto Righthert	...	...	iiij. s.
„ Henr de Haregreue	...	...	ij. s.
„ Rog fit Robti	...	...	...	ij. s. iiij. đ.
„ Wilto fit Hug	...	...	...	vj. s.
„ Rogo Spark	...	...	...	ij. s.

Sm^a. xlij. s. iiij. đ. pb.

Waultre
[Wavertree]

Đ Rico de Wauertre	...	...	xiiij. đ. q^a.
„ Alan le Hogge ...	...	...	xiij. đ. q^a.
„ Adam le Hogge	...	...	xij. đ. ob.
„ Adam fit Edi	...	...	ij. s. viij. đ.
„ Wilto de Haukeslegh ...	...	xix. đ. ob.
„ Wilto fit Dandy	...	...	xix. đ. ob.

Sm^a. ix. s. iij. đ. pb.

Bedeford
[*Bedford*]

Ð Johe de Vaulton	...	...	ij. s. iiij. d.
„ Thom̃ de Shuttlesworth		...	ij. s. v. d.
„ Rog̃o de Warton		...	ij. s.
„ Wilto le Crouther	...	...	ij. s. viij. d.
„ Johe de Wirhale	...	...	ij. s. vij. d.
„ Ad̃ de Morleghes	...	...	iiij. s. viij. d.
„ Adam del grene	...	...	v. s. iiij. d.
„ Wilto de Byrom	...	...	ij. s. viij. d.
„ Ric̃ fit Robi	...	...	xv. d.
„ Wilto fit Joh^ne [*sic*]	...	...	xij. d.

Sm^a. xxvj. s. xj. d. pb.

Maghhale
[*Maghull*]

Ð Ric̃o le Cartwright	...	...	ij. s.
„ Ric̃o de Rynacres	...	...	xx. d.
„ Thom̃ fit Elcok	...	...	xvj. d.
„ Henr̃ Carpent̃	...	...	xij. d.
„ Robto ffox	...	...	xij. d.
„ Wilto fit Pauli	...	...	xij. d.
„ Johe fit Simon	...	...	xij. d.

Sm^a. ix. s. pb.

Thorneton
[*Thornton*]

Ð Robto le Molineux	...	...	ij. s. iiij. d.
„ Marg̃ia relicta Simon	...	....	xvj. d.
„ Wilto fit Ric̃i	...	...	xvj. d.
„ Robto fit Thome	...	...	iij. s. iiij. d.
„ Adam fit Thom̃	...	...	xij. d.
„ Gilbto de Tarleton	...	...	xij. d.
„ Hug̃oe fit Wilti	...	...	ij. s.
„ Johe de Horsshaghe	...	...	ij. s.
„ Wilto Spendeloue	...	...	xvj. d.

Sm^a. xv. s. viij. d. pb.

Rauenesmeł
[*Ravens Meols*]

Đ Rič̃o de Dodelegħ	...	...	xx. đ.
„ Rič̃o le Raye	...	...	...	xvj. đ.
„ Wilło fił Rič̃i	...	...	x. đ.
„ Wilło fił Joħis	...	...	...	xij. đ.
„ Roḡo fił Joħis	...	...	...	xij. đ.
„ Roƀto Broun	...	...	...	xij. đ.
„ Roƀto de Aynolesdale	...	...	xiiij. đ.
„ Adam de Aynollesdale	..	xij. đ.
„ Wilło de Dodelegh	...	...	xij. đ.
„ Adam Banast̃r	...	...	...	xx. đ.

Sm^a. xj. ß. viij. đ. pƀ.

Ecclestoñ
[*Eccleston*]

Đ Alañ de Ecclestoñ	...	...	v. ß.
„ Rič̃o de Stanyhirst	...	...	iij. ß. v. đ.
„ Adam fił Roḡi	...	...	iiij. ß.
„ Wilło del Spen	...	...	...	iij. ß. xj. đ.
„ Roḡo fił Aleẋi	...	...	...	iij. ß.
„ Roƀto cłico	...	...	...	iiij. ß.
„ Henr̃ de Hale	...	...	...	iij. ß. iiij. đ.

Sm^a. xxvj. ß. viij. đ. pƀ.

Keùłdeley
[*Cuerdley*]

Đ Wilło de Lynacre	...	...	iij. ß. iiij. đ.
„ Rič̃o de Plumptoñ	...	...	iiij. ß.
„ Rič̃ fił Wilłi	...	...	...	ij. ß. iiij. đ.
„ Joħe de Bury	...	...	...	ij. ß. iiij. đ.
„ Alan fił Ade	...	...	...	v. ß.
„ Adam fił Benedc̃i	...	...	...	v. ß.
„ Thom̃ fił Rič̃i	...	...	...	iiij. ß.
„ Roƀto de Balshagh	...	...	...	iiij. ß.

Sm^a. xxx. ß. pƀ.

Crosseby þua
[*Little Crosby*]

Ð Nicħo Blundelt	...	...	v. ß. ij. đ.
„ Joħe de Hyndelegħ	...	...	v. ß. x. đ. qª.
„ Henr̃ Bercar̃	...	...	iij. ß. vj. đ. qª.
„ Riĉo fit Wilti	...	...	iiij. ß.
„ Roƀto Page	...	...	iij. ß. v. đ.
„ Roƀto fit Wilti	...	...	xvj. đ. oƀ.
„ Roᷠo fit Henr̃	...	...	xiiij. đ.
„ Adam fit Bymne	...	...	xvj. đ.

Smª. xxv. ß. x. đ. þƀ.

Seftoñ
[*Sephton*]

Ð Wilto de Molineux	...	...	iiij. ß.
„ Roƀto del Ridynge	...	...	iiij. ß.
„ Wilto Ade [*sic*]	...	...	iij. ß. iiij. đ.
„ Riĉo de Holand	...	...	iij. ß.
„ Adam Gresse	...	...	iij. ß. iiij. đ.
„ Roƀto fit Riĉi	...	...	v. ß. viij. đ.
„ Henr̃ de Grenolf	...	...	iij. ß. xj. đ. qª.
„ Wilto de Holond	...	...	iij. ß. xj. đ. qª.
„ Thoñ le Demand	...	...	iij. ß. xj. đ.
„ Wiltmo Sharþ	...	...	iij. ß. xj. đ.

Smª. xxxix. ß. oƀ. þƀ.

Lydyate
[*Lydiate*]

Ð Gilƀto de Lidyate	...	...	ij. ß. ij. đ. oƀ.
„ Roƀto de Wolfalt	...	...	iiij. ß. viij. đ.
„ Roƀto le Harpour	...	...	iiij. ß. iiij. đ.
„ Alañ de Halsale	...	...	iiij. ß. xj. đ. oƀ.
„ Elia de Okeshaghe	...	...	xij. đ.
„ Riĉo de Wolfalt	...	...	x. đ.
„ Alañ fit Henr̃	...	...	x. đ.
„ Adam del Halgħ	...	...	vj. ß. ij. đ. oƀ.

Smª. xxv. ß. oƀ. þƀ.

Rayneford
[*Rainford*]

D Riĉo de Lathum	...	...	ij. s. ij. đ.
„ Alañ fil Dande	...	...	iij. s.
„ Wilłο de Rayneford	...	...	ij. s. vj. đ.
„ Roḡo del Berne	...	...	iiij. s.
„ Marḡ de ffoureokshaghe	...	...	ij. s.
„ Adam fil Joħis	...	...	iij. s. v. đ.
„ Adam de Haynesarm̄	...	...	iij. s. v. đ.
„ Adam le Cropper	...	...	iij. s. vj. đ.

Smᵃ. xxiiij. s. pb.

Kirkeby
[*Kirkby*]

D Riĉo Maideñ	...	...	...	iij. s. j. đ. ob. qᵃ.
„ Riĉo fil Henr̃	...	...	...	iiij. s. ij. đ. ob. qᵃ.
„ Riĉo fil Thom̃	...	...	...	iij. s. ijđ. qᵃ.
„ Wilł fil Alañ	...	...	...	iiij. s. ix. đ. qᵃ.
„ Roƀto de Ingeswaith	...	...	vj. s. ij. đ.
„ Roḡo de Melling	...	...	iiij. s. ob.
„ Joħe Tirehare	...	...	...	ij. s.
„ Henr̃ fil Riĉi	...	...	...	xij. đ. ob.
„ Joħe fil Riĉi	...	...	...	vj. s. j. đ.

Smᵃ. xxxiiij. s. iiij. đ. pb.

Pembertoñ
[*Pemberton*]

D Adam de Pemƀtoñ	...	...	iij. s. iij. đ.
„ Henr̃ de Pemƀtoñ	...	...	iij. s.
„ Huḡ de Pemƀtoñ	...	...	ij. s. viij. đ.
„ Roƀto Carpenꝰ	...	...	iij. s. j. đ.
„ Thom̃ fil Huḡ	...	...	iij. s.
„ Adam de Wynstaneslegħ	...	xij. đ.
„ Huḡ Spark	...	...	...	xij. đ.
„ Joħ del Legħ	...	...	...	xij. đ.

Smᵃ. xviij. s. pb.

fforneby
[*Formby*]

D Adam de fforneby	...	...	iij. š.
„ Thoñ Beek	...	...	xvj. đ.
„ Wilło le Ray	...	...	xviij. đ.
„ Wilło Mulł	...	...	ij. š. xj. đ.
„ Wilło de Longetoñ	...	...	iij. š. vj. đ.
„ Roбto fił Roği	...	...	xij. đ.
„ Adam fił Gilбti	...	...	xij. đ.
„ Wilło de Aynolsdale	...	...	xij. đ.
„ Rađo fił Roği	...	...	xij. đ.
„ Joñe de Wygan	...	...	iij. š. ix. đ.

Sm^a. xx. š. pб.

Sonky cū Penketħ
[*Sankey with Penketh*]

D Jordañ de Penketħ	...	...	iij. š.
„ Riĉo Penketħ	...	...	ij. š. vj. đ.
„ Henŕ de Whitfeld	...	...	xviij. đ.
„ Aleẍ de Barwe	...	...	xviij. đ.
„ Riĉo de Asshtoñ	...	...	iiij. š. iiij. đ.
„ Joñe del Birches	...	...	v. š.
„ Riĉo de Gatelondlegħ	...	...	v. š.
„ Henŕ le Colt	...	...	v. š.
„ Riĉo fił Simoñ	...	...	iij. š. ij. đ.

Sm^a. xxxj. š. pб.

Bothull
[*Bootle*]

D Wilło Bareheued	...	...	ij. š. iiij. đ.
„ Joñe fił Roği	...	...	xx. d.
„ Adam del Grenes	...	...	iij. š.
„ Wilło le Shepeherd	...	...	xij. đ.
„ Henŕ de Bothulł	...	...	ij. š.
„ Joñe de Wirhale	...	...	ij. š.
„ Riĉi fił Hugōis	...	...	ij. š.

Sm^a. xiiij. š. pб.

Kirkedale
[*Kirkdale*]

Đ Adam de Irlond	...	...	iij. ꞩ.
„ Wilł Cissoꞃ	...	...	ij. ꞩ. v. đ.
„ Adam fił Hayne	...	...	ij. ꞩ.
„ Henꞃ fił Stepħi	...	...	xviij. đ.
„ Wilł fił Roƀti	...	...	x. đ.
„ Henꞃ fił Roƀi	...	...	xij. đ.
„ Joħe fił Roꞡi	...	...	x. đ.
„ Wilło de Whiteby	...	...	ix. đ.

Smᵃ. xij. ꞩ. iiij. đ. pƀ.

Wyndhulł
[*Windle*]

Đ Riꞓo fił Roƀi de Collay	...	iij. ꞩ. iij. đ. qᵃ.
„ Riꞓ de Wysshagħ	...	iiij. ꞩ. oƀ. qᵃ.
„ Joħe Baroun	...	iiij. ꞩ.
„ Wilł de de Waltoñ [*sic*]	...	v. ꞩ. iiij. đ.
„ Riꞓo de Legħ	...	ij. ꞩ.
„ Riꞓo de Aldecroft	...	ij. ꞩ.
„ Robto de Grouk	...	ij. ꞩ.
„ Adam. Burtays	...	xvj. đ.

Smᵃ. xxiiij. ꞩ. pƀ.

Mellyng
[*Melling*]

Đ Roƀto de Molineux	...	...	xxiij. đ.
„ Roƀto de Bothulł	...	...	iiij. ꞩ.
„ Nicħo de Bothulł	...	...	ij. ꞩ.
„ Thoɱ Wylde	...	...	xij. đ.
„ Ađ de Bothulł	...	...	xviij. đ.
„ Joħe fił Henꞃ	...	...	v. ꞩ. vij. đ.
„ Roƀto fre eius	...	...	v. ꞩ.
„ Wilło fił Bertrami	...	...	v. ꞩ.
„ Roƀto le Sleghe	...	...	v. ꞩ.

Smᵃ. xxxj. ꞩ. pƀ.

Lathū

[*Lathom*]

Ð Henr̄ de Wittoñ	...	...	ij. ꝸ. x. ð.
„ Roƀto de Taldeford	...	...	ij. ꝸ. v. ð.
„ Adam del Kar ...	...	...	ij. ꝸ. viij. ð.
„ Roƀto de Cruce	...	...	iiij. ꝸ. viij. ð.
„ Joñe de Cruce ...	...	...	x. ð.
„ Adam de Burscogħ	...	...	ij. ꝸ. vïij. ð. qᵘ.
„ Simone de ffairclogħ	...	...	iiij. ꝸ.
„ Aleẍ de ffairclogħ	...	...	ij. ꝸ. iiij. ð.
„ Rič̃o de Burscogħ	...	...	ij. ꝸ. vj. ð. oƀ. qᵃ.
„ Adam de Warinwroo	...	...	ij. ꝸ. ix. ð.
„ Adam Pawesone	...	...	ij. ꝸ. viij. ð.
„ Thoм̃ Dandisone	...	...	iiij. ꝸ. viij. ð
„ Simoñ de Wolmore	...	...	v. ꝸ. xj. ð.
„ Rič̃o del Kar ...	...	...	v. ꝸ.
„ Raðo de Kartmalŧ	...	...	v. ꝸ.
„ Joñe de Burscoghe	...	...	v. ꝸ.

Smᵃ. lx. ꝸ. pƀ.

Halsale

[*Halsall*]

Ð Gilƀto de Halsale	...	...	vij. ꝸ. oƀ.
„ Roƀto Dollan ...	...	...	iiij. ꝸ. ix. ð. oƀ.
„ Adam Walshcroft	...	...	iiij. ꝸ. oƀ.
„ Simone fiŧ Rič̃i	...	...	iiij. ꝸ. ix. ð. oƀ.
„ Adam Bercar̄ ...	...	...	iiij. ꝸ. iij. ð.
„ Roᵷ Bercar̄	...	...	iiij. ꝸ. vj. ð. oƀ.
„ Adam fiŧ Roᵹi ...	...	...	ij. ꝸ. iiij. ð.
„ Wilŧo le Oxherd	...	...	iiij. ꝸ.
„ Roƀto fiŧ Rič̃i ...	...	...	ij. ꝸ. qᵃ.
„ Simoñ de Teulond	...	...	ij. ꝸ. qᵃ.
„ Wilŧo fiŧ Roᵹi ...	...	...	xviij. ð.
„ Roᵷ fil Roᵷ	...	...	xix. ð.

Smᵃ. xliiij. ꝸ. pƀ.

Bullinge cū Winstanlegh
[Billinge with Winstanley]

Ð Roƀto de Huytoñ	...	...	ij. ẛ.
„ Roḡo de Winstanlegh	...	...	ij. ẛ.
„ Wilƚo de Bullinge	...	...	ij. ẛ.
„ Ri͂co de Crokehurst	...	...	ij. ẛ.
„ Henꝛ̃ fiƚ Henꝛ̃	...	...	ij. ẛ.
„ Adam fiƚ Olot	...	...	xviij. đ.
„ Adam de Leght	...	...	xviij. đ.
„ Adam fiƚ Hancok	...	...	xxiij. đ.

Smᵃ. xiiij. ẛ. xj. đ. pƀ.

Paar
Parr]

Ð Adam de Par	...	...	ij. ẛ. viij. đ.
„ Ri͂co de Laghok	...	...	iij. ẛ. viij. đ.
„ Petꝛ̃ de Laghok	...	...	ij. ẛ. iiij. đ.
„ Ri͂co fiƚ Wilke	...	...	ij. ẛ.
„ Alañ fiƚ Gilƀti	...	...	xx. đ.
„ Wilƚo fiƚ Wilƚi	...	...	xx. đ.
„ Adam del Heth	...	...	xij. đ.
„ Wilƚo fiƚ Wilƚi fiƚ Rađi	...	...	xij. đ.

Smᵃ. xvj. ẛ. pƀ.

Pynyngton
[Pennington]

Ð Ri͂co de Bradeshaghe	...	...	ij. ẛ. iiij. đ.
„ Ri͂co de Pynyngton	...	...	xvj. đ.
„ Roḡo del ffermhed	...	...	ij. ẛ.
„ Rađo fiƚ Agñ	...	...	vj. ẛ. iiij. đ.
„ Ri͂co del Wode	...	...	ix. đ.

Smᵃ. xij. ẛ. ix. đ. pƀ.

Orelt
[Orrell]

Ð Henꝛ̃ de Orelt	...	...	ij. ẛ.
„ Thom̃ del Egge	...	...	ij. ẛ.
„ Roƀto Carpentaꝛ̃	...	...	xij. đ.
„ Johe fiƚ Dode	...	...	xiij. đ.

Smᵃ. vj. ẛ. j. đ. pƀ.

Hale
[*Hale*]

Đ Roƀto de Irland	... ...	xvj. đ.
„ Roƀto le Rider ...	... ...	xiiij. đ. oƀ.
„ Roǥ de Kulchith	... ...	xiiij. đ. oƀ.
„ Joħe de Irland ...	... ...	ij. ꝭ. ij. đ. oƀ.
„ Joħe de Holond	... ...	xviij. đ. oƀ.
„ Rĩco del Doustes	... ...	xviij. đ. oƀ.
„ Roƀto del Bonk	... ...	xiij. đ.
„ Rĩco del Bonk ...	... ...	xxij. đ. oƀ.
„ Roƀto del Egħe	... ...	xiij. đ.
„ Thurstano de Bradelegħ	...	xxij. đ. oƀ.
„ Joħe le Spenꝭ ...	... ...	xxij. đ. oƀ.
„ Joħe del Wode ...	... ...	xxij. đ. oƀ.
„ Joħe fił Ade Capp̃li	... ...	ij. ꝭ. vij. đ.
„ Rĩco fił Elene ...	... ...	xxij. đ. oƀ.
„ Roǥo Short ...	... ...	ij. ꝭ. iiij. đ.
„ Roƀto del Milne	... ...	xvj. đ. qᵃ.
„ Ađ fił Ade ...	... ...	ij. ꝭ. iiij. đ.
„ Roǥo le Mayresone	... ...	xx. đ.
„ Adam fił Wiłłi	... ...	xiiij. đ. oƀ.
„ Alañ fił Wiłłi ...	... ...	xij. đ.
„ Roƀto del Shaghe	... ...	v. ꝭ.
„ Joħe de Orełł ...	... ...	v. ꝭ.
„ Joħe fflour ...	... ...	v. ꝭ.
„ Roǥ de Boltoñ ...	... ...	v. ꝭ.
„ Rĩco le ffermon	... ...	xj. đ. qᵃ.

Smᵃ. liiij. ꝭ. pƀ.

Ayntre
[*Aintree*]

Đ Henr̃ de Athertoñ	... ...	iij. ꝭ. x. đ. oƀ. qᵃ.
„ Roǥo del Rydingge	...	xviij. đ.
„ Nicħo de Ayntr̃	... ...	xiij. đ. qᵃ.
„ Huǥ Tatelok ...	... ...	xj. đ.
„ Rĩco fił Wiłłi ...	... ...	ij. ꝭ. vj. đ.
„ Joħe de Nateby	... ...	xiij. đ.
„ Roƀto fił Roǥi ...	... ...	xij. đ.

Smᵃ. xij. ꝭ. pƀ.

Waltoñ
[*Walton-on-the-Hill*]

Ð Roɓto del Rys ...	...	...	iiij. ꝯ. vj. đ.
„ Wilto fił Madoci	...	...	iij. ꝯ. vj. đ.
„ Joħe del Brigge	...	...	ij. ꝯ.
„ Wilto de Penrich	...	...	iij. ꝯ.
„ Riõo le Wodeward	...	...	ij. ꝯ.
„ Riõo fił Joħis ...	...	...	iij. ꝯ.
„ Gilɓto fił Roɓti	...	...	iiij. ꝯ.
„ Riõo de Kekwike	...	...	ij. ꝯ.
„ Riõo Bullok	...	...	ij. ꝯ.
„ Wilto fił Roɓti ...	...	...	iij. ꝯ.
„ Joħe Welan	...	...	ij. ꝯ.

Smᵃ. xxxj. ꝯ. pɓ.

Westeley
[*West Leigh*]

Ð Wilto de Vrmestoñ	...	...	xx. đ.
„ Riõo de Bradeshagħ	...	...	ix. đ. qᵃ.
„ Alicia de Lathū	...	...	viij. đ ŏ.
„ Roᵹo Pose ...	...	...	viij. đ. ŏ.
„ Adam Becke ...	...	...	viij. đ. qᵃ.
„ Roɓto Graybred	...	...	viij. đ. qᵃ.
„ Roɓto le Priest ...	...	...	v. ꝯ. j. đ. qᵃ.

Smᵃ. x. ꝯ. iiij. đ. pɓ.

Wynquik cū Hulm̃
[*Winwick with Hulme*]
[No names.]

Smᵃ Wapentacħ. iiij. ˣˣ xiiij. łi. x. ꝯ. vij. đ. oɓ. qᵃ. pɓ

Et cvij. ꝯ. de xᵃ. Burᵹ de Wygan ⁊ Liuerpol. pɓ.

Wapentachiū de Salfordshir

[HUNDRED OF SALFORD.]

Salford
[*Salford*]

D Adam Irnefot	...	...	ij. s.
„ Johe de Oldefeld	...	...	ij. s.
„ Thom̃ de Pilkyntoñ	...	...	xvj. d.
;„ Wilto Tinctore	...	...	xvj. d.
„ Adam fit Henr̃	...	...	xvj. d.
„ Johe de Johe de Pilkyntoñ [*sic*]			xvj. d.
„ Thom̃ fit Galfri	...	...	iij. s. iij. d.
„ Wilto fit Thom̃	..	...	iij. s. iij. d.
„ Adam de Penhiltoñ	...	...	iij. s.
„ Johe le Carter	...	...	iij. s. ij. d.

Sm. xxij. s. pb.

Blakerode
[*Blackrod*]

D Matho del Birches	...	...	ij. s. viij. d.
„ Johe de Grimefford	...	...	xj. d.
„ Johe fit Henr̃	...	...	xvj. d.
„ Rico Mariot	...	...	xij. d.
„ Hug̃ le Coup	...	...	xiij. d.
„ Wilto del Hult	...	...	ij. s.

Sm. ix. s. pb.

Radecliue
[*Radcliffe*]

D Wilto fit Agñ	...	...	iij. s. j. d.
,, Alañ de Bradeshagh	...	...	iij. s. j. d.
„ Rico Letissone	...	...	ij. s. j. d.
„ Wilto de Grenehurst	...	...	ij. s. j. d.
„ Alex fit Henr̃	...	...	xvj. d.
„ Henr̃ le Taillor	...	...	x. d.
„ Adam Knot	...	...	x. d.

Sm. xiij. s. iiij. d. pb.

Chadertoñ
[*Chadderton*]

Ɖ Margia relicta Wilti de Chadre-toñ	... ...	ij. s. vj. đ.
„ Robto fil Helewys	... ...	xxiij. đ.
„ Adam fil Amie	... ...	xvj. đ.
„ Henr de Boultoñ	... ...	ix. s. viij. đ.
„ Rico de Okedeñ	... ...	ij. s. ij. đ.
„ Rico Shakelok	... ...	xiiij. đ.
„ Rico fil Henr	... ...	xij. đ.
„ Adam de Scolecrofte	... ...	xv. đ.

Smᵃ. xxj. s. pb.

Stretford
[*Stretford*]

Ɖ Hugõe Emnesone	... .	xvij. đ. ob.
„ Adam fil Thom	... ...	xvj. đ.
„ Rico Derlinge	... ...	xvij. đ. qᵃ.
„ Robto fil Henr	... ...	xvj. đ. ob. qᵃ.
„ Matilt relicta Wilti	... ...	ij. s. vij. đ. ob.
„ Johe Molendinar	... ...	v. s.
„ Rico fil Margie	... ...	v. s.
„ Johe fil Thom	... ...	ij. s.
„ Rico fil Thom	... ...	xxj. đ.

Smᵃ. xxij. s. pb.

Butterworth
[*Butterworth*]

Ɖ Rico de Byroun	... ...	v. s. viij. đ. ob.
„ Adam de Belefeld	... ...	v. s. vij. đ. ob.
„ Adã de Turnagh	... ...	ij. s.
„ Wilto le Wilde	... ...	xxiij. đ.
„ Henr de Belefeld	... ...	ix. đ.
„ Henr de Buttworth	... ...	ij. s.

Smᵃ. xviij. s. pb.

Ruyton
[*Royton*]

Ɖ Rog fil Johanne	... ...	ij. s.
„ Adam le ffaukonner	... ...	xvj. đ.

D Thom̃ de Prestewich ... ... ij. s.
„ Roḡo fit Thom̃ ... ... xvj. d.
„ Wilto de Ruytoñ ... ... xij. d.
„ Ad̄ Molend̄ ... ... xvj. d
„ Robto le ffaukonner ... ... xij. d

Sm̃ª. x. s. pb.

Cromton

[*Crompton*]

D Johe de Chethm ... ... ij. s.
„ Emma relicta Thom̃ ... ij. s. viij. d
„ Wills fit Elene ... xvj. d
„ Ratto de Gartesside ... ij. s.
„ Roḡo fit Johis ... xij. d
„ Henr̃ de Clegge ... xij. d
„ Adam del Wroo ... xij. d
„ Thom̃ del Wroo ... xij. d

Sm̃ª. xij. s. pt.

Oldom

[*Oldom*]

D Huḡ le Crouther ... ... v. s.
„ Johe de Holm ... ... iij. s.
„ Robto de Cromptoñ ... ... iij. s.
„ Henr̃ del Legh ... ... xvj. d.
„ Adam del ffairhalghes ... ... xij. d.
„ Wilto de Oldom ... ... xij. d.
„ Robto de Sholghre ... ... xij. d.
„ Rico de Grenacres ... ... xij. d.

Sm̃ª. xvj. s. iiij. d. pb.

Roynton

[*Rivington*]

D Robto de Pilkintoñ ... ... iij. s.
„ Ad̄ fit Robti ... ... xij. d
„ Wilto de Brodehurst ... ... xij. d

Ð Wilło de Gameleslegħ ... xij. đ.
   „   Wilło de Gameleslegħ senioř... xij. đ.
   „   Joħe de Erlegħ ... ... xij. đ.
   „   Joħe fił Mabilł ... ... xx. đ.

Sm^a. x. ʒ. pɓ.

Redicħ
[*Reddish*]

Ð Jorđ fił Joħis ... ... xxij. đ.
   „   Roɓto le Taillour ... ... xxj. đ.
   „   Henř Cłico ... ... xviij. đ.
   „   Joħe de Langelegħ ... ... xxj. đ.
   „   Joħe de Redicħ ... ... ix. đ.
   „   Matħo fił Emne ... ... xiiij. đ.
   „   Adam fił Ede ... ... xiiij. đ. oɓ.
   „   Aleẋ del Knolł ... ... ix. ʒ. iiij. đ.
   „   Joħe del Egge ... ... viij. đ. oɓ.

Sm^a. xx. ʒ. pɓ.

Asshtoñ
[*Ashton under Line.*]

Ð Joħe de Asshtoñ ... ... v. ʒ. vij. đ.
   „   Ričo de Claideñ ... ... ij. ʒ. v. đ.
   „   Hugõe del Heye ... ... xx. đ.
   „   Aleẋ de Chadertoñ ... ... xx. đ.
   „   Henř de Mostoñ ... ... xviij. đ. oɓ.
   „   Thoɱ de Shepelegħ ... ... xix. đ.
   „   Adam fił Eue ... ... xij. đ. oɓ.
   „   Ričo le Reue ... ... xx. đ.
   „   Roɓto fił Riči ... ... iiij. ʒ.
   „   Adam Twynteringe ... ... iiij. ʒ.
   „   Henř de Waterhouses ... ... viij. ʒ.
   „   Wilło de Rylegħ ... ... iiij. ʒ.
   „   Roɓto de Bartoñ ... ... vj. ʒ.
   „   Ričo de Bromyhurst ... ... iiij. ʒ.
   „   Roɓto Tvdy ... ... vj. ʒ. ix. đ.

Sm^a. liiij. ʒ. pɓ.

Lostok cū Romworth
[Lostock with Rumworth]

Đ Adam Coler	...	...	...	xx. đ.
„ Johe fił Riči	...	...	...	xvj. đ.
„ Wilło de Aynesworth	...		...	xij. đ.
„ Johe fił Robti	...	...		iiij. ȿ.
„ Alex del Birches		...	...	ij. ȿ.
„ Henr̃ de Windhull		...	...	ij. ȿ.
Wilł fił Robti	...		...	ij. ȿ.

Sm̄ª. xiiij. ȿ. pb̄.

Spotlond
[Spotland]

Đ Ričo de Baumford	...	...	iij. ȿ.
„ Galfr̃ le Hayward	...	...	xvj. đ.
„ Robto de Heghlegh	...	...	iij. ȿ.
„ Johe de Wolstonholm̄	...	...	iiij. ȿ.
„ Wilło le Wolfe	...	...	ix. ȿ. iiij. đ.
„ Robto le Haiward		...	ij. ȿ. j. đ.
„ Galfr̃ de Heghlegh	...	...	v. ȿ.
„ Adam de Bradelegh	...	...	iij. ȿ. iij. đ.
„ Wilło de Craweshagh	...	...	iij. ȿ.

Sm̄ª. xxxiiij. ȿ. pb̄.

Bury
[Bury]

Đ Margꝯia de Radecliue	...	...	vij. ȿ.
„ Johe de ffenton̄	...	...	iij. ȿ.
„ Thom̄ de Werberton̄	...	...	ij. ȿ. iiij. đ.
„ Wilło Kay	...	...	iij. ȿ. iiij. đ.
„ Ričo de Notehogh	...	...	ij. ȿ.
„ Ađ fił Robti	...	...	vij. ȿ.
„ Johe fił Mathi	...	...	vij. ȿ.
„ Rogꝯ de Walmeslegh	...	...	ij. ȿ.
„ Wilło de Bury	...	...	ij. ȿ. iiijđ.
„ Johe de Routesthorn̄	...	...	ij. ȿ.
„ Wilło le Mordrmer	...	...	ij. ȿ.

Sm̄ª. xl. ȿ. pb̄.

D

Hunresfeld
[Hundersfield]

Ᵽ Henr̄ de Wordhult	...	...	iiij. s. v. đ. qᵃ.
„ Ađ de Birdeshult	...	...	iij. s. vj. đ. qᵃ.
„ Wilto del Shore	...	...	iiij. s. viij. đ.
„ Matħo de Kirkeshagħ	...	...	iiij. s. ij. đ. qᵃ.
„ Cristiañ de Bukkelegħ		...	iiij. s. ij. đ. qᵃ.
„ Henr̄ Tyrry	...	...	iiij. s. vj. đ.
„ Henr̄ de Slaueden̄	...	...	xij. đ.
„ Adam de Hegħlegħ	...	...	xviij. đ.
„ Roḡo ded [*sic*] Ernelegh		...	xij. đ.
„ Wilt Ony	...	...	xij. đ.

Smᵃ. xxx. s. pb̄.

Castelton
[Castleton]

Ᵽ Nicħo del Slak	...	...	ij. s. j. đ. ob̄.
„ Roḡo de Birdeshult	...	...	xx. đ. qᵃ.
„ Henr̄ del Slak	...	...	xx. đ. qᵃ.
„ Joħe de Kirkedale	...	...	iiij. s.
„ Joħe de Birdeshult	...	...	x. đ. ob̄.
„ Joħe de Holden̄	...	...	x. đ. ob̄.
„ Nicħo de Castelton̄	...	...	x. đ. ob̄.
„ Wilto le Mercer	...	...	x. đ. ob̄.

Smᵃ. xiij. s. pb̄.

Wythinton
[Withington]

Ᵽ Roḡo de Barlowe	...	...	xvij. s. iiij. đ.
„ Thoм̃ fit Jorđi	...	...	xvij. s. iiij. đ.
„ Joħe de Wythinton̄	...	...	xij. s.
„ Rič̃o fit Rob̄ti de Hyde		...	xij. s. iiij. đ.
„ Matħo Dauy	...	...	ij. s. ix. đ.
„ Joħe fit Thoм̃	...	...	ij. s vj. đ.
„ Henr̄ del Egge	...	...	ij. s. vj. đ.
„ Thoм̃ del Egge	...	...	ij. s. vj. đ.

Smᵃ. lxix. s. iij. đ. pb̄.

Mamcestr̃
[*Manchester*]

Đ Adam de Radecliue	...	...	iij. s̃. ij. đ.
„ Henr̃ Butt̃rinde	...	...	iij. s̃. ob̃.
„ Rog̃o fit Hug̃	...		xxj. đ.
„ Adam fit Rīcĩi	...	...	xv. đ.
„ Joħe Cissor̃	...	...	x. đ.
„ Adam Gore	...	...	xj. đ.
„ Wilto de Chorletoñ	...		ij. s̃.
„ Robto de Briggelegħ	...		ij. s̃.
„ Hugõe del Hult	..	...	xv. đ. ob̃.
„ Thom̃ de Bexwik	...	...	iij. s̃. vij. đ. ob̃.
„ Henr̃ de Oldom	. .	...	iiij. s̃. iij. đ.
„ Alex̃ le Widousone	...	...	iij. s̃. j. đ.
„ Robto del Hirne	...	...	xij. đ.
„ Robto fit Hugõis	...	...	x. s̃.
„ Alex̃ fit Ede	...	...	iij. s̃.
„ Joħe fit Joħis le Hunte		...	iiij. s̃. ix. đ. ob̃.

Sm^a. xlvj. s̃. pb̃.

Bartoñ
[*Barton upon Irwell*]

Đ Thom̃ de Hulm̃	...	...	iiij. s̃.
„ Rĩco de Crosseshagħ	...	...	iiij. s̃. ij. đ. ob̃.
„ Rog̃ de Westelegħ	...	...	ij. s̃. ij. đ.
„ Rĩco le Walsħ	...	...	ij. s̃. viij. đ.
„ Adam fit Rog̃i	...	...	xiiij. đ.
„ Thom̃ Braybon	...	...	xij. đ.
„ Gilbto de Bromihurst	...	...	v. s̃.
„ Rĩco de Neweham	...	...	v. s̃.
„ Joħe del Croft	...	...	ij. s̃.
„ Wilto de Brunlegħ	...	...	ix. đ. ob̃.
„ Wilto de Brounlegħ	...	...	ij. s̃.

Sm^a. xxx. s̃. pb̃.

Hetoñ cũ Haliwelle
[*Heaton with Halliwell*]

Đ Wilto Barfot	...	...	xij. đ.
„ Joħe de Asphult	...	...	xij. đ.

D 2

Đ Riĉo fił Wilłi ... ... xij. đ.

„ Henr̃ de Brodefeld ... ... xij. đ.

„ Adam de Whithalgh ... ... xij. đ.

„ Johe le Wolf ... ... v. s̃.

„ Meurik del Brodefeld ... ... xij. đ.

„ Adam de Ecclis ... ... xij. đ.

„ Roƀto de Hetoñ ... ... xij. đ.

Smª. xiij. s̃. pƀ.

Middeltoñ
[*Middleton*]

Đ Adam de Hopwode ... ... viij. s̃. iiij. đ.

„ Elia de Aynesworth ... ... v. s̃. ij. đ.

„ Alañ de Brounehilł ... ... v. s̃.

„ Adam de Boultoñ ... ... ij. s̃.

„ Wilło de Longelegh ... ... viij. s̃.

„ Henr̃ de Stakehilł ... ... iij. s̃.

„ Gilƀto de Chorltoñ ... ... ij. s̃. vj. đ.

„ Riĉo de Hengandechadre ... iij. s̃.

„ Johe de Kirkeyard ... ... iij. s̃.

Smª. xl. s̃. pƀ.

Pilkyntoñ
[*Pilkington*]

Đ Roƀto le Gateler ... ... xvij. đ. oƀ.

„ Roĝ le Suker ... ... xviij. đ.

„ Roĝo de Neweham ... ... xvij. đ.

„ Johe del Birches ... ... xxj. đ. oƀ.

„ Roƀto de Ecclis ... ... xij. s̃. vij. đ.

„ Henr̃ fił Gilƀti ... ... xviij. đ.

„ Roƀto del Rodes ... ... xvj. đ.

„ Adam Dyemogh ... ... xj. đ.

„ Johe del Blakebrok ... ... ix. đ.

Smª. xxiij. s̃. iiij. đ. pƀ.

Totyngton
[*Tottington*]

Đ Adam de Routhesthorñ ... iij. s̃.

„ Roƀto del Ewode ... ... iij. s̃. iiij. đ.

Ð Jordañ fił Roɓti   ...   ...   iij. ſ.
,, Matilł de Grenehalgħ ...   ...   iij. ſ.
,, Adam de Routhesthorn Junioř   xx. đ.

Smª. xiiij. ſ. pɓ.

Chethªm
[*Cheetham*]
Ð Roɓto del Birches   `...   ...   ij. ſ.
,, Adam del Held   ...   ...   xviij. đ.
,, Adam del Egge   ...   ...   xij. đ.

Smª. iiij. ſ. vj. đ. pɓ.

Penhiltoñ
[*Pendleton*]
Ð Henř de Boltoñ   ...   ...   xx. đ.
,, Riĉo del Wode   ...   ...   xx. đ.
,, Roɓto de Penhiltoñ   ...   ...   xviij. đ.
,, Thoħ de Penhiltoñ   ...   ...   xij. đ.
,, Joħe le Łorde ...   .   xij. đ.
,, Henř Cłico   ...   ...   ij. ſ.
,, Riĉo de Linhales   •...   ...   ij. ſ.
,, Wiłło le Minour   ...   ...   xij. đ.
,, Ađ le Hayward   ...   ...   xx. đ.

Smª. xiij. ſ. vj. đ. pɓ.

Boultoñ
[*Bolton-le-Moors*]
Ð Joħe de Thonge   ...   ...   ij. ſ. viij. đ.
,, Adam de Esherwode ...   ...   ij. ſ.
,, Roɓto de Cromptoñ   ...   ...   ij. ſ.
,, Wiłł de Thonge   ..   ...   xx. đ.
,, Thoħ del Hułł   ...   ...   ij. ſ.
,, Adam fił Thoħ   ...   ...   xx. đ.
,, Joħe de Sharples   ...   ...   iiij. ſ.
,, Nicħo del Wode   ...   ...   xiiij. đ.
,, Henř de Esherwode   ...   ...   xiiij. đ.
,, Riĉo Carpenẗ ...   .   x. đ.
., Thoħ le Bouker   ...   ...   x. đ.

Smª. xx. đ. pɓ.

Halghtoñ
[*West Houghton*]

Đ Wilto de Rylondes	...	...	iij. s.
„ Johe de Vrmestoñ	...	...	xviij. đ.
„ Robto de Chaydok	...	...	xx. đ. qᵃ.
„ Robto de Rylondes	...	...	xviij. đ. ob.
„ Adam de Romworthe	...	...	xx. đ. qᵃ.
„ Johe le Sire	...	...	xij. đ.
„ Johe Turnour	...	...	xij. đ.
„ Rĩco le Sire	...	...	x. đ.
„ John le Broune	...	...	x. đ.

Smᵃ. xiij. s. j. đ. pb.

Clifton
[*Clifton*]

Đ Rĩco le Reve	...	...	xij. đ.
„ Elia de Penhulbury	...	...	xvj. đ.
„ Adam le Workeslegh	...	...	íj. s. ij. đ.
„ Alex fit Rogi	...	...	xviij. đ.

Smᵃ. vj. s. pb.

Harewode
[*Harwood*]

Đ Wilto de Haliwalle	...	...	xix. đ.
„ Wilto Somre	...	...	xvij. đ.
„ Henr̃ Doggesone	...	...	xx. đ.
„ Alaln fit Henr̃	...	...	ij. s.
„ Henr̃ de Bradeshagh	...	...	xvj. đ.
„ Rogo le Kirkemon	...	...	xiiij. đ.
„ Rĩco fit Johis	...	...	xij. đ.
„ Wilto Kimbbok	...	...	xj. đ.

Smᵃ. xj. s. j. đ. pb.

fflixtoñ
[*Flixton*]

Đ Rĩco le Valentin	...	...	ij. s. viij. đ. ob.
„ Henr̃ del Wode	...	...	xxij. đ.
„ Wilto del Berne	...	...	ij. s. viij. đ.

Ᵽ Riĉo fił Roƀi ... ... ij. ꝛ.

„ Joħe de Botħn ... ... xix. đ. oƀ.

Smᵃ. x. ꝛ. x. đ. pƀ.

Penhulbury
[*Pendlebury*]

Ᵽ Huḡ de Athirtoñ ... ... xxiij. đ.

„ Henꞃ ffabꞃ ... ... ix. đ.

„ Wiłło fił Thom̃... ... ... x. đ.

„ Joħe de Penhulton ... ... ix. đ.

„ Aleẍ fił Thom̃ ... ... ix. đ.

Smᵃ. v. ꝛ. pƀ.

Hultoñ
[*Hulton*]

Ᵽ Henꞃ de Workesległ ... ... iij. ꝛ. j. đ. oƀ.

„ Wałto fił Gilƀti ... ... xix. đ. oƀ.

„ Riĉo de Cleworthe ... ... xvij. đ. oƀ.

„ Riĉo le Drake ... ... xiiij. đ.

„ Roƀto le Wyse ... ... xj. đ.

„ Thom̃ Huddemogħ ... ... xj. đ. oƀ.

„ Riĉo le Kempe ... ... x. đ.

Smᵃ. x. ꝛ. j. đ. pƀ.

Workeslegħ
[*Worsley*]

Ᵽ Riĉo de Workeslegħ ... ... vj. ꝛ.

„ Roƀto de Workeslegħ ... ... ij. ꝛ. ij. đ. oƀ.

„ Henꞃ de Shakreslegħ ... ... ij. ꝛ. j. đ. oƀ.

„ Hugoñ fił Joħis ... ... xvj. đ.

„ Adam Silcoksone ... ... xij. đ.

„ Riĉ le Cartwright ... ... xij. đ.

„ Wiłło de Chaidok ... ... xij. đ.

„ Riĉo le Nailer ... ... xij. đ.

„ Wiłło fił Anđr ... ... iij. ꝛ.

„ Roḡo de Haselhurst ... ... xvj. đ.

Smᵃ. xx. ꝛ. pƀ.

Prestewich
[*Prestwich*]

Đ Adam le Hirdmon	...	...	xxj. đ. oƀ.
„ Joħe le Barũ	...	...	iij. ȿ. iiij. đ.
„ Henr̃ fit Thom̃	...	...	iij. ȿ. ij. đ. oƀ.
„ Wilło le Couherd	...	...	xvij. đ. oƀ.
„ Wilło fit Elie	...	...	xvij. đ. oƀ.
„ Galfr le Coke	...	...	xvj. đ. oƀ.
„ Roƀto fit Gille	...	...	xvj. đ. oƀ.

Smª. xiiij. ȿ. pƀ.

Turtoñ
[*Turton*]

Đ Wilło de Broxhop̃	...	...	ij. ȿ. vj. đ.
„ Wilło Hawelł	...	...	xxij. đ. oƀ.
„ Roƀto le Coke	...	...	xvij. đ. oƀ.
„ Joħne de Birchewoode	...	ij. ȿ. iiij. đ.
„ Adam le Wolfe	...	...	xxj. đ.
„ Roḡo fit Jorđ	...	...	xij. đ.
„ Roğ del Clif	...	...	x. đ.
„ Hugōe de Eggeworthe	...	xv. đ.

Smª. xiij. ȿ. pƀ.

Hetoñ Norreis
[*Heaton Norris*]

Đ Joħe Blewet	...	...	ij. ȿ. ij. đ.
„ Wilło le Prestesmon	...	...	xxj. đ.
„ Adam Page	...	...	iiij. ȿ. j. đ.
„ Wilło le Coke	...	...	xxj. đ. oƀ.
„ Wilło del Brigge.	...	...	viij. đ. oƀ.
„ Roƀto del Boure	...	...	xij. đ.
„ Roƀto le Norreis	...	...	xij. đ.

Smª. xij. ȿ. vj. đ. pƀ.

Eggewortħ
[*Edgeworth*]

Đ Joħe Entwisell	...	...	iiij. ȿ. ij. đ.
„ Roƀto fit Elie	...	...	xij. đ.
„ Roğ de Eggewortħ	...	...	xvj. đ.

Ð Joħe de Birchewode ... ... xij. đ.

„ Elia de Quernedoñ ... ... x. đ.

„ Matħo del Roche ... ... xiiij. đ.

Smᵃ. ix. ⁸. vj.ʼđ. pᵬ.

Vrmestoñ

[*Urmston*]

Ð Joħe de Trafford ... ... iiij. ⁸. iij. đ.

„ Galfꝝ de Vrmestoñ ... ... ij. ⁸. vj. đ.

„ Roᵬto de Glasebrok ... ... xij. đ.

„ Riĉo fił Henꝝ ... ... xij. đ.

„ Adam de Irwelham ... ... xij. đ.

Smᵃ. ix. ⁸. ix. đ. pᵬ.

Asphułł

[*Aspull*]

Ð Henꝝ de Asphułł ... ... iij. ⁸.

„ Henꝝ del fforde ... ... xij. đ.

„ Roᵬto del Mylne ... ... xvj. đ.

„ Hugōe de Orełł ... ... xj. đ.

„ Joħe del fforde ... ... x. đ.

Smᵃ. vij. ⁸. pᵬ.

Ð Roᵬto de Bulhalgħ p catałł suis
in diu)sis locis ... ... vj. ⁸. viij. đ.

Smᵃ. vj. ⁸. viij. đ.

Chorletoñ

[*Chorlton*]

Ð Roᵬto de Trafford ... ... iij. ⁸. iiij. đ.

Smᵃ. iij. ⁸. iiij. đ.

Smᵃ. Wapentacħ. xxxix. łi. iiij. ⁸. pᵬ.

Wapentacħ de Leplondsħir.

[HUNDRED OF LEYLAND.]

Chernok Richt
[*Charnock Richard*]

Đ Ričo de Haliwalle Caꝑlto	...	ij. ઙ. iiij. đ.
„ Wilŧo del Rydinge	... ...	ij. ઙ. iiij. đ.
„ Roɓto fit Joħis ...	... ...	ij. ઙ.
„ Joħe de Derbishiř	... ...	xij. đ.
„ Roɓto de Wallehulŧ	... ...	xij. đ.
„ Henř le Colt	... ...	ij. ઙ.
„ Adam de Amoundrenesse	...	xvj. đ.
„ Henř del Hoŧm	... ...	xij. đ.
„ Rađo Trigge	... ..	xiij. đ.
„ Adam de Asshhou	... ...	xij. đ.
„ Joħe del Ridinge	... ...	xij. đ.
„ Ađ fit Thom̃	... ...	xij. đ.

Sm ͣ. xvij. ઙ. j. đ. pɓ.

Parua Hole
[*Little Hoole*]

Đ Nicħo le Botiller	... ...	iij. ઙ.
„ Ranulpħ de Singelton ...	...	iij. ઙ.
„ Joħe Justice	... ...	xij. đ.
„ Ričo Brawles	... ...	xij. đ.
„ Wilŧo de ffisshwik	... ...	xij. đ.

Sm ͣ. ix. ઙ. pɓ.

Becanshou cū Heskeitħ
[*Becconsall with Hesketh*]

Đ Adam de Heskaitħ	... ...	ij. ઙ.
„ Roɓto fit Henř ...	... ...	xij. đ.
„ Wilŧo fit Wilŧ ...	... ...	xij. đ.
„ Adam Mody	... ...	xij. đ.
„ Roɓto fit Joħis ...	... ...	xij. đ.
„ Wilŧo fit Wilŧi Senioř ...	...	xij. đ.

Đ Wilło fił Joħis ...　　...　　...　xij. đ.
„ Joħe fil Riči　...　　...　　...　xij. đ.
„ Thoñ fił Henř ...　　...　　...　xij. đ.

Smᵃ. x. ꝯ. pƀ.

Andretoñ
[*Anderton*]
Đ Wilło de Andretoñ　　...　　. . iij. ꝯ.
„ Henř le Grayne　　...　　...　iij. ꝯ.
„ Wilło del ffritħ ...　　...　　...　xvj. đ.
„ Wilło fił Thoñ　　...　　...　xij. đ. oƀ.
„ Wilło fił Jorđi ...　　...　　...　xij. đ.
„ Thoñ Lyghtfot　　...　　...　xij. đ.

Smᵃ. x. ꝯ. iij, đ. oƀ. pƀ.

Brethertoñ
[*Bretherton*]
Đ Adam Banastř ...　　...　　...　iij. ꝯ.
„ Roƀto de Thorꝑ　　...　　...　ij. ꝯ. viij. đ.
„ Wilł Banastř　...　　...　　...　ij. ꝯ.
„ Joħe Banastř　...　　.,　　...　ij. ꝯ. viij. đ.
„ Joħe de Tarletoñ　　...　　...　ij. ꝯ.
„ Joħe del Car　...　　...　　...　ij. ꝯ.
„ Wilło de Haselingdeñ ...　　...　ij. ꝯ. viij. đ.
„ Joħe de Rugħford　　...　　...　ij. ꝯ.
„ Joħe Carpenꝑ　...　　...　　...　ij. ꝯ.
„ Ričo de Heskyn　　...　　...　ij. ꝯ.
„ Wilł fił Thoñ ...　　...　　...　xij. đ.
„ Ričo del Lache ...　　...　　...　xij. đ.

Smᵃ. xxv. ꝯ. pƀ.

Hogħwike cū ffaringtoñ
[*Howick with Farington*]
Đ Wilło de ffaringtoñ　　...　　...　iij. ꝯ.
„ Thoñ de Noteshaghe ...　　...　iij. ꝯ.
„ Wilło de Hogħwike　...　　...　ij. ꝯ. vj. đ.
„ Wilło fił Ecke ...　　...　　..　xij. đ.
„ Joħe fił Rič　...　　...　　...　iij. ꝯ.

Đ Henr̃ fil Roḡi de ffaringtoñ ... iij. ˢ. vj. đ.

„ Johe de ffarintoñ ... ... iij. ˢ.

„ Wilł de Buddeworth ... ij. ˢ.

„ Joħ fil Isabelł ... ... ij. ˢ.

Smᵃ. xxiij. ˢ. pb.

Claitoñ

[*Clayton le Woods*]

Đ Adam de Claitoñ ... ... v. ˢ.

„ Johe fil Thoᷓ ... ... xviij. đ.

„ Gilbto de Swynney ... iij. ˢ.

„ Warino fil Thoᷓ ... ... ij. ˢ.

„ Robto de Clayton ... ... ij. ˢ.

„ Johe Lombe ... ... ij. ˢ.

„ Johe de la More ... ... ij. ˢ.

„ Henr̃ le Webester ... ... xij. đ.

Smᵃ. xviij. s. vj. đ. pb.

Wythinhulł cū Rotheleswortħ

[*Withnell with Rothelsworth*]

Đ Adam del Bergħ ... ... ij. ˢ.

„ Adam fil Roḡi ... ... xvj. đ.

„ Roḡo de Rotheleswortħ ... xxj. đ.

„ Wilło Molenđ ... ... x. đ.

„ Riõo fil Robi de Withinhulł ... xvj. đ.

„ Riõo Same ... ... ix. đ.

Smᵃ. viij. ˢ. pb.

Heth Chernok

[*Heath Charnock*]

Đ Riõo le Perpount ... ... xviij. đ.

„ Henr̃ de Asshou ... ... xvj. đ.

„ Adam fil Henr̃ ... ... xx. đ.

„ Wilło del Strete ... ... xx. đ.

„ Adam del ffairhurst ... ... xij. đ.

„ Johe del Slak ... ... ij. ˢ. iiij. đ.

„ Roḡo del Halle ... ... iiij. ˢ.

„ Huḡ le Milner ... ... ix. đ.

Ð Riĉo fit Raði ... ... ix. đ.

„ Wilło le Taillour ... ... xij. đ.

Smᵃ. xvj. ʃ. pƀ.

Hotoñ

[*Hutton*]

Ð Roƀto fit Roği de Bradeforð ... ij. ʃ.

„ Roƀto fit Coci ... ... xvj. đ.

„ Henᵳ Bermantilł ... ... xxij. đ.

„ Wilło Cłico ... ... xij. đ.

„ Joħ fit Anoᵳ ... ... xij. đ.

„ Alañ fit Abel ... ... x. đ.

„ Adam del Snape ... ... xvj. đ.

„ Wilło Gederpeny ... ... xij. đ.

„ Thoɱ fit Joħ ... ... xij. đ.

„ Henᵳ fit Patricii ... ... xij. đ.

„ Wilło Bretoñ ... ... xij. đ.

Smᵃ. xiii. ʃ. iiij. đ. pƀ.

Hogħtoñ

[*Hoghton*]

Ð Riĉo de Hogħtoñ ... ... ij. ʃ.

„ Joħe de Hogħtoñ ... ... xx. đ.

„ Wałto le Carter ... ... xiij. đ.

„ Wilło Spendeloue ... ... ix. đ.

„ Henᵳ de Brundeñ ... ... ix. đ.

„ Henᵳ fit Henᵳ ... ... ix. đ.

Smᵃ. vij. ʃ. pƀ.

Moudeslegħ

[*Mawdesley*]

Ð Roƀto de Bisphᵃm ... ... ij. ʃ.

„ Joħe de Hole ... ... ij. ʃ.

„ Henᵳ fit Huğ ... ... ij. ʃ.

„ Joħe de Birkyn ... ... xij. đ.

„ Riĉo fit Að ... ... ij. ʃ.

„ Roğ fit Huğ ... ... xij. đ.

„ Wariñ Banastᵳ ... ... xvij. đ.

Đ Adam fił Huḡ ...   .   ij. s̍.
„ Adam de Depedale   ...   ...   ij. s̍.

Sm^a. xv. s̍. v. đ. p̄b̄.

Crostoñ
[*Croston*]

Đ Joħe fił Wariñ ...   .   xx. đ.
„ Wilło fił Joħis ...   .   xiiij. đ.
„ Wilło fił Roƀti ...   .   ij. s̍. ij. đ.
„ Rañ fił Geruas̍ ...   .   ij. s̍.
„ Adam le fferour   ...   ...   ij. s̍.
„ Wilło de Prestoñ   ...   ...   xv. đ.
„ Wilło fił Rič̄i ...   .   xiiij. đ.
„ Thom̄ de Bulk ...   .   ij. s̍.
„ Rič̄ fił Roƀi   ...   .   ij. s̍.

Sm^a. xv. s̍. v. đ. p̄b̄.

Longetoñ
[*Longton*]

Đ Thom̄ fił Matilł   ...   ...   iij. s̍.
„ Wilło fił Thom̄ ...   .   iij. s̍.
„ Joħe fił Roƀti ...   .   ij. s̍.
„ Adam de Caterhale   ...   ...   ij. s̍.
„ Wilło del Halle   ...   ...   xviij. đ.
„ Petro de Riselegħ   ...   ...   xviij. đ.
„ Thom̄ fił Roƀti ...   .   xviij. đ.
„ Adam de Ballepulł   ...   ...   xviij. đ.
„ Wilło fił Roƀi ...   .   xviij. đ.
„ Joħe del Berne ...   .   xvj. đ.
„ Rič̄o fił Ađ   ...   .   xvj. đ.
„ Wilło faƀr   ...   .   xij. đ.
„ Warino de Mora   ...   ...   xvj. đ.
„ Roḡo fił Joħis ...   .   xvj. đ.
„ Roƀto Busshelł ...   .   xviij. đ.
„ Joħe fił Henr̄ ...   .   xviij. đ.
„ Adam fił Roƀti...   ...   ...   xiij. đ.
„ Huḡ Busshell ...   .   xij. đ.

Sm^a. xxix. s̍. p̄b̄.

Penworthᵃm

[*Penwortham*]

D҃ Joħe de Cliffe ... ... ij. �. iiij. đ.

„ Wilło del Scales ... ... x. đ.

„ Thom̃ de Twershagħ ... ... xij. đ.

„ Ric̃o de Roley ... . xij. đ.

„ Joħe Kaynok ... ... xviij. đ.

„ Adam Russelł ... ... xij. đ.

„ Aleẋ de Marehalgħ ... ... xvj. đ.

Smᵃ. ix. ꝰ. pḃ.

Wheltoñ cū Hepay

[*Wheelton with Heapey*]

D҃ Ric̃o del fforde ... ... xviij. đ.

„ Hug̃ del Kulnekar ... ... iij. ꝰ.

„ Adam de Shakerlegħ ... ... xviij. đ.

„ Adam fił Joħis ... ... xij. đ.

„ Adam Mody ... ... xij. đ.

„ Wilło de Withenhulł ... ... xij. đ.

Smᵃ. ix. ꝰ. pḃ.

Tarletoñ

[*Tarleton*]

D҃ Ric̃o fił Joħis ... ... ij. ꝰ.

„ Johanna de Graystok ... ... ij. ꝰ.

„ Roḃto fił Ađ ... ... xviij. đ.

„ Ric̃o fił Wilłi ... ... xx. đ.

„ Adam de Thwershagħ ... ... ij. ꝰ.

„ Joħe fił Wilłi ... ... xx. đ.

„ Joħe fił Wilłi Junioꝛ ... ... iij. ꝰ.

„ Joħe le ffermon ... ... iij. ꝰ.

„ Adam fił Wilłi ... ... ij. ꝰ.

„ Roḃto de Miłton ... ... ij. ꝰ.

Smᵃ. xx. ꝰ. x. đ. pḃ.

Perbald

[*Parbold*]

D҃ Lucia de Perbald ... ... ij. ꝰ.

„ Stepħo fił Simoñ ... ... xij. đ.

Đ Joħe fit Riĉi ... ... xij. đ.

„ Henr̃ Rawe ... ... ij. ꝑ.

„ Wilł fit Hancok ... ... xij. đ.

„ Riĉo del Walle ... ... xij. đ.

„ Robto fabr ... ... xij. đ.

„ Wilł del Crok ... ... xij. đ.

Smᵃ. x. ꝑ. pb.

Rughford

[*Rufford*]

Đ Joħe de Heskaitħ ... ... v. ꝑ. viij. đ

„ Wilło de Rughford ... ... iiij. ꝑ. vj. đ.

„ Joħe Carpentar̃ ... ... xij. đ.

„ Joħe le Waterward ... ... v. ꝑ. vj. đ.

„ Robto de Horskar ... ... v. ꝑ.

Smᵃ. xx. ꝑ. viij. đ. pb.

Chorlegħ cū Bispham

[*Chorley with Bispham*]

Đ Huḡ de Kulm̃leghe ... ... xij. đ.

„ Adam fit Wilłi ... ... xv. đ.

„ Adam le Wodeward ... ... ij. ꝑ.

„ Roḡ fit Wilł ... ... ij. ꝑ.

„ Wilł Broun ... ... xx. đ.

„ Roḡ de Bispham ... ... ij. ꝑ. iiij. đ.

„ Simoñ de Skallayclogħ ... iij. ꝑ.

„ Joħe fit Elie ... ... ij. ꝑ. viij. đ.

„ Wilło fit Herberd ... ... ij. ꝑ.

„ Robto le Taillour ... ... ij. ꝑ.

„ Wilło fit Elie ... ... ij. ꝑ.

„ Thoñ de Bispham ... ... ij. ꝑ.

Smᵃ. xxiij. ꝑ. xj. đ. pb.

Standissħ cū Longetr̃

[*Standish with Langtree*]

Đ Joħe de Standissħ ... ... iiij. ꝑ.

„ Thoñ de Longetr̃ ... ... ij. ꝑ. viij. đ.

Ð Thom̃ de Ecclistoñ ... ... ij. s̃.

„ Roƀto de Pynyntoñ ... ... ij. s̃.

„ Wilto de Birlegħ ... ... xij. đ.

„ Henr̃ de Standissħ ... ... ij. s̃. vj. đ.

„ Roƀto de Derwalleshaghe ... iij. s̃.

„ Thom̃ del Mire ... ... ij. s̃.

„ Roƀto de Derbyshire ... ... ij. s̃. iiij. đ.

Sm̃ᵃ. xx. s̃. vj. đ. pƀ.

Coppehult cū Worthintoñ

[*Coppul with Worthington*]

Ð Wilto de Worthintoñ ... ... iij. s̃.

„ Joħe de Cophult ... ... iij. s̃.

„ Joħe de Chisenhale ... ... iiij. s̃.

„ Joħe de Derbyshire ... ... iiij. s̃.

„ Roğo de Chisenhale ... ... iij. s̃.

„ Adam le Taillour ... ... xvj. đ.

„ Wilto fit Roƀti ... ... iiij. s̃.

„ Roƀto de Prestecote ... ... ij. s̃.

„ Thom̃ de Vggenhale ... ... xvj. đ.

„ Henr̃ ffairweder ... ... xvj. đ.

Sm̃ᵃ. xxvij. s̃. pƀ.

Ecclistoñ cū Heskyn

[*Eccleston with Heskin*]

Ð Roƀto de Heskyn ... ... ij. s̃.

„ Ričo de Heskyn ... ... ij. s̃.

„ Roğ del Persones ... ... ij. s̃.

„ Wilto de Claitoñ ... ... iij. s̃.

„ Wilto de Armetridiñg ... ij. s̃.

„ Ađ fit Adam ... ... xij. đ.

„ Huğ le Presteson ... ... ij. s̃.

„ Thom̃ fit Riči ... ... iiij. s̃.

„ Henr̃ Carpentar̃ ... ... v. s̃.

„ Henr̃ del Wode ... ... xij. đ.

„ Thom̃ del Eues ... ... xij. đ.

E

D Wilło del Brokhouses ...   ...   xij. đ.

„ Adam Wympesone   ...   ...   xij. đ.

Smª. xxvij. ꞩ. pƀ.

Sheuintoñ
[*Shevington*]

D Rogꝰ de Hultoñ   ...   ...   xviij. đ.

„ Henr̄ de Hultoñ   ...   ...   xij. đ.

„ Henr̄ Carpenꝙ ...   .   xviij. đ.

„ Rico de Heye ...   .   xviij. đ.

„ Thom̄ Carpenꝙ ...   .   ij. ꞩ.

„ Robto de Prestecote   ...   ...   xij. đ.

„ Henr̄ Proudfot ...   .   v. ꞩ. iiij. đ.

„ Adam Kempe ...   .   xviij. đ.

„ Wilło Lemynge   ...   ...   xviij. đ.

Smª. xvj. đ. ix. đ. pƀ.

Hole Magnª
[*Much Hoole*]

D Thurstañ de Norťhlegh   ...   ij. ꞩ. iiij. đ.

„ Joħe de Croft   ...   .   ij. ꞩ.

„ Wilł fił Riči   ...   .   ij. ꞩ.

„ Joħe le Coke   ...   .   xviij. đ. oƀ.

„ Rico fił Joħis ...   .   ij. ꞩ.

„ Joħ de Burscogh   ...   ...   xvj. đ.

„ Joħe fił Riči   ...   .   xij. đ.

„ Rico fił Thom̄ ...   .   xij. đ.

„ Wilło de Pemƀton   ...   ...   xvj. đ.

Smª. xiiij. ꞩ. vj. đ. oƀ. pƀ.

Wrightintoñ
[*Wrightington*]

D Rico Banastr̄   ...   .   iiij. ꞩ. ij. đ.

„ Adam de Derbyshir̄   ...   ...   xij. đ.

„ Eđo de Riggeby   ...   ...   xxj. đ.

„ Simoñ de Wrightintoñ   ...   xviij. đ.

„ Alañ de Riggeby   ...   ...   xiiij. đ.

„ Robto del Clogh   ...   ...   xiiij. đ.

Đ Henř de Tunlegħ ... ... xviij. đ.

„ Nicħo de Tunstalt ... ... xxij. đ.

„ Warino de Heskyn ... ... xviij. đ.

„ Roƀto fabro ... ... xij. đ.

„ Wilƭo de Tunlegħ ... ... ij. ſ.

„ Wilƭo de Dwerihouse ... ... iij. ſ. ij. đ.

„ Henř le Draper ... ... iij. ſ. ij. đ.

„ Galfř Banastř ... ... xvj. đ.

„ Wilƭo fiƭ Roƀi ... ... xv. đ.

„ Ađ fiƭ Simoñ ... ... xv. đ.

„ Riĉ de Wynquik ... ... xv. đ.

Smᵃ. xxix. ſ. pƀ.

Kerdeñ
[*Cuerden*]

Đ Wilƭo de Whithalgħ ... ... v. ſ.

„ Adam fiƭ Alañ ... ... ij. ſ.

„ Joħe Lenmon ... ... ij. ſ.

„ Wilƭo Warde ... ... ij. ſ.

„ Riĉo de ffaldeworthinges ... xij. đ.

„ Elia de Kerdeñ ... ... xij. đ.

„ Thoɱ fiƭ Roǥ ... ... xij. đ.

Smᵃ. xiiij. ſ. pƀ.

Vlnes Waltoñ
[*Ulnes Walton*]

Đ Wilƭ de Waltoñ ... ... iij. ſ.

„ Joħe de Croft ... ... ij. ſ. vj. đ.

„ Walƭo Molenđ ... ... iij. ſ.

„ Roǥ fiƭ Roǥi ... ... iij. ſ. vj. đ.

„ Joħe de Brethertoñ ... ... iij. ſ.

„ Riĉo de Couhilƭ ... ... ij. ſ.

„ Roƀto de Hepay ... ... xij. đ.

„ Riĉo de Goldburñ ... ... xij. đ.

„ Wilƭ fiƭ Thoɱ ... ... xij. đ.

Smᵃ. xx. ſ. pƀ.

E 2

Burnehilt
[*Brindle*]

Ð Riĉo le Wodeward	...	...	xxij. đ.
„ Robto Medico ...	...	...	xxiij. đ.
„ Rogo Bark	...	...	ix. đ.
„ Wilto de Coleuyle	...	...	ix. đ.
„ Johe de Wythinhult	...	...	xvj. đ.
„ Johe de Deneholm̃	...	...	xv. đ
„ Riĉo fit Beñ	...	...	xiiij. đ.
„ Wilto del Mersh	...	..	xv. đ.
„ Robto de Burnehult	...	...	ij. s.

Sm*. xij. s. iij. đ. pb.

Whithull in bosco
[*Whittle in the Wood*]

Ð Walto le Wogher	...	...	ij. s.
„ Johe del Bonk ...	...	...	ij. s.
„ Robto Coco	...	...	ij. s.
„ Wilto del Crok	...	...	ij. s. iiij. đ.
„ Johe fit Wilti ...	...	...	xx. đ.
„ Robto fabr	...	...	xij. đ.
„ Johe le Wodeward	...	...	xij. đ.
„ Wilto Robtmogh	...	...	xij. đ.
„ Wilto fit Robti	...	...	xij. đ.

Sm*. xiiij s. pb.

Leylond
[*Leyland*]

Ð Adam de Andretoñ	...	...	iij. s.
„ Henr̃ fit Wilti ...	...	...	ij. s.
„ Johe de ffaldeworthinges	...	ij. s. iiij. đ.
„ Robto le Spiser	...	...	iij. s.
„ Thom̃ fit Henr̃	...	...	ij. s. ij. đ.
„ Thom̃ fit Riĉi ...	...	...	ij. s.
„ Thom̃ Toppynge	...	...	ij. s.
„ Wilto del Knoll	...	...	xij. đ.
„ Johe del Blakelache	...	...	xij. đ.

Sm*. xviij. s. vj. đ. pb.

Dokesbuꝛ cū Adlintoñ
[*Duxbury with Adlington*]

Ð Thoм̃ de Adlyntoñ	...	...	ij. ꝯ. ij. đ. oƀ.
„ Wilƚo del Burgħ	...	...	ij. ꝯ. ij. đ. oƀ.
„ Joħn de Adlyntoñ	...	...	xiiij. đ.
„ RoꝪ de Anlasargħ	...	...	xiiij. đ.
„ Wilƚo fiƚ Ric̃i	...	...	xiiij. đ.
„ Ric̃ fiƚ Hugōis	...	...	xiiij. đ.
„ Adam de Shaddeswode		...	xviij. đ. oƀ.
„ Roƀto del Burgħ	...	...	xviij. đ. oƀ.
„ Wilƚ fiƚ Micħis	...	...	xviij. đ.
„ Ric̃ de Haliwalle	...	...	xviij. đ.
„ Wilƚ del Strete	...	...	xij. đ.

Sm̃ᵃ. xvj. ꝯ. ij. đ. ꝑƀ.

Eukestoñ
[*Euxton*]

Ð MarꝪia de Holand	...	...	ij. ꝯ. viij. đ.
„ RoꝪ le Spenser	...	...	iij. ꝯ.
„ Joħe de Ermetridinge	...	...	iij. ꝯ.
„ RoꝪ le Graine	...	...	iij. ꝯ. iiij. đ.
„ Thurstañ de Hindeley		...	ij. ꝯ. viij. đ.
„ Wilƚ del Ermetridinge		...	ij. ꝯ.
„ Gilƀto de Grayne	...	...	xvj. đ.
„ Rađo fiƚ Hawiꝯ	...	...	ij. ꝯ.
„ Henꝛ fiƚ Walti	...	...	xvj. đ.
„ Roƀto de Mertoñ	...	...	xx. đ.

Sm̃ᵃ. xxiij. ꝯ. ꝑƀ.

Whithulƚ Waleys
[*Welsh Whittle*]

Ð Thoм̃ de Suttoñ	...	...	ij. ꝯ. j. đ.
„ Adam de la Legħe	...	...	xiiij. đ.
„ Ric̃o Molenđ	...	...	ij. ꝯ.
„ Thoм̃ le Perpount	...	...	xij. đ.
„ Henꝛ del Heye	...	...	xij. đ.

Sm̃ᵃ. vij. ꝯ. iij. đ. ꝑƀ.

Sm̃ᵃ. Wapentacħ xxviij. ƚi. x. ꝯ. v. đ.

Wapentachiũ de Amoundrenesse.

[HUNDRED OF AMOUNDERNESS.]

Prestoñ
[*Preston*]

Burgus taẍ ad. x.^{am}

Đ Adam de Bury	...	...	v. ꝰ.
„ Roƀto de Horwich	...	...	iij. ꝰ.
„ Albređ fił Roƀti	...	...	iiij. ꝰ.
„ Johe del Wych	...	...	iiij. ꝰ. oƀ.
„ Galfř de Hacounshou	...	...	iij. ꝰ.
„ Wilło faƀr	...	...	iij. ꝰ.
„ Johe de Asshtoñ	...	...	ij. s.
„ Aleẍ Marescalł	...	...	ij. ꝰ.
„ Johe fił Tille	...	...	iiij. ꝰ.
„ Agñ relicť Johis de Prestoñ	...	iij. ꝰ. iiij. đ.
„ Wilło Pałi	...	...	iij. ꝰ.
„ Wilło de Holand	...	...	iij. ꝰ. iiij. đ.
„ Henř le Shermon	...	...	iij. ꝰ. viij. đ.
„ Albređ fił Ade	...	...	ij. ꝰ. oƀ.
„ Roğo del Wych	...	...	xij. đ.
„ Wilło fił Mirre	...	...	ij. ꝰ. vj. đ.
„ Adam del Wych	...	...	xviij. đ.
„ Nicho fił Galfř	...	...	xvij. đ.
„ Johe de Laylond	...	...	xviij. đ.

Smᵃ. liij. ꝰ. iiij. đ. pƀ.

Gairstang
[*Garstang*]

Đ Tho῀ de Balryg῀	...	...	v. ꝰ. viij. đ.
„ Roƀto de Hide	...	...	ij. ꝰ. j. đ.
„ Agñ relicta Laurenc̃	...	xij. đ. oƀ.
„ Roğ fił Ricĩ	...	...	ij. ꝰ. viij. đ. oƀ. qᵃ.
„ Rañ del Bonk	...	...	xviij. đ.
„ Tho῀ fił Laurenc̃	...	...	iij. ꝰ. ij. đ. oƀ.

Ð Adam fil̃ Thoɱ   ...   ...   ij. s̃. iij. đ.

„ Adam fil̃ Laurenc̃   ...   ...   xiij. đ. oƀ.

„ Wilło fil̃ Alic̃   ...   .   ij. s̃. vj. đ.

„ Ric̃o de Routheclife   ...   ...   xvj. đ. oƀ.

„ Joħe Rider   ...   .   iij. s̃. v. đ.

„ Wilło le Hine   ...   ...   xij. đ. qᵃ.

„ Galfr fil̃ Walɫi   ...   ...   ij. s̃. xj. đ.

„ Joħe de Kendale   ...   ...   xvj. đ.

„ Henr̃ de Balrike   ...   ...   ij. s̃. xj. đ.

„ Ric̃ fil̃ Roƀi   ...   ...   iij. s̃. oƀ. qᵃ.

„ Adam faƀr   ...   ...   ij. s̃. v. đ. oƀ. qᵃ.

„ Thoɱ del Stubbe   ...   ...   xij. đ. oƀ.

„ Wilło fil̃ Bymme   ...   ...   xxij. đ.

„ Wilło Spynke   ...   ...   xij. đ. oƀ.

„ Nicħo del Bakhous   ...   ij. s̃. iiij. đ.

„ Joħe fil̃ Roği   ...   ...   ij. s̃. iiij. đ. qᵃ.

„ Roğo Vnderwode   ...   ...   xxij. đ.

„ Gilƀto Sparwe   ...   ...   ij. s̃. ij. đ. oƀ.

„ Wilło fil̃ Joħis   ...   ...   iij. s̃. ij. đ. oƀ.

„ Henr̃ Sidskirte   ...   ...   ij. s̃. viij. đ. oƀ. qᵃ.

„ Adam Sutore   ...   ...   ij. s̃. ix. đ. oƀ. qᵃ.

„ Wilło de Stokburgge   ...   ...   ij. s̃. v. đ. oƀ. qᵃ.

„ Roƀto del fforde   ...   ...   xix. đ. oƀ.

„ Joħe fil̃ Tille   ...   ...   iij. s̃. iij. đ.

„ Henr̃ fil̃ Roƀti   ...   ...   xvij. đ. oƀ.

„ Roğo fil̃ Ade   ...   ...   iij. s̃. vij. đ.

„ Isold vx̃ Joħis Skrite   ...   xvij. đ. oƀ. qᵃ.

„ Hankin le Masoun   ...   ...   ij. s̃. j. đ.

„ Thoɱ Molenđ   ...   ...   xx. đ.

„ Joħe de Halghtoħ   ...   iiij. s̃. xj. đ. oƀ.

„ Ric̃o faƀr   ...   ...   ij. s̃. iiij. đ.

„ Galfr del ffilde   ...   ...   ij. s̃. ij. đ. oƀ. qᵃ.

„ Galfr Wynter   ...   ...   ij. s̃. oƀ.

„ Adam Lyrikan   ...   ...   iiij. s̃. iiij. đ.

„ Jurđo fil̃ Nicħi   ...   ...   iiij. s̃. iiij. đ.

„ Roğ le Bakester   ...   ...   xij. đ. oƀ.

Smᵃ. c. s̃. xj. đ. pƀ.

Stalmynne cū Staynolł
[*Stalmine with Stanall*]

Đ Joħe Decano	...	...	... ij. ₴.
„ Robto Molenđ ...	...	...	xvj. đ.
„ Adam fił Jordañ	...	...	ij. ₴.
„ Walťo fił vidue...	...	...	iiij. ₴.
„ Joħe Arlegħ	...	...	... ij. ₴.
„ Joħe fił Jacoby ...	...	...	iij. ₴.
„ Wilło fił Riĉi	...	...	... iij. ₴.
„ Wilło Pacok	...	...	... xvj. đ.
„ Riĉo fił Huḡ	...	...	... xvj. đ.

Smᵃ. xx. ₴. pb.

Grenolł cū Thisteltoñ
[*Greenhalgh with Thistleton*]

Đ Joħe de Askebrek	...	...	ij. ₴. vj. đ.
„ Wilł fił Ađ	...	...	... ij. ₴.
„ Joħe fił Wilłi	...	...	... ij. ₴. vj. đ.
„ Wilło de Birches	...	...	xviij. đ.
„ Wilło de Routhecliue ...	...	xviij. đ.
„ Riĉo fił Dode	...	...	... ij. ₴. x. đ.
„ Joħe fił Joħis	...	...	... ij. ₴. ij. đ.
„ Wilło de Cornay	...	...	ij. ₴. x. đ.
„ Roḡ de Thisteltoñ	...	...	ij. ₴. ij. đ.

Smᵃ. xx. ₴. pb.

Alstoñ cū Hodersale
[*Alston with Hothersall*]

Đ Riĉo de Hoghtoñ	...	...	vj. ₴. viij. đ.
„ Robto de Hodersale	...	...	xij. đ.
„ Robto fił Wilłi ...	...	...	xiij. đ.
„ Riĉo de Balghhołm	...	...	xix. đ.
„ Adam de Ellale	...	...	xiiij. đ.
„ Joħe de Ribbelcesŧr	...	...	xj. đ.
„ Joħe ñł Robti ...	...	...	xj. đ.

Smᵃ. xiij. ₴. iiij. đ.

Barton
[*Barton*]

Đ Wilło del Erlesgate	...	...	ij. ꝭ. vj. đ.
„ Adam fił Dode	...	...	v. ꝭ.
„ Rog̃o Wawayn	...	...	ij. ꝭ.
„ Gilbto del Halle	...	...	iij. ꝭ.
„ Wilło le Coudeler	...	...	iij. ꝭ.
„ Robto de Walton	...	...	ij. ꝭ.
„ Joħe le Coudeler	...	...	ij. ꝭ. ij. đ.
„ Henr̃ de Singelton	...	...	xvj. đ.
„ Hugõe de Holugħford	...	xij. đ.
„ Robto de Skipton	...	...	xij. đ.
„ Hugõc de Billesburgh	...	...	xij. d.

Smᵃ. xxiiij. ꝭ. pb.

Etheliswike
[*Elswick*]

Đ Wilło del ffilde	...	...	iij. ꝭ. ij. đ.
„ Robto fił Joħis	...	...	iij. ꝭ. vj. đ.
„ Hugõe fił Pauli	...	...	iij. ꝭ.
„ Joħe del Howes	...	...	ij. ꝭ.
„ Wilło fił Ađ	...	...	ij. ꝭ. ix. đ.
„ Ricõo fił Riči	...	...	xx. đ.
„ Ricõo fił Hug̃	...	...	xij. đ.
„ Adam fił Rog̃i	...	...	ij. ꝭ. xj. đ.

Smᵃ. xx. ꝭ. pb.

Þua Eccliston cũ Layrbrek
[*Little Eccleston with Larbrick*]

Đ Ricõo del Crosse	...	...	iij. ꝭ.
„ Thurstan de Layrbrek	...	ij. ꝭ. iiij. đ.
„ Wilło fił Matħi	...	...	ij. ꝭ. iiij. đ.
„ Wilło fił Rog̃i	...	...	xij. đ.
„ Joħe fabr	...	...	xvj. đ.
„ Ricõo del Kirke	...	...	xij. đ.
„ Rog̃o fił Wilł	...	...	xvj. đ.
„ Ricõo fił Wilłi	...	...	xij. đ.

Smᵃ. xiij. ꝭ. iiij. đ. pb.

Grimesargħ cū Brokholes
[*Grimsargh with Brockholes*]

Đ Wilło de Grimesargħ	...	...	xx. đ.
„ Thoɱ de Hide	...	...	ij. ꝯ.
„ Adam de Brokholes	...	...	ij. ꝯ.
„ Wilło de Brokholes	...	...	xviij. đ.
„ Riċ de Eccleshulł	...	...	xvj. đ.
„ Adam del ffilde	...	...	xiiij. đ.
„ Wilło Piscatoꝛ	...	...	xiiij. đ.
„ Rađo Albyn.	...	...	xij. đ.

Smᵃ. xj. ꝯ. x. đ. pɓ.

Lee
[*Lee*]

Đ Riċo de Hoghtoñ	...	...	v. ꝯ. iiij. đ.
„ Adam fił Agñ	...	...	ij. ꝯ.
„ Joħe fił Amoꝛ	...	...	xv. đ.
„ Roɓto ffraunceis	...	...	xiij. đ.
„ Henꝛ de Chernok	...	...	xij. đ.
„ Roɓto fił Roɓti	...	...	x. d.

Smᵃ. xj. ꝯ. vj. đ. pɓ.

Caꝑhale
[*Catterall*]

Đ Lora de Caterhale	...	...	v. ꝯ.
„ Henꝛ de Rowale	...	...	ij. ꝯ.
„ Edɱo de Wedacre	...	...	ij. ꝯ.
„ Henꝛ fił Gilɓti	...	...	iij. ꝯ. v. đ. oɓ
„ Rađo fullone	...	...	ij. ꝯ.
„ Joħe fil Rađi	...	...	iij. ꝯ. iiij. đ.
„ Wilło de Tarletoñ	...	...	xv. đ. oɓ.

Smᵃ. xx. ꝯ. j. đ. pɓ.

Claghtoñ
[*Claughton*]

Đ Henꝛ de ffetherby	...	...	iij. ꝯ.
„ Joħe de Mirescogħ	...	...	ij. ꝯ.
„ Adam fił Galfr	...	...	xij. đ.

Ɖ Joħe le Reder ... ... xij. đ.
„ Roƀto del Bonk ... ... xij. đ.
„ Joħe de Staunford ... ... xvj. đ.
„ Wilƚo de Whitingh m ... ... xij. đ.
„ Joħe de Heghᵃm · ... ,... xij. đ.
„ Roƀto de Mirescogħ ... ... xij. đ.
„ Galfr fiƚ Wilƚi ... ... xij. đ.

Smᵃ. xiij. ꝸ. iiij. đ. pƀ.

Ethelistoħ
[*Elston*]

Ɖ Wilƚo de Ethelistoħ ... ... ij. ꝸ.
„ Petro de Dodhulƚ ... ... ij. ꝸ. ij. đ.
„ Wilƚo de Grenehurst ... ... ij. ꝸ.
„ Thom̃ de Broghtoħ ... ... ij. ꝸ.
„ Henr̃ de Querndoun ... ... xx. đ.
„ Wilƚ de Halghtoħ ... ... xx. đ.
„ Wilƚo de Akesħagh ... ... xiiij. đ.
„ Roƀto fiƚ Ričī ... ... xij. đ.
„ Rič̃o de Ingole ... ... xii. đ.

Smᵃ. xiiij. ꝸ. viij. đ. pƀ.

Gosenargħ
[*Goosnargh*]

Ɖ Joħe de Gosenargħ ... ... vj. ꝸ. viij. đ.
„ Wilƚo de Grenehilles ... ... viij. ꝸ.
„ Matilƚ de Mideltoħ ... ... v. ꝸ. iiij. đ.
„ Henr̃ de Gosenargh ... ... iiij. ꝸ.
„ Joħe de Coure ... ... iij. ꝸ. iiij. đ.
„ Rič̃o Bercar̃ ... ... v. ꝸ. viij. đ.
„ Rič̃o del Kirke ... ... v. ꝸ.
„ Rič̃o le Porter ... ... iiij. ꝸ. ij. đ.
„ Rič̃o de Grenehilles ... ... ix. đ.

Smᵃ. xliij. ꝸ. pƀ.

Hordorñ cū Nutoñ
[*Hardhorn with Newton*]

Ɖ Joħe fiƚ Nicħi ... ... iij. ꝸ.
„ Wilƚo faƀr ... ... xviij. đ.

Ð Roƀto fił Henr̄ ...	...	...	iij. ſ.
„ Henr̄ fił Joħis ...	...	...	ij. ſ. vj. đ.
„ Wilło Carpentar̄	...	...	ij. ſ.
„ Henr̄ fił Henr̄ ...	...	...	xviij. đ.
„ Alex̃ de Neutoñ	...	...	iij. ſ.
„ Adam del Pulł ...	...	...	xviij. đ.
„ Joħe de la More	...	...	iij. ſ.
„ Adam de Taldrestath ...	...	...	iij. ſ.
„ Wilło Broun	...	...	ij. ſ.
„ Wilło Tillesone	...	...	ij. ſ.

Smᵃ. xxviij. ſ. pƀ.

Riggeby
[*Ribby with Wray*]

Ð Joħe del Bonk ...	...	...	ij. ſ.
„ Joħe Curtais	...	...	ij. ſ.
„ Jordõ fił Thom̃ ...	...	...	ij. ſ. ij. đ. oƀ.
„ Riͨo de Plimptoñ	...	...	xx. đ.
„ Alañ le Palmer	...	...	xij. đ.
„ Joħe fił Jorđi	...	...	xij. đ.
„ Joħe fił Wilłi	...	...	xiij. đ. qᵃ.
„ Adam de Mora	...	...	xij. đ. qᵃ.
„ Wilło fił Thom̃	...	...	ij. ſ. ij. đ.

Smᵃ. xiiij. ſ. ij. đ. pƀ.

Brinȳge cū Kelgmesargħ
[*Bryning with Kellamergh*]

Ð Rogõ Culban	...	...	iij. ſ.
„ Adam de Sharples	...	...	iij. ſ.
„ Alañ fił Ađ	...	...	iij. ſ.
„ Wilło del Castelł	...	...	iij. ſ.
„ Ađ fił Ađ	...	...	v. ſ.
„ Adam Page	...	...	xij. đ.

Smᵃ. xviij. ſ. pƀ.

Billesburgħ
[*Bilsborough*]

Ð Wilło de Cotom	...	...	v. ſ. viij. đ.
„ Joħe del Yate ...	...	...	ij. ſ. v. đ. oƀ.

Đ Huḡ de Billesburgħ ... ... ij. s̄. xj. đ.

„ Ričo de Morlegħ ... ... xvij. đ.

„ Roƀto fił Anoł ... ... xviij. đ.

„ Roƀto le Skirmer ... ... xij. đ. oƀ.

Smᵃ. xv. s̄. pƀ.

Singeltoñ Magnᵃ cū parua
[*Great and Little Singleton*]

Đ Thom̄ fił Jorđi ... ... iiij. s̄.

„ Wiłło fił Roƀti ... ... iij. s̄.

„ Roƀto fił Riči ... ... ij. s̄.

„ Roƀto de Warthebrek ... ... iij. s̄.

„ Wiłło fił Thom̄ ... ... ij. s̄.

„ Thom̄ fił Roḡi ... . ij. s̄.

„ Adam fił Thom̄ ... ... ij. s̄.

„ Wiłło de Etheliswik ..: ... ij. s̄.

Smᵃ. xx. s̄. pƀ.

Westebi cū Plumptoñ
[*Westby with Plumpton*]

Đ Adam fił Jorđi ... ... xvj. đ.

„ Rič fił Alañ ... ... xvj. đ.

„ Roƀto du Marrais ... ... ij. s̄. ij. đ.

„ Adam Bercał ... ... xvj. đ.

„ Joħe de Plumptoñ ... ... xvj. đ.

„ Rič Sweteglee ... ... xij. đ.

„ Adam de Mithoꝑ ... ... xij. đ.

„ Roƀto le Carter ... ... ij. s̄.

„ Wiłło de Plumptoñ ... ... xij. đ.

„ Roƀto del Craḡ ... ... x. đ.

Smᵃ. xiij. s̄. iiij. đ. pƀ.

Wartoñ
[*Warton*]

Đ Thom̄ de Singeltoñ ... ... v. s̄. viij. đ.

„ Roƀto de Wartoñ ... ... iiij. s̄.

„ Wiłł fił Wiłłi ... ... iij. s̄. ij. đ.

„ Adam del Pułł ... ... iij. s̄.

Đ Adam fit Joħis ...   .   ij. ꝟ.
„ Thoɱ del Halle   ...   ...   · ij. ꝟ.
„ Riꝯ fit Henꝝ   ...   ...   xviij. đ.
„ Joħ fit Rogi   ...   ...   xiiij. đ.

Smᵃ. xxij. ꝟ. vj. đ. pƀ.

Eccliston̄ Magnᵃ
[*Great Eccleston*]

Đ Joħe de Carleton̄   ...   ...   ij. ꝟ.
„ Joħe Pacok   ...   ...   iij. ꝟ.
„ Rog le White   ...   ...   iij. ꝟ.
„ Wilto le Warenđ   ..   ...   ij. ꝟ.
„ Riꝯ de Glasebrok   ...   ...   ij. ꝟ.
„ Riꝯ del Halle   ...   ...   xviij. đ.
„ Joħ fit Rogi   ...   ...   xviij. đ.
„ Joħ Pacok Junioꝝ   ...   ...   xij. đ.

Smᵃ. xvj. ꝟ. pƀ.

Asshton̄
[*Ashton*]

Đ Laurenꝯ Trauers   ...   ...   iij. ꝟ.
„ Eđo de Haidok   ...   ...   iij. ꝟ.
„ Thoɱ fit Dauyd   ...   ...   xviij. đ.
„ Joħe fit Riꝯi   ...   ...   xij. đ.
„ Joħe fit Alan̄   ...   ...   xij. đ.
„ Joħe de Sunderlond   ...   ...   xij. đ.
„ Henꝝ fit Elie   ...   ...   xij. đ.

Smᵃ. xj. ꝟ. vj. đ. pƀ.

Halghton̄
[*Haighton*]

Đ Joħe de Bolton̄   ...   ...   xiij. đ. oƀ.
„ Joħe de Blakeburn̄   ...   ...   xij. đ.
„ Wilto de Etheliston̄   ...   ...   xviij. oƀ.
„ Ceciƚ relicta Henꝝ   ...   ...   xij. đ.
„ Wiƚt fit Galfr   ...   ...   xij. đ.
„ Wiƚt fit Amie   ...   ...   xvij. đ.
„ Joħe fit Walꝯi   ...   ...   xv. đ.
„ Gilƀto fit Walꝯi   ...   ...   xx. đ.
„ Nicħo Cissoꝝ   ...   ...   xij. đ.

Smᵃ. xj. ꝟ. pƀ.

Wodeplumptoñ
[Woodplumpton]

Đ Gilƀto de Morhalle	...	...	iij. ꝸ.
„ Joħe de Rediford	...	...	ij. ꝸ.
„ Roƀto· de Cherneley	...	...	ij. ꝸ.
„ Ricõ fiꞇ Matħi	...	...	iij. ꝸ.
„ Wilꞇo del Kar	...	...	ij. ꝸ.
„ Wilꞇo fiꞇ Ade	...	...	ij. ꝸ.
„ Roƀto Skryuin	...	...	iij. ꝸ.
„ Henꞃ de Grenolf	...	...	ij. ꝸ.
„ Joħ del Lache	...	...	iij. ꝸ.
„ Roƀto del Karhouses	...	...	ij. ꝸ.
„ Aꝺ de Wirhale	...	...	ij. ꝸ.
„ Wilꞇ de Grenholꞇ	...	...	ij. ꝸ.
„ Henꞃ fiꞇ Malle	...	...	ij. ꝸ.
„ Wilꞇo fiꞇ Thom̃	...	...	ij. ꝸ.
„ Henꞃ de Rediford	...	...	ij. ꝸ.
„ Wilꞇ Cherneley	...	...	ij. ꝸ.
„ Roƀto del Kar	...	...	ij. ꝸ.
„ Ricõ de Neusom	...	...	ij. ꝸ.

Smᵃ. xl. ꝸ. pƀ.

Inskiꝑ cū Sourby
[Inskip with Sowerby]

Đ Roǧo le ffleccher	...	...	ij. ꝸ. v. ꝺ. qᵃ.
„ Wilꞇo Emnesone	...	...	iij. ꝸ. vj. ꝺ.
„ Tristram̃ Daa	...	...	xij. ꝺ. qᵃ.
„ Ricõ del Halle	...	...	ij. ꝸ.
„ Wilꞇo de Sourby	...	...	iij. ꝸ.
„ Wilꞇo fiꞇ Thom̃	...	...	ij. ꝸ. iiij. ꝺ.
„ Wilꞇ de Shagħ	...	...	xx. ꝺ.
„ Joħe Wynter	...	...	xxij. ꝺ. oƀ.
„ Wilꞇ fiꞇ Hugõis	...	...	xiiij. ꝺ.
„ Joħ de Sourby	...	...	ij. ꝸ.
„ Ricõ de Inskiꝑ	...	...	xij. ꝺ.

Smᵃ. xxij. ꝸ. pƀ.

Carletoñ
[*Carleton*]

Ᵽ Joħe fit Thoᵐ	...	...	...	iij. ꝭ.
„ Nicħo de Haihołm	...	...	ij. ꝭ.
„ Roƀto Capło	...	...	...	ij. ꝭ. vj. đ.
„ Joħe Banner	...	...	...	xvj. d.
„ Joħ fit Jakes	...	...	...	xvj. đ.
„ Godith de Carletoñ	...	...	xiij. đ.
„ Riõo faƀr	...	...	...	xij. đ.
„ Thoᵐ fit Nicħi	...	...	...	xviij. đ.
„ Riõo Coderussħ	...	...	xv. đ.
„ Adam del Halle	...	...	ij. ꝭ.
„ Riõo Molenđ	...	...	...	xij. đ.
„ Henr̃ le Daa	...	...	...	xij. đ.

Smᵃ. xix. ꝭ. pƀ.

Neutoñ
[*Newton*]

Ᵽ Wilło fit Vnwyn	...	...	xviij. đ.
„ Riõo le Bolour	...	...	ij. ꝭ. ij. đ.
„ Joħe le ffrenkissħ	...	...	xiiij. đ.
„ Joħe le Stayninge	...	...	ij. ꝭ. vij. đ. ob.
„ Riõo fit Hawisie	...	...	xxij. đ.
„ Wilło de Cotouₘ	...	...	ij. ꝭ.
„ Wilł fit Wilłi	...	...	...	ij. ꝭ. vij. đ. ob.
„ Nicħo de Neutoñ	...	...	ij. ꝭ. ij. đ.
„ Adam fit Joħ	...	...	...	ix. đ.
„ Wilło fit Riõi	...	...	...	ix. đ.

Smᵃ. xvij. ꝭ. vj. đ. pƀ.

ffrekiltoñ
[*Freckleton*]

Ᵽ Roƀto de ffrekiltoñ	...	...	ij. ꝭ.
„ Rađo de ffrekiltoñ	...	...	ij. ꝭ.
„ Roƀto de Hodersale	...	...	ij. ꝭ.
„ Wilł fit Wilłi	...	...	...	iij. ꝭ.
„ Roƀto fit Micħis	...	...	ij. ꝭ.
„ Wilło Dikemon	...	...	ij. ꝭ. iiij. đ.

Đ Wilło de Mithoƥ ... ... ij. s. vj. đ.

„ Riĉo de Kendale ... ... iij. s.

„ Nicħo Busshelt ... ... ij. s.

„ Thom̃ de la More ... ... ij. s.

„ Joħe de la More ... ... ij s.

„ Riĉo fił Marg̃ie ... ... xvj. đ.

Smᵃ. xxvj. s. ij. đ. pƀ.

Preshoū cū Hacounshou
[Preesall with Hackinsall]

Đ Wilło de Hacounshou ... ... ij. s. qᵃ.

„ Joħ de Asshtoñ ... ... xx. đ. oƀ.

„ Joħe de Hacounshou ... ... xvj. đ. qᵃ.

„ Wilł fił Stepħi ... ... iij. s. vij. đ. oƀ.

„ Wilło le Pynder ... ... ij. s. viij. đ. oƀ.

„ Riĉo de Northbrok ... ... iij. s. iiij. đ.

„ Wilło Sharƥ ... ... iij. s. iiij. đ.

„ Joħe fił Joħis ... ... xvj. đ.

„ Joħe fił Rog̃i ... ... ij. s. v. đ.

„ Roƀto fił Simoñ ... ... ij. s.

Smᵃ. xxiij. s. x. đ. pƀ.

Rybbeltoñ
[Ribbleton]

Đ Rađo fił Riĉi ... ... ij. s.

„ Wałto de Wresdale ... ... xx. đ.

„ Adam Albam ... ... xviij. đ.

„ Rog̃ Hullesone ... ... xiiij. đ.

„ Rog̃o de Ribbeltoñ ... ... ij. s. j. đ.

„ Henr̃ fił Simoñ ... ... xviij. đ.

„ Wilło fił Gilƀti ... ... xiiij. đ.

„ Adam le Bole ... ... xij. đ. qᵘ.

Smᵃ. xij. s. j. đ. qᵘ. pƀ.

Hameltoñ
[Hambleton]

Đ Henr̃ le Por̃tmogħ ... ... ij. s.

„ Wilł fił Beñ ... ... xx. đ.

F

Đ Wilł de Beseley ... ... ij. ꝭ.

  „ Ađ le Swon ... ... ij. ꝭ.

  „ Wilł de Gilbtholm̃ ... ... ij. ꝭ.

  „ Robto de Carltoñ ... ... ij. ꝭ.

  „ Riĉo de Mithoꝑ ... ... ij. ꝭ.

  „ Wilło de Stalmynne ... ... xvj. đ.

Sm̆ᵃ. xv. ꝭ. pᵬ.

Lythũ
[Lytham]

Đ Adam Braciatoꝛ ... ... vj. ꝭ. iiij. đ.

  „ Galfr de ffanseby ... ... iiij. ꝭ. j. đ.

  „ Joħ fił Matilł ... ... ij. ꝭ. ij. d.

  „ Thom̃ le Coke ... ... iij. ꝭ. v. đ.

  „ Henꝛ de Mithoꝑ ... ... iiij. ꝭ. viij. đ.

  „ Riĉo de Mithoꝑ ... ... xj. đ.

  „ Joħe le Bernegrayne ... ... xvij. đ.

Sm̆ᵃ. xxiij. ꝭ. pᵬ.

Mertoñ
[Great Marton]

Đ Thom̃ le Molineux ... ... ij. ꝭ.

  „ Robto de Marisco ... ... ij. ꝭ. j. đ. oᵬ.

  „ Micħ fił Thom̃ ... ... xij. đ.

  „ Thom̃ Russelł ... ... iij. ꝭ.

  „ Robto Rudde ... ... xij. đ.

  „ Adam Ctico ... ... iij. ꝭ.

  „ Riĉo de Hestholm ... ... v. ꝭ. x. đ.

  „ Anabilł uꝝ Wilłi ... ... iij. ꝭ.

  „ Joħe de Mertoñ ... ... iij. ꝭ. j. đ. oᵬ.

  „ Robto fił Robti ... ... ij. ꝭ. vij. đ.

Sm̆ᵃ. xxvj. ꝭ. viij. đ. pᵬ.

Whitinghᵃm
[Whittingham]

Đ Adam fił Aleꝝ ... ... xviij. đ.

  „ Matił vꝝ Aleꝝ ... ... xviij. đ. oᵬ. qᵃ.

Đ Alicia de Singeltoñ ... ... ij. s̃. xj. đ. ob̃. qᵃ.

„ Henr̃ fiꞇ Warini ... ... iij. s̃.

„ Rañ de Singeltoñ ... ... iij. s̃.

„ Wilꞇo de Graistok ... ... ij. s̃. vij. đ.

„ Thoꞥ de Singeltoñ ... ... ij. s̃.

„ Rico de ffisshwik ... ... ij. s̃. ob̃. qᵃ.

„ Rico fiꞇ Amlie ... ... ij. s̃. iiij. đ.

„ Wilꞇo de Whitingham ... ... ij. s̃. x. đ. ob̃. qᵃ.

Smᵃ. xxiiij. s̃. pb̃.

Broghtoñ
[*Broughton*]

Đ Thoꞥ de Singeltoñ ... ... xxiij. đ. qᵃ.

„ Wilꞇ del Halle ... ... xvj. đ.

„ Wilꞇ de Prees ... ... ij. s̃. ij. đ. õ. qᵃ.

„ Adam de Singeltoñ ... ... ij. s̃. iiij. đ. qᵃ.

„ Thoꞥ de Whitacre ... ... xvj. đ.

„ Wilꞇ de Singeltoñ ... ... xij. đ.

„ Rico de Ingolhed ... ... ij. s̃. ij. đ. ob̃. qᵃ.

„ Wilꞇ de la More ... ... iij. s̃.

„ Wilꞇ Bolroun ... ... xij. đ.

„ Johe de Waltoñ ... ... ij. s̃. iiij. đ.

„ Ađ fiꞇ Rog̃i ... ... ij. s̃. viij. đ.

„ Adam de Whitacr̃ ... ... iij. s̃.

„ Wilꞇ del Sik ... ... ij. s̃. iij. đ.

Smᵃ. xxvj. s̃. viij. đ. pb̃.

Vprotheclife
[*Upper Rawcliffe*]

Đ Rico fiꞇ Rog̃i ... ... iij. s̃.

„ Adam Pacok ... ... iij. s̃.

„ Adam Cissor̃ ... ... iij. s̃.

„ Adam de Sotheworth ... ... xvj. đ

„ Johe Birewath ... ... xx. đ.

„ Henr̃ de ffortoñ ... ... xvj. đ.

Smᵃ. xiij. s̃. iiij. đ. pb̃.

F 2

Latoñ cũ Warthebrek
[Layton with Warbreck]

Đ Thoм̃ del Bonk...	...	...	iij. ꝝ. ij. đ.
„ Micħe del Pulт	...	...	vj. ꝝ. viij. đ.
„ Adam Cay	...	...	ij. ꝝ.
„ Joħ le Shepherd...	...	...	iij. ꝝ. j. đ.
„ Adam fiт Joħis	...	...	ij. ꝝ. viij. đ.
„ Nicħo le Taillor...	...	...	iij. ꝝ. viij. đ.
„ Joħe fiт Roği	...	...	ij. ꝝ. ix. đ.
„ Wilтo fiт Thoм̃	...	...	xij. đ.

Sm*. xxv. ꝝ. pᵬ.

Pultoñ
[Poulton le Fylde]

Đ Wilт de Ecclistoñ	...	...	vj. ꝝ.
„ Adam le Knyght	...	...	iiij. ꝝ. ij. đ.
„ Roᬏto de Pultoñ	...	...	ij. ꝝ.
„ Joħe Page	...	...	ij. ꝝ.
„ vicaꝝ de Pultoñ...	...	...	ij. ꝝ. viij. đ.
„ Roᵍ de Pultoñ	...	...	ij. ꝝ. vj. đ.
„ Roᵍ Abelт	...	...	ij. ꝝ.
„ Nicħo de Pultoñ	...	...	xij. đ.
„ Adam del Crosse	...	...	x. đ.
„ Adam fiт Simoñ	...	...	x. đ.
„ sᬏtaxatoꝛ dc̃e ville de fine ꝑ t*ns			iij. ꝝ. iiij. đ.

Sm*. xxvij. ꝝ. iiij. đ. pᬏ.

Treueles
[Treales]

Đ Wilтo fiт Roği	...	...	iij. ꝝ.
„ Thoм̃ fiт Jorđi	...	...	ij. ꝝ. ij. đ.
„ Jorđo fiт Jorđi	...	...	ij. ꝝ. ij. đ.
„ Benedicto de Treueles ...	...	ij. ꝝ. iiij. đ.
„ Ađ fiт Gilᬏti	...	...	ij. ꝝ. iiij. đ.
„ Ric̃o fiт Joħis	...	...	ij. ꝝ.
„ Ric̃o fiт Wilтi	...	...	ij. ꝝ.
„ Adam fiт Thoм̃	...	...	xij. đ.

Ð Riĉo le Harper ...   .   xviij. đ.
„ Joħe de Treueles   ...   ...   xviij. đ.
„ Adam fit Jorđi ...   .   xviij. đ.
„ Roɓti fit Ade   ...   ...   xviij. đ.

Smᵃ. xxiij. ȿ. pɓ.

Cliftoñ
[*Clifton*]

Ð Nicħo de Catford   ...   ...   xxj. đ.
„ Riĉo de Threlfalt   ...   ...   ij. ȿ. iij. đ.
„ Wilt Sutoř   ...   ...   xvj. đ.
„ Riĉ le Walker ...   .   iij. ȿ.
„ Thoᵐ fit Ade ...   .   ij. ȿ. viij. đ.
„ Brounrobyn [*sıc*]   ...   ...   ij. ȿ.
„ Adam Vnwyn ...   .   ij. ȿ.
„ Adam fit Dode ...   .   ij. ȿ.
„ Adam fit Ađ   ...   ...   ij. ȿ.
„ Wilt de Brinynğ   ...   ...   iij. ȿ.

Smᵃ. xxij. ȿ. pɓ.

Wethetoñ cū Prees
[*Weeton with Prees*]

Ð Adam le Grayne   ...   ...   ij. ȿ. viij. đ.
„ Roɓto de Swartebrek ...   ...   ij. ȿ. viij. đ.
„ Adam fit Riĉi ...   .   ij. ȿ. iiij. đ.
„ Wilt de Riggeby   ...   ...   ij. ȿ. ix. đ.
„ Wilt de Mithoꝑ   ...   ...   ij. ȿ. vij. đ.
„ Joħ de Swartbrek   ...   ...   ij. ȿ.
„ Roɓto Prees   ...   ...   ij. ȿ.
„ Adam de Rowale   ...   ...   xiiij. đ.
„ Wilt de Mithoꝑ   ...   ...   ij. ȿ. ij. đ.
„ Joħ de Ellale ...   .   ij. ȿ. ij. đ.
„ Wilt de Hale ...   .   xviij. đ.

Smᵃ. xxiiij. ȿ. pɓ.

Outrothe clife
[*Out Rawcliffe*]

Ð Thoᵐ fit Alani ...   .   iiij. ȿ.
„ Roğ de Routheclife   ...   ...   iij. ȿ.

Đ Alañ de Preshou ... ... iij. ꝑ.
„ Henr̃ fabr̃ ... ... iij. ꝑ. vj. đ.
„ Wilto fit Elie ... ... ij. ꝑ. vj. d.
„ Joħe fit Roƀti ... ... ij. ꝑ.
„ Wilł de Eccliston̄ ... ... xij. đ.
„ Rog̃ de Morebrek ... ... xij. đ.
„ Joħe de Layrbrek ... ... ij. ꝑ.
„ Roƀto fit Riči ... ... xx. đ.
„ Ric̃o Lestrange ... ... ij. ꝑ.
„ Wilł de Halle ... ... xij. đ.

Smᵃ. xxvj. ꝑ. viij. đ. pƀ.

Neusom
[*Newsham*]

Đ Adam Pygot ... ... xvj. đ.
„ Henr̃ de Pulton̄ ... ... xiiij. đ.
„ Joħe le Hunter ... ... xij. đ.
„ Adam de Neusom ... ... xij. đ.
„ Henr̃ fit Wilłi ... ... xij. đ.

Smᵃ. v. ꝑ. vj. đ. pƀ.

Thorneton̄
[*Thornton le Fylde*]

Đ Alinor̃ de Thorneton̄ ... ... xvj. đ. oƀ. qᵃ.
„ Wilto le Swon ... ... xv. đ. oƀ.
„ Joħe de Staynolł ... ... ij. ꝑ. v. d. qᵃ.
„ Thoñ fit Riči ... ... iij. ꝑ. ij. đ.
„ Thoñ de Thorneton̄ ... ... iiij. ꝑ.
„ Batty de Brun ... ... iij. ꝑ. ij. đ.
„ Ric̃o de Ellale ... ... xv. đ.
„ Wilto Alotessone ... ... xiij. đ.
„ Wilto Proudfot ... ... xiij. đ.
„ Ric̃o fit Rog̃i ... ... xiij. đ.
„ Joħ fit Joħis de Heton̄ ... ... xiij. đ.

Smᵃ. xxj. ꝑ. oƀ. pƀ.

Mithelargħ cū Westsū
[*Medlar with Wesham*]

Ð Gilƀto de Mithelargħ ... ... ij. s. vj. đ.
 „ Waŧto de Mithelargħ ... ... xij. đ.
 „ Wilŧ le Harper ... ... ij. s.
 „ Alex̃ de Mithelargħ ... ... ij. s.
 „ Roƀto de Lynhoŧm ... ... ij. s.
 „ Joħe fiŧ Rogĩ ... ... ij. s. vj. đ.
 „ Roƀto fiŧ Ađ ... ... ij. s.
 „ Thoñ de Wolfalŧ ... ... ij. s.
 „ Joħe garcõe Cecilie ... ... ij. s.

Smᵃ. xviij. s. pƀ.

ffisshwik
[*Fishwick*]

Ð Simoñ fiŧ Ade ... ... xij. đ. oƀ. qᵃ.
 „ Wilŧo [fiŧ] Ricĩ ... ... ij. s. oƀ.
 „ Cristiana relicta Nicħi de Burgh xviij. đ.
 „ Ricõ de ffisshwik ... ... xiiij. đ. oƀ.
 „ Ricõ fiŧ Alani ... ... xij. đ.
 „ Hug̃ de ffisshwik ... ... xiiij. đ. qᵃ.

Smᵃ. viij. s. pƀ.

Kirkehⁿm
[*Kirkham*]

Ð Ricõ le Harpouř ... ... iij. s.
 „ Thoñ le Harpour ... ... ij. s. vj. đ.
 „ Joħe le Wadder ... ... iij. s. vj. đ.
 „ Roƀto. Trusseloue ... ... ij. s. j. đ. oƀ.
 „ Wilŧo de Westsum ... ... xij. đ.
 „ Roƀto le Harpour ... ... iij. s.
 „ Waŧto de Herford ... ... ix. đ.
 „ Thoñ del Halle ... ... ix. đ.
 „ Joħe Pride ... ... xj. đ.

Smᵃ. xvij. s. vj. đ. oƀ. pƀ.

Bispham cū Northbrek
[*Bispham with Norbreck*]

Ð Alinor fit Joħis ...	...	...	xij. đ.
„ Thom̃ de Eccliston̄	...	...	ij. s.
„ Wilt del Pult ...	...	...	xij. đ.
„ Adam̃ fit Ađ ...	...	...	iij. s.
„ Wilto de Singelton̄	...	...	iiij. s.
„ Henr̃ de Dutton̄	...	...	iij. s.
„ Joħe fit Ađ ...	...	...	ij. s.
„ Joħe le White ...	...	...	xviij. đ.
„ Adam de Lithū	...	...	ij. s.
„ Wilt le Poniour	...	...	xvj. đ.
„ Joħ del Bonk ...	...	...	xiiij. đ.

Sm*. xxij. s. pƀ.

Sm*. Wapentacħ. lj. ƚi. iiij. s. x. đ. qᵘ.
Et. liij. s. iiij. đ. de xᵃ. Burgi de Preston̄.

𝕬𝖆𝖕𝖊𝖓𝖙𝖆𝖈𝖍𝖎ū 𝖉𝖊 𝕭𝖑𝖆𝖈𝖐𝖇𝖚𝖗𝖓𝖘𝖍𝖎r̃.

[HUNDRED OF BLACKBURN.]

Merlay
[*Great Mearley*]

Ð Rico fit Ađ Noelt	...	...	ij. s. ij. đ.
„ Joħe Maunselt ...	...	...	ij. s.
„ Rico fit Roği Noelt	...	...	x. đ.

Sm*. v. s. pƀ.

Alueth*m
[*Altham*]

Ð Joħe de Aluetham	...	...	iij. s.
„ Henr̃ de Hindehult	...	...	xx. đ.
„ Joħe fit Wilti ...	...	...	xij. đ.
„ Joħe fre eius ...	...	...	ix. đ.
„ Roƀto de Shipyn	...	...	x. đ.
„ Wilt de Hoghton̄	...	...	ix. đ.
„ Rico de Alueth*m	...	...	ij. s.

Sm*. x. s. pƀ.

Dounom
[*Downham*]

Ð Hugõe de Dounom	...	...	ij. s. iiij. đ.
„ Wilto Bythewelle	...	...	ij. s. viij. đ.
„ Riĉo fit Petr̃	...	...	iij. s.
„ Robto de Louthian	...	...	xij. đ.
„ Adam le Skynnersone		...	xij. đ.
„ Riĉo Galt	...	...	iij. s.
„ Henr̃ fit Alex̃	...	...	xij. đ.

Smª. xiiij. s. pb.

Cliderhou
[*Clitheroe*]

Ð Robto de Cliderhou	...	...	vj. s.
„ Gilbto de Russhton	...	...	iij. s.
„ Johe fit Alex̃	...	...	vj. s.
„ Johe fit Riĉi	...	...	vj. s.
„ Johe fit Wilti	...	...	ij. s. viij. đ.
„ Wilto le Taillour	...	...	ij. s. iiij. đ.
„ Wilto de Wisewalle	...	...	xvj. đ.
„ Riĉ Coy ...	...	...	ij. s. iiij. đ.
„ Riĉ fit Riĉi	...	...	ij. s. iiij. đ.
„ Adam Russelt	...	...	iij. s.
„ ·Wilt Wherdray	...	...	ij. s.

Smª. xxxvij. s. pb.

Chatteburñ
[*Chatburn*]

Ð Johe fit Riĉi	...	...	ij. s.
„ Adam fit Thom̃	...	...	ij. s.
„ Thom̃ fit Rog̃	...	...	ij. s.
„ Adam le Cok	...	...	xviij. đ. ob.
„ Robto fit Petr̃	...	...	xviij. đ. ob.

Smª. ix. s. j. đ. pb.

Worstoñ
[*Worston*]

Ð Johe de Angrum	...	...	ij. s.
„ Joh fit Michecok	...	...	ij. s.

Đ Riĉo del Lathes	...	...	xviij. đ.
„ Wilł fił Thoɱ	...	...	ij. s. j. đ.
„ Wilł fił Ađ	...	...	xviij. đ.

Smᵃ. ix. s. j. đ. pɓ.

Chircħ
[*Church*]

Đ Nicħo de Chircħ	...	...	xvj. đ.
„ Ađ de Wallebonk	...	...	xvj. đ.
„ Adam fił Stepħi	...	...	xij. đ.
„ Stepħo de Chircħ	...	...	xiiij. đ.
„ Henr̃ Molenđ	...	...	iij. s. ij. đ.

Smᵃ. viij. s. pɓ.

Cliuacħ
[*Cliviger*]

Đ Gilɓto de la Leghe	...	...	iiij. s.
„ Ađ fabr̃	...	...	...	xvj. đ.
„ Henr̃ fił Roɓti	...	...	iij. s.
„ Wilło Hardere	...	...	ij. s.
„ Henr̃ de Calueknolł	...	...	iij. s.
„ Roɓto fił Stepħi	...	...	ij. s.

Smᵃ. xv. s. iiij. đ. pɓ.

Haselindeñ
[*Haslingden*]

Đ Adam de Holdeñ	...	...	ij. s.
„ Joħe de Balshaghe	...	...	ij. s. viij. đ.
„ Roɓto fił Awarđ	...	...	xvj. đ.
„ Adaɱ fił Roɓi	...	...	xij. đ.
„ Ađ fił Simoñ	...	...	xij. đ.
„ Roɓto fił Reginalđ	...	...	xij. đ.

Smᵃ. ix. s. pɓ.

Osbaldestoñ
[*Osbaldeston*]

Đ Thoɱ de Osbaldestoñ	...	...	ij. s. iiij. đ.
„ Wilł de Osbaldestoñ	...	...	xj. đ.
„ Joħ le Broune	...	...	xiij. đ.

Smᵃ. iiij. s. iiij. đ. pɓ.

Baldrestoñ
[*Balderstone*]

·Ð Riĉo de Baldrestoñ	...	...	xx. đ.
„ Wilł de Smalley	...	...	ix. đ. ob.
„ Riĉ fił Joħ	...	...	xij. đ.
„ Riĉ de Wardhulł	...	...	x. đ.
„ Joħe de Westewode	...	...	xv. đ.
„ Thoñ de Wardhulł	...	...	ij. š. j. đ. ob.

Smª. vij. š. viij. đ. pb.

Keûdale
[*Cuerdale*]

Ð Joħe de Keûdale	...	...	ij. š.
„ Riĉo de Stihołm	...	...	xij. đ.
„ Joħ fił Gilbti	...	...	iij. š.
„ Henŕ fił Thoñ	...	...	xvj. đ.
„ Henŕ del Cliffe	...	...	xij. đ.
„ Robto garcõe Riĉi	...	...	xvj. đ.
„ Wilł del Bothe	...	...	ij. š. ij. đ.

Smª. xj. š. x. đ. pb.

Simoundestoñ
[*Simonstone*]

Ð Nicħo de Holdeñ	...	...	iiij. š.
„ Joħe de Simoundeston	...	ij. š.
„ Joħe de Eghes	...	...	ix. đ.
„ Roĝo fił Alot	...	...	ix. đ.
„ Roĝ de Whitacŕ	...	...	ix. đ.
„ Simoñ fił Roĝi	...	...	ix. đ.

Smª. ix. š. pb.

Parua Harewode
[*Little Harwood*]

Ð Henŕ de Claitoñ	...	...	iij. š.
„ Joħe Page	...	...	xij. đ.
„ Riĉo de Couhulł	...	...	xvj. đ.
„ Wilło del Bothe	...	...	xv. đ.

Smª. vj. š. vij. đ. pb.

Penhiltoñ Magna cū pua
[*Great and Little Pendleton*]

Ð Wiłło de Bilingtoñ	...	...	ij. ß.
„ Wiłł del Gerner	...	...	xij. đ.
„ Adam de Morlegh	...	...	xij. đ.
„ Stepho del Ridding	...	...	xij. đ.
„ Adam le Baker	...	...	xij. đ.
„ Wiłł de Derwent	...	...	xij. đ.
„ Reginald de Whallay	...	...	xij. đ.

Smª. viij. ß. pƀ.

Haptoñ
[*Hapton*]

Ð Adam de Briddestwiselł		...	iij. ß.
„ Johe de Shuttlesworth		...	xij. đ.
„ Joħ de Haptoñ		...	xij. đ.
„ Ric̃ del Heye	...	...	ij. ß. vj. đ.
„ Joħ del Eghes	...	...	ij. ß.
„ Alañ del Childres		...	iij. ß.
„ Rog̃ de Aluetham		...	ij. ß. vj. đ.

Smª. xv. ß. pƀ.

Brunlay
[*Burnley*]

Ð Oliver̃ de Stanesfelđ	...	...	ij. ß. viij. đ.
„ Johe de la Leghe	...	...	xxiij. đ.
„ Johe de Dunnokshagh		...	iij. ß. x. đ.
„ Ric̃o del Brigge	...	...	ij. ß. v. đ.
„ Ric̃o de Plesingtoñ	...	...	xviij. đ. oƀ.
„ Adam le Parker	...	...	xix. đ.
„ Roƀto del Holnis	...	...	xviij. đ.
„ Reginałđ de Coudeñ	...	...	ij. ß. oƀ.
„ Gilƀto del Halle	....	...	xviij. đ.

Smª. xix. ß. pƀ.

Padiham
[*Padiham*]

Ð Ric̃o de Whitacr̃	...	...	xvj. đ.
„ Ric̃o del Wode	...	...	xvj. đ.

Đ Wilł de Mikelbrok ... ... xij. đ.
„ Thom̃ fił Henr̄ ... ... xxj. đ.
„ Roǧ le Ledbeter ... ... xvj. đ.
„ Adam de Angrum ... ... ij. ꝭ.
„ Henr̄ fił Johis ... ... xv. đ. oƀ.

Sm̃ꝰ. x. ꝭ. oƀ. pƀ.

Plesintoñ
[*Pleasington*]

Đ Johe de Wynkedlegh ... ... iiij. ꝭ.
„ Johe de Copphulł ... ... ij. ꝭ.
„ Roǧ fił Elie ... ... xx. đ.
„ Henr̄ del Ewode ... ... xvj. đ.
„ Henr̄ de Plesintoñ ... ... x. đ.
„ Aleẍ de Thoonge ... ... xij. đ.
„ Huǧ Redylegh .. .. xij. đ.

Sm̃ꝰ. xj. ꝭ. x. đ. pƀ.

Samlesbur̄
[*Samlesbury*]

Đ Wilło ffaƀr ... ... iij. ꝭ. iiij. đ.
„ Henr̄ Loteby ... ... iij. ꝭ.
„ Henr̄ de Smalley ... ... iij. ꝭ.
„ Joh Hardegray ... . iij. ꝭ. iiij. đ.
„ Aleẍ Deuyas ... ... iij. ꝭ. ij. đ. oƀ
„ Adam fił Rici ... ... iij. ꝭ. iiij. đ.
„ Gilƀto del Cliffe ... ... xiiij. đ.
„ Nicho del Dene ... ... xvj. đ. oƀ.
„ Adam de Ethelistoñ ... ... ij. ꝭ. oƀ.
„ Roƀto fił Roƀti ... ... xiiij. đ. oƀ.
„ Roƀto de Hale ... ... iiij. ꝭ.
„ Joh fił Roƀti ... . ij. ꝭ.
„ Wilł del Coppedhurst ... ... ij. ꝭ.
„ Wilło fił Thom̃ ... ... ij. ꝭ. iiij. đ.
„ Adam fił Roǧi ... ... xvj. đ. oƀ.
„ Adam de Coppedhurst ... xv. đ. oƀ.

Sm̃ꝰ. xxxviij. ꝭ. pƀ.

Leuesay
[*Livesey*]

Ð Henr̃ le Walssħ	...	...	iij. s̃. viij. đ
„ Adam del Ewode	...	...	iij. s̃. viij. đ.
„ Roƀto del Knolt	...	...	iiij. s̃. iiij. đ.
„ Roǧo de Dewyhirst	...	...	ij. s̃.
„ Henr̃ fit Ric̃i	...	...	ij. s̃. iiij. đ.
„ Nicħo del Ewode	...	...	xij. đ.
„ Adam de Liuesay	...	...	xij. đ.

Sm̃ᵃ. xviij. s̃. pƀ.

Walton in the Dale
[*Walton le Dale*]

Ð Joħe de Longetoñ	...	...	xiiij. s̃.
„ Henr̃ Banastr̃	...	...	iij. s̃.
„ Wilt Banastr̃	...	...	iij. s̃.
„ Huǧ de Haidok	...	...	xij. đ.
„ Joħe de Waltoñ	...	...	iij. s̃.
„ Alex̃ de Longeley	...	...	ij. s̃.
„ Galfr̃ Banastr̃	...	...	iij. s̃.
„ Adam de Balshagħ	...	...	iij. s̃.
„ Joħe de Blakeburñ	...	...	xij. đ.
„ Joħe de Glendoñ	...	...	xij. đ.
„ Joħ de Hanshaghe	...	...	xij. đ.
„ Jacobo de Lostok	...	...	iij. s̃.
„ Joħe del Ridinǧ	...	...	ij. s̃.
„ Henr̃ fit Henr̃	...	...	xij. đ.
„ Wilt de Coluile	...	...	ij. s̃.
„ Adam de Wyndibonk	...	...	xviij. đ.
„ Wilt Gerstan	...	...	xviij. đ.

Sm̃ᵃ. xlvj. s̃. pƀ.

Oswaldestwyselt
[*Oswaldtwisle*]

Ð Adam de Haworth	...	...	xviij. đ.
„ Adam de ffoxhulbonk	...	...	xvj. đ.
„ Thom̃ de Prestewich	...	...	ij. s̃. ix. đ.

Đ Simon Sharp̃ ... ... ij. s. iiij. đ.
„ Roḡ de Catlowe ... ... ij. s. vj. đ.
„ Alañ de Kenian ... ... xx. đ.

Smᵃ. xij. s. pƀ.

Aghtoñ
[*Aighton*]

Đ Adam de Winkedlay ... ... iiij. s. iiij. đ.
„ Joñe de Bailegħ ... ... iij. s. iiij. đ.
„ Riĉo fit Gilƀti ... ... iij. s. iiij. đ.
„ Wilt del Knolt ... ... ij. s.
„ Adam le Taillour ... ... ij. s.
„ Riĉ de Bury ... ... ij. s. viij. đ.
„ Riĉo de Liuesay ... ... iij. s.
„ Rađo de Baylegħ ... ... xxij. đ.
„ Roƀto de Clyderhou ... ... iiij. s.
„ Wilt fit Elie ... ... xv. đ. oƀ.
„ Riĉo fit Tille ... ... ij. s. vj. đ.
„ Wilto fit Roƀti ... ... ij. s. vj. đ.
„ Henr̃ del Asshes ... ... xx. đ.
„ Joñe de Dodehull ... ... xvj. đ.
„ Henr̃ de Hacounshou ... ... ij. s. iiij. đ.
„ Joñe Fox ... ... xxiij. đ.

Smᵃ. xl. s. oƀ. pƀ.

Salebur̃
[*Salesbury*]

Đ Ađ de Cliderhou ... ... ij. s.
„ Henr̃ del Brok ... ... xij. đ.
„ Roƀto Dunsy ... ... xij. đ.
„ Riĉo de Tyndyhed ... ... ij. s.

Smᵃ. vj. s. pƀ.

Huncote
[*Huncoat*]

Đ Wilt de Briddestwyselt ... ij. s.
„ Wilt de Bakestondeñ ... ... xij. đ.
„ Riĉo de Huncote ... ... xiiij. đ.
„ Wilto fit Huḡ ... ... xij. đ.

Ð Gilƀto fił Nicħi ...   .   xij. đ.

„ Wilł le Mercer ...   .   xij. đ.

„ Roƀto de Wysewalle ...   ...   xij. đ.

Smᵃ. viij. ઠ. ij. đ. pƀ.

Chipin
[*Chipping*]

Ð Riĉo fił Að   ...   .   xxiij. đ.

„ Riĉo del Karscele   ...   ...   ij. ઠ. j. đ. oƀ.

„ Wilł Scot   ...   .   v. ઠ.

„ Adam fił Roƀ ...   .   xviij. đ.

„ Wilło fil Rađi ...   .   xviij. đ.

„ Roƀto fił Roƀti ...   .   iij. ઠ. ij. đ.

„ Roƀto de Yolstones   ...   ...   ij. ઠ.

„ Nicħo del Brenaund   ...   ...   xxij. đ.

„ Að fił Stepħi   ...   .   xvi. đ.

„ Rađo fił Wilłi ...   .   v. ઠ.

„ Rađo de Helm̃ ...   .   ix. đ.

„ Riĉo del Halle ...   .   xiij. đ.

„ Wilł de Helm̃ ...   .   x. đ.

„ Stepħo de Rauenshagh   ...   xij. đ.

Smᵃ. xxix. ઠ. oƀ. pƀ.

Brerclif cũ Extwiselł
[*Briercliffe with Extwistle*]

Ð Adam de Walleshagħ ...   ...   ij. ઠ. vj. đ.

„ RoꝘ Carpenꝯ   ...   .   xviij. đ.

„ Henr̃ Swapeltrot   ...   ...   xij. đ. oƀ.

„ Roƀto le Mon ...   .   ij. ઠ. vj. đ.

„ Roƀto de Brereclif   ...   ...   ij. ઠ. vj. đ.

„ Gilƀto le Mon ...   .   ij. ઠ.

„ Huꞡ del falł ...   .   ij. ઠ.

„ Adam fił Joħ ...   .   ij. ઠ.

Smᵃ. xvj. ઠ. oƀ. pƀ.

Harewode Magna
[*Great Harwood*]

Ð Joħe de Heskeith   ...   ...   vj. ઠ.

„ Wilło le Dene ...   .   xx. đ.

Ɖ Rado fił Henr̃ ... ... xx. đ.
„ Wilł de Ourom ... ... iij. s̃. iiij. đ.
„ Henr̃ fił Rič̃i ... ... ij. s̃.
„ Wilło fił Ađ ... ... ij. s̃.
„ Rog̃ le Lewed ... ... xij. đ.
„ Rič̃ de Kekshaghe ... ... xij. đ.
„ Wilło del Ridding̃ ... ... xx. đ.
„ Adam le Sklater ... ... xj. đ.
„ Joħ Magħeles ... ... xj. đ.
„ Wilło del Wode ... ... x. đ.

Sm̃ᵃ. xviij. s̃.

Bylyngton
[*Billington*]

Ɖ Wilło fił Oliu̇i ... ... iij. s̃. iiij. đ.
„ Joħe de Bradhull ... ... iiij. s̃. j. đ. ob̃.
„ Rog̃o de Longefeld ... ... ij. s̃. viij. đ.
„ Joħ fił Rog̃i ... ... iij. s̃. j. đ.
„ Wilł fił Daukyn ... ... ij. s̃. ix. d.
„ Rog̃ fabr ... ... ix. đ.
„ Rob̃to de Snoddeswortħ ... xj. đ.
„ Wilło fił Rađi ... ... xvij. d.

Sm̃ᵃ. xix. s̃. ob̃. pb̃.

Claitoñ s̃r Moras
[*Clayton le Moors*]

Ɖ Henr̃ de Claitoñ ... ... ij. s̃. iiij. đ.
„ Rob̃to fił Henr̃ ... ... xij. đ.
„ Wilł de Whitfeld ... ... x. đ.
„ Rič̃ de Claitoñ ... ... x. đ.
„ Willo de Harpersone ... ... x. đ.
„ Adam fił Rog̃ ... ... x. đ.

Sm̃ᵃ. vj. s̃. viij. d. pb̃.

Netherderwenđ
[*Nether Darwen*]

Ɖ Alex̃ de Turtoñ... ... ... ij. s̃.
„ Adam fił Jorđi ... ... ij. s̃.

Đ Henr̃ de Monkes ... ... xxj. đ.
„ Adam Stridhom ... ... xvj. đ.
„ Joħ de Onnūclogh ... ... xvj. đ.
„ Joħe de Witton ... ... xvj. đ.
„ Adam Blakhed ... ... xij. đ.

Smᵃ. x. ſ. ix. đ.

Thorndelegħ cū Whetelegħ
[*Thornley with Wheatley*]
Đ Thom̃ de Knolł ... ... xviij. đ.
„ Ričo de Bradeley ... ... xij. đ.
„ Thom̃ de Grenehilł ... ... xvj. đ.
„ Ričo Dawesone ... ... xx. đ.
„ Swano fił Cristiañ ... ... xiiij. đ. oƀ.
„ Wilło del Toun ... ... iij. ſ.
„ Huḡ de Mittoñ ... ... iij. ſ. iiij. đ.
„ Ričo de Grenehilł ... ... ij. ſ.
„ Roƀto de Bradelegħ ... ... xx. đ.
„ Ričo fił Huḡ ... ... xvj. đ.

Smᵃ. xviij. ſ. oƀ. pƀ.

Blakeburñ
[*Blackburn*]
Đ Joħe de Coule ... ... ij. ſ. iij. đ. qᵃ.
„ Alañ de Westshagħ ... ... ij. ſ. vj. đ. oƀ.
„ Wilł fił Roƀti ... ... ij. ſ. iij. đ.
„ Matilł de Redelegħ ... ... ij. ſ. oƀ.
„ Henr̃ Mimmyñḡ ... ... xx. đ. oƀ. qᵃ.
„ Elia de ffagheside ... ... xvij. đ.
„ Elia de Ridelegħ ... ... xij. đ. oƀ. qᵃ.
„ Joħe del Mercs ... ... ij. ſ. ij. đ.
„ Adam le Vacher ... ... xxiij. đ.
„ Henr̃ de Haukeshagħ ... ... xij. đ. qᵃ.
„ Henr̃ fił Alič ... ... xiij. đ. qᵃ.
„ Ričo fił Alañ ... ... xiiij. đ.
„ Wilł Page ... ... xiiij. đ.

Smᵃ. xxj. ſ. x. đ. qᵃ. pƀ.

Russhtoñ
[*Rishton*]

Ɖ Juoñ del Holt	...	...	...	xx. đ.
„ Roƀto de Turtoñ	...	...	xx. đ.
„ Henr̃ de Russhtoñ	...	...	xvj. đ.
„ Ađ de Whithagħ	...	...	iiij. ȿ. x. đ.
„ Joħe de Couhilt	...	...	xij. đ.
„ Henr̃ fit Juonis	...	...	x. đ.
„ Riĉo Hert	...	...	...	x. đ.
„ Roƀto Warde	...	...	...	x. đ.

Smᵃ. xiij. ȿ. pƀ.

ffolrige
[*Foulrige*]

Ɖ Joħ de Reued	...	...	...	iij. ȿ. iiij. đ.
„ Roƀto de Bukshagħ	...	...	ij. ȿ.
„ Riĉo de Monkerode	...	...	ij. ȿ.
„ Joħ de Leghecroft	...	...	ij. ȿ. x. đ.
„ Riĉo del Shaghe	...	...	iiij. ȿ.
„ Joħe faƀr	...	...	...	ij. ȿ.
„ Adam de ffolrige	...	...	xij. đ.

Smᵃ. xviij. ȿ. ij. đ. pƀ.

Melaire cū Ecclishult
[*Mellor with Eccleshill*]

Ɖ Adam de Turtoñ	...	...	iij. ȿ. iiij. đ.
„ Riĉo de Shorrok	...	...	ij. ȿ. iiij. đ.
„ Alañ Bond	...	...	...	xvj. đ.
„ Gilƀto de Cokerlegħ	...	...	xiiij. đ. ob.
„ Adam de Huntingdeñ	...	...	xij. đ.
„ Riĉo de Gorlache	...	...	xij. đ.
„ Wilt fit Huȝ	...	...	xij. đ.
„ Joħ de Holoñ	...	...	xij. đ.

Smᵃ. xij. ȿ. ij. đ. ob. pƀ.

Merclesdeñ
[*Marsden*]

Ɖ Riĉo de Waynwright	...	...	ij. ȿ. vij. ȿ. q.
„ Roƀto de Catlow	...	...	ij. ȿ.

G 2

Đ Wilło le ffissher	...	...	iij. s. iij. đ.
„ Rič fił Ađ	...	...	ij. s. vj. đ.
„ Rič le Turnour	...	...	ij. s.
„ Adam le Hunter	...	...	ij. s. vj. đ.
„ Adam de Catlowe	...	...	ij. s. vj. đ.
„ Thom de Brereclif	...	...	xxj. đ.
„ Adam Bete	...	...	xvj. đ.

Sm^a. xx. s. vj. đ. q^a. pb.

Oułderwenđ
[*Over Darwen*]

Đ Wilło le Baroñ	...	...	iiij. s.
„ Joħ fił Vghtrith	...	...	xviij. đ.
„ Ričo de Alstoñ	...	...	iiij. s.
„ Nicħo del Crosse	...	...	xij. đ.
„ Rič fił Bymne	...	...	xx. đ.
„ Rog le Taillour	...	...	xiiij. đ.

Sm^a. xiij. s. iiij. đ. pb.

Wlipsħ cū Dynkedlegħ
[*Wilpshire with Dinkley*]

Đ Rogo de Dynkedlegħ	...	...	ij. s.
„ Adam fabr	...	..	xiiij. đ.
„ Adam del Dewyhirst	...	...	xvj. đ.
„ Wilł del Brigge	...	...	xv. đ.
„ Henr fił Walłi	...	...	ij. s. ij. đ. ob.
„ Joħe fił Cłici	...	...	xv. đ.

Sm^a. ix. s. ij. đ. ob. pb.

Claiton in the Dale
[*Clayton le Dale*]

Đ Adam le Blakeburñ	...	...	iij. s. ij. đ.
„ Joħe fił Gilbti	...	...	xij. đ.
„ Thom de Huntingdeñ	...	...	ij. s. vj. đ.
„ Joħ de Balshaghe	...	...	xviij. đ.
„ Henr de Huntingdeñ	...	...	xviij. đ.
„ Matħo de Whallay	...	...	xvj. đ.

Sm^a. xj. s. pb.

Wisewalt
[*Wiswall*]

Ð Riĉo fił Henr̃	...	...	...	ij. ꝭ. v. đ.
„ Adam Molenđ	...	...	...	xv. đ.
„ Henr̃ fił Galfr	...	...	...	xx. đ.
„ Wilło Scot	...	...	...	xvj. đ.
„ Adam fił Riĉi	...	...	...	ix. đ.
„ Roꝯ del Wode	...	...	...	viij. đ. oꝧ.
„ Henr̃ fił Ađ	...	...	...	x. đ.

Smᵃ. viij. ꝭ. xj. oꝧ.

Colne
[*Colne*]

Ð Joħe del Holt	...	...	...	ij. ꝭ. viij. đ.
„ Wilło Altencotes		...	...	ij. ꝭ.
„ Ađ Molenđ	...	...	...	iij. ꝭ. v. đ. oꝧ.
„ Roꝧto ꝑpõito	...		...	xij. đ.
„ Joħe de Kelbrok		...	...	iij. ꝭ.
„ Micħe le Walker		...	...	xvj. đ.
„ Wilł le Dryuer		...	...	xxiij. đ.
„ Riĉo Molenđ		...	...	ij. ꝭ.
„ Nicoħo del Bothe		...	...	ij. ꝭ. j. đ.
„ Wilło de Emot		...	...	xij. đ.

Smᵃ. xx. ꝭ. v. d. oꝧ. ꝕꝧ.

Worthestorñ
[*Worsthorn*]

Ð Wilło de Windhulł		...	...	xviij. đ.
„ Wilło del Hallestudes		...	...	xv. đ.
„ Joħe fił Riĉi	...		...	ix. đ. oꝧ.
„ Roꝯ de Windhulł		...	...	xvj. đ.
„ Matħo fił Henr̃	...		...	ij. ꝭ.
„ Roꝧto Tenaunt		...	...	xiiij. đ.
„ Roꝧto del Hallestudes		...	...	xij. đ.

Smᵃ. ix. ꝭ. oꝧ. ꝕꝧ.

Duttoñ
[*Dutton*]

Đ Henr̃ de Claitoñ	...	...	ij. ß.
„ Joñe de Claitoñ	...	...	ij. ß.
„ Thom̃ de Dodehult	...	...	iiij. ß.
„ Henr̃ de Huntingdeñ	...	...	ij. ß.
„ Wilt fit Wilti	...	...	xviij. đ.
„ Wilt de Blakekeburñ [*sic*]	...	xv. đ. oꝗ.
„ Wilto Motoñ	...	...	ix. đ.
„ Ric̃o del Asshes	...	...	xij. đ.
„ Wilt de Huntingdeñ	...	...	xj. đ.

Sm^a. xv. ß. v. đ. oꝗ. ꝗꝗ.

Mittoñ Hentherñ ⁊ Coldecotes
[*Mitton, Henthorn, & Coldcoates*]

Đ Johanna de Coldecotes	...	ij. ß.
„ Auicia de Hentherñ	...	...	xv. đ.
„ Ric̃ fit Alañ	...	...	xij. đ. oꝗ.
„ Ric̃ de Whallay	...	...	xiij. đ.
„ Wilt de Mittoñ	...	...	xij. đ.
„ Henr̃ fit Roꝗto	...	...	xiij. đ.

Sm^a. vij. ß. v. đ. oꝗ. ꝗꝗ.

Reuid
[*Read*]

Đ Alicia del Clogħ	...	...	ij. ß.
„ Joñe de Stanlawe	...	...	ij. ß. ij. đ.
„ Joñe del Holt	...	...	xvj. đ.
„ Ric̃ fit Alañ	...	...	xij. đ.
„ Adam de Lyntoñ	...	...	ix. đ.
„ Adam fit Roꝗ	...	...	ix. đ.

Sm^a. viij. ß. ꝗꝗ.

Ribbelcestr̃
[*Ribchester*]

Đ Roꝗto Motoñ	...	...	...	vj. ß. iiij. đ. oꝗ.
„ Roꝗto ffraunceis	...	...	iiij. ß. viij. đ.

Ð Roƀto fiɫ Wilɫi ... ... vj. ꝫ. oƀ.

„ Adam de Ribbelcestr̃ ... ... iij. ꝫ. iiij. đ.

„ Thoɱ [fil] Georgii ... ... iij. ꝫ. viij. đ.

„ Ađ fiɫ Ađ ... ... iij. ꝫ.

„ Joħ del Brok ... ... xvj. đ.

„ Ric̃ Motoñ ... ... xiij. đ. qᵃ.

„ Ric̃o de Chipindale ... ... xiij. đ.

„ Ric̃o fiɫ Simoñ ... ... xij. đ.

„ Henr̃ Motoñ ... ... xij. đ.

„ Joħe fiɫ Wilɫ ... ... xviij. đ.

„ Henr̃ de Kerdeñ ... ... iij. ꝫ.

„ Wilɫo de Dillewortħ ... ... ix. đ.

Smᵃ. xxxvij. ꝫ. x. đ. qᵃ. pƀ.

Wyttoñ
[*Witton*]

Ð Roƀto de Radecliue ... ... ij. ꝫ.

„ Galfr̃ del Egħes ... ... xx. d.

„ Ric̃o fiɫ Simoñ ... ... xij. đ.

„ Roƀto de Bullynḡ ... ... xvj. đ.

Smᵃ. vj. ꝫ. pƀ.

Twyseltoñ
[*Twiston*]

Ð Ric̃o de Grenacres ... ... ij. ꝫ. vi. đ.

„ Adam le fforster ... ... xviij. đ.

„ Wilɫ le fforster ... ... xij. đ.

Smᵃ. v. ꝫ. pƀ.

Whallay
[*Whalley*]

Ð Joħe de Whallay ... ... ij. ꝫ. vj. đ.

„ Ric̃o le Baker ... ... xij. đ.

„ Thurstano cɫrico ... ... xviij. đ.

Smᵃ. v. ꝫ. pƀ.

Smᵃ. Wapentacħ xxxvij. ɫi. xiij. ꝫ. j. đ. qᵃ.

Wapen̄ de Lonesdale.

[HUNDRED OF LONSDALE.]

Lanc̄
[*Lancaster*]

Burḡ tax̄ ad xam.

D Adam fiƚ Simon̄	... ...	v. s̄.
„ Adam le Purser	... ...	viij. s̄.
„ Joħe le Mercer ...	... ...	viij. s̄.
„ Hug̃ le Lister ...	... ...	v. s̄.
„ Thom̄ le Mason	... ...	iiij. s̄.
„ Joħe le Ken ...	... ...	v. s̄.
„ Robto de Bolroun	... ...	vj. s̄.
„ Alan̄ fiƚ Magri ...	... ...	iiij. s̄. vj. đ.
„ Joħe fiƚ Joħis Laurence	...	iiij. s̄.
„ Joħe de Lodlawe	... ...	vj. s̄.
„ Joħe de Caton̄ ...	... ...	ij. s̄. x. đ.
„ Joħe le Sklater	... ...	v. s̄.

Sma. lxiij. s̄. iiij. đ. pƀ.

Caton̄ cū Claghton̄
[*Caton with Claughton*]

D Joħe de Lytindale	... ...	ij. s̄. vj. đ. oƀ.
„ Adam de Claghton̄	... ...	ij. s̄. x. đ. oƀ
„ Rog̃ le Walker ...	... ...	iij. s̄. ij. đ.
„ Joħe fiƚ Isolđ ...	... ...	iij. s̄. viij. đ.
„ Joħe fiƚ Ađ ...	... ...	ij. s̄. ix. đ.
„ Ric̄o fiƚ Godetħ	... ...	ix. s̄.
„ Joħe de Huddesbank ...	...	ix. s̄.
„ Joħ fiƚ Batti ...	... ...	iiij. s̄.
„ Adam del Crag̃	... ...	xx. đ.
„ Joħe del grene...	... ...	v. s̄.
„ Joħ de Leek ...	... ...	v. s̄.
„ Wiƚƚ fiƚ Rog̃ ...	... ...	xvj. d.
„ Wiƚƚ fiƚ Thom̄ ...	... ...	xij. đ.

Sma. *lj. s̄. pƀ.*

Mideltoñ
[*Middleton*]

Ð Wilł de Burgħ ... ... x. đ.
„ Thoм̃ de Rigmayden ... ... x. đ.
„ Roǧ de Pynnymoᷓ ... ... xvj. đ.
„ Wilło fił Roƀti ... ... x. đ.
„ Joħe Brewes ... ... x. đ.
„ Wilł Chapmon ... ... xvj. đ.

Smᵃ. vj. ſ. pƀ.

Tathᵃm cū Irby
[*Tatham cum Ireby*]

Ð Thoм̃ Dreperaa ... ... ij. ſ.
„ Riᴄ̃o fił Wilłi ... ... ij. ſ.
„ Roƀto fforestaᷓ ... ... · ij. ſ. vj. đ.
„ Joħ fił Stepħi ... ...· ij. ſ. vj. đ.

Smᵃ. ix. ſ. pƀ.

Leek
[*Leck*]

Ð Huǧ fił Wilłi ... ... iij. ſ.
„ Joħe de Toddegilł ... ... iij. ſ.
„ Wilło le Spenſ ... ... xij. đ.
„ Riᴄ̃o de Crauen ... ... xij. đ.
„ Thoм̃ fił Joħ ... ... xij. đ.

Smᵃ. ix. ſ. pƀ.

Skertoñ
[*Skerton*]

Ð Elia dę Bemound ... ... xvj. đ.
„ Joħ faƀr ... ... xij. đ.
„ Roƀto p̃p̃õito ... ... xij. đ.

Smᵃ. iij. ſ. iiij. đ. pƀ.

Whityntoñ
[*Whittington*]

Ð Roƀto Daues ... ... ij. ſ. j. đ.
„ Adam fił Beñ ... ... xxj. đ.

Ð Wilł Scot	...	... ...	xxj. đ.
„ Thom̃ Collan	...	... ...	ij. s̃. viij. đ.
„ Wilł fił Simoñ	...	... ...	ij. s̃. ij. đ.
„ Adam del Mire		... ...	xix. đ.

Sm̃ᵃ. xij. s̃. pƀ.

Ellale
[*Ellel*]

Ð Thom̃ de Slene	...	... ...	ij. s̃. vj. đ.
„ Roƀto del graunge	...	... ...	ij. s̃. v. đ. oƀ.
„ Roƀto de ffisshwik	...	...	ij. s̃.
„ Hug̃ del fflaskes	...	...	ij. s̃. vj. đ. oƀ.
„ Adam fił Jorđ	...	... ...	iij. s̃. oƀ.
„ Joñ fił Henr̃	...	... ...	ij. s̃. ij. đ.
„ Joñ le Turnour	...	... ...	ij. s̃. oƀ.
„ Ađ Carpenť	...	... ...	iij. s̃. oƀ.
„ Thom̃ fił Gilƀti	...	... ...	ij. s̃. viij. đ.
„ Gilƀto de Bolroñ	...	... ...	ij. s̃. oƀ.

Sm̃ᵃ. xxiiij. s̃. vj. đ. pƀ.

Vrsewik
[*Urswick*]

Ð Simoñ fił Rič̃i	...	... ...	xiij. đ.
„ Wilł fił Roƀti	...	... ...	xij. đ.
„ Alañ de Boltoñ	...	... ...	vj. s̃. ix. đ.
„ Wilł fił Joñ	...	... ...	v. s̃.
„ Roƀto Carpenť	...	... ...	ij. s̃. ij. đ.
„ Thom̃ fił Rog̃i	...	... ...	xviij. đ.
„ Henr̃ Garlaunđ	...	... ...	xviij. đ.
„ Joñ fił Wilł	...	... ...	ij. s̃. vj. đ.
„ Adam Bellard	...	... ...	xxiij. đ.
„ Micħe fił Rog̃i	...	... ...	x. đ.
„ Micħ fił Thom̃	...	... ...	xij. đ.
„ Joñ Derlinge	...	... ...	xvj. đ.
„ Wilł Rabayn	...	... ...	xvj. đ.

Sm̃ᵃ. xxviij. s̃. pƀ.

Burgħ
[*Burrow*]

Đ Ric̃ del Hołm	...	...	...	ij. ß.
„ Wilł Kerling	...	...	...	ij. ß.
„ Wilł fił Joħ	...	...	...	ij. ß.
„ Rog̃ fił Joħ	...	...	...	ij. ß.
„ Joħ fił Wilł	..	...	...	xij. đ.
„ Joħ fił Ede	...	...	...	ij. ß.

Smᵃ. xj. ß. pb̃.

Sline cū Hest
[*Slyne with Hest*]

Đ Joħ fił Elie	...	...	...	xij. đ.
„ Rađo de Slyne	...	...	...	xij. đ.
„ Adam Cissore	...	...	...	xij. đ.
„ Nicħo p̃põito	...	...	...	xij. đ.
„ Wilł de Crauen	...	...	...	ij. ß.
„ Wilł fił Adam	...	...	...	xij. đ.
„ Wilło Persoñ	...	...	...	xviij. đ.
„ Thoñ de Hest	...	...	...	xviij. đ.

Smᵃ. x. ß. pb̃.

Kirkeby Irlitħ
[*Kirkby Ireleth*]

Đ Joħe de Kirkeby	...	...	iij. ß. j. đ. qᵃ.
„ Joħ de Boltoñ	...	...	xvj. đ. ob̃.
„ Joħe fił Matħi	...	...	xv. đ. ob̃. qᵃ.
„ Joħ de Pulł	...	...	xij. đ. ob̃.
„ Thoñ del Waynesgate		...	xiiij. đ.
„ Alañ fił Wilłi	...	...	xij. đ. ob̃.
„ Rob̃to de Coltoñ	...	...	xix. đ. ob̃. qᵃ.
„ Joħ de Gretebrek	...	...	xvj. đ. ob̃.
„ Ric̃o Baseb̃ron	...	...	xvj. đ.
„ Matho fił Gilb̃ti	...	...	xij. đ.
„ Adam de Coltoñ	...	...	xj. đ.
„ Wilł de Gretebrek	...	...	xj. đ. ob̃. qᵃ.
„ Rog̃ de Cornay	...	...	viij. đ. ob̃. qᵃ.

Đ Joħ de Burghdale ... ... xxj. đ. qᵃ.
„ Roᵍ de Grenedale ... ... xvj. đ. oƀ.
„ Wilł de Soutergate ... ... xj. đ. oƀ. qᵃ.

Smᵃ. xxj. ꞩ. j. đ. oƀ. qᵃ. pƀ.

Penyngtoñ
[*Pennington*]

Đ Henr̃ de Loftscales ... ... xiij. đ.
„ Joħ de Kertemelł ... ... xiij. đ.
„ Wilł fił Roḡi ... ... iij. ꞩ.
„ Adam del Grenes ... ... ix. đ.
„ Joħ fił Roḡi ... ... ix. đ.

Smᵃ. vj. ꞩ. viij. đ. pƀ.

Lees
[*Leece*]

Đ Alex le Couherd ... ... ij. ꞩ. j. đ.
„ Wilł Bercar̃ ... ... ij. ꞩ. v. đ. oƀ.
„ Thom̃ Derlyng ... ... ij. ꞩ. x. đ.
„ Joħ le Hunter ... ... xiij. đ.
„ Joħe fił Dande ... ... xv. đ.
„ Adam le Palfraimon ... ... ij. ꞩ. ij. đ.
„ Alañ Dynyer ... ... ij. ꞩ.
„ Thom̃ del Lund ... ... ij. ꞩ. j. đ.
„ Adam Derlyng ... ... ij. ꞩ. j. đ.
„ Wilł de Salthouses ... ... ij. ꞩ. vj. đ.
„ Adam le Prestesmon ... ... xxiij. đ. oƀ.
„ Roƀto Carectar̃ ... ... xiij. đ. oƀ.
„ Wilł fił Joħis ... ... iiij. ꞩ. iiij. đ. oƀ.

Smᵃ. xxviij. ꞩ. pƀ.

Pulton Bare cū Thorishołm
[*Poulton le Sands and Bare with Torrisholme*]

Đ Joħ Walleys ... ... iiij. ꞩ.
„ Joħe de Pultoñ ... ... ij. ꞩ.
„ Wilł Placeden ... ... iij. ꞩ.
„ Wilł fił Gilƀti ... ... iiij. ꞩ.

Ð Joħe de Bare ... ... ij. ꝝ.
„ Thoɱ de Greneholɱ ... ... ij. ꝝ.
„ Joħe Sabyn ... . ij. ꝝ.
„ Thoɱ de Kertmelł ... ... ij. ꝝ.

Smᵃ. xx. ꝝ. pƀ.

Scotford
[*Scotforth*]
Ð Rañ le Gentilł ... ... iij. ꝝ. j. đ.
„ Joħ de Balrigge ... ... ij. ꝝ. viij. đ.
„ Hawiꝝ de Balroun ... ... iij. ꝝ. j. đ.
„ Joħ de ffourneis ... ... xij. đ.
„ Joħ fił Wilł ... ... xvj. đ.
„ Henꝝ de Balriꝝ ... ... xx. đ.
„ Joħ fił Alani ... ... ij. ꝝ.
„ Joħ fił Ade ... ... xvj. đ.

Smᵃ. xvj. ꝝ. ij. đ. pƀ.

Vluerestoñ
[*Ulverston*]
Ð Nicħo de Broghtoñ ... ... iiij. ꝝ. xj. đ. oƀ. qᵃ.
„. Wilło de Osmoundrelawe ... vj. ꝝ. iij. đ. oƀ. qᵃ.
„ Thoɱ Sele ... ... viij. ꝝ. iij. đ.
„ Ađ de Lees ... ... iij. ꝝ. x. đ. oƀ.
„ Adam Belle ... ... iij. ꝝ. ij. đ.
„ Thoɱ del Trees ... ... iij. ꝝ. viij. đ.
„ Simoñ fił Matilł ... ... iij. ꝝ. vj. đ. oƀ. qᵃ.
„ Thoɱ de Ridmerthwait ... ij. ꝝ. viij. đ. qᵃ.
„ Riĉo fił Gunnyld ... ... iij. ꝝ. vj. đ. oƀ.
„ Joħ del Bonk ... ... iij. ꝝ.
„ Beñ de Gaytscale ... ... ij. ꝝ. iij. đ. qᵃ.
„ Adam de Skelwath ... ... ij. ꝝ. x. đ. oƀ.
„ Joħ fił Roꝿ ... ... xx. đ. oƀ. qᵃ.
„ Roꝿ Elterwatꝝ ... ... xvij. đ. oƀ.
„ Adam de Stablcheruy ... ij. s. iij. đ. qᵃ.
„ Roꝿ de Cammpaigne ... ... ij. ꝝ. iiij. đ. oƀ. qᵃ.
„ Adam de Todhoubonk ... xiiij. đ. oƀ.
„ Adam fił Dande ... ... xiiij. đ.

Đ Ric̃ de Salthouȝ	...	...	ij. ȿ. viij. đ.
„ Joħ fit Cristiañ ...	...	...	xxiij. đ. oƀ.
„ Alañ fit Ric̃	...	...	xxiij. đ.
„ Wilt Scopemun	...	...	xvj. đ. oƀ.
„ Joħ le Swon	...	...	xx. đ. oƀ. qᵃ.
„ Adam fit Nicħi	...	...	iiij. ȿ. ij. đ.
„ Adam fit Ric̃i ...	...	...	xj. đ. qᵃ.
„ Adañ de Mirewraa	...	...	v. ȿ. j. đ.
„ Thom̃ Belle	...	...	v. ȿ. j. đ.
„ Wilt fit Wilti ...	...	...	iij. ȿ. iiij. đ.

Smᵃ. iiij. ti. vj. ȿ. viij. đ. pƀ.

Haltoñ
[*Halton*]

Đ Joħ del Scales ...	...	...	ij. ȿ. iiij. đ.
„ Joħ de la More	...	...	ij. ȿ. x. đ.
„ Beatric̃ vidua ...	...	...	iiij. ȿ.
„ Wilt de Steresacre	...	...	xij. đ.
„ Thom̃ del Howe	...	...	xij. đ.
„ Ric̃ de Berdesay	...	...	xx. đ.
„ Simōe de Grisdale	...	...	ij. ȿ. ij. đ.

Smᵃ. xv. ȿ. pƀ.

Kerneford cū Berwik
[*Carnforth with Borwick*]

Đ Nicħo Staffult ...	...	...	ij. ȿ.
„ Thom̃ Sprentlope	...	...	ij. ȿ.
„ Roƀto de Wasshyntoñ	...	...	iij. ȿ.
„ Adam fit Thom̃...	...	...	iij. ȿ. viij. đ.
„ Adam Staffult ...	...	...	xij. đ.
„ Ađ Ctico	...	...	xij. đ.
„ Thom̃ Broñ	...	...	ij. ȿ. iiij. đ.
„ Thom̃ Grindebofe	...	...	xj. đ.

Sm. xvj. ȿ. pƀ.

Aldyngham
[*Aldingham*]

Đ Wilto Buntynge	...	...	ij. ȿ. qᵃ.
„ Micħe Ramage...	...	...	ij. ȿ. qᵃ.

Đ Thoᵐ fił Wałti... ... ... xvj. đ. oᵬ.

„ Henᷓ fił Giłᵬti ... ... xvj. đ.

„ Alañ fił Wiłł ... ... xviij. đ.

„ Roᵍ fił Dande ... ... xviij. đ.

„ Roᵬto Quynfel ... ... ij. ᵹ. ix. đ.

„ Wiłł del Scales... ... ... xxi. đ. oᵬ.

„ Ađ Alkes ... ... ij. ᵹ.

„ Adam Derlinge ... ... ij. ᵹ. ij. đ. oᵬ.

„ Thoᵐ del Cote... ... ... iij. ᵹ. ij. đ.

„ Thoᵐ le Sᴶiaunt ... ... xvj. đ.

„ Wiłł fił Wiłł ... ...· ... ij. ᵹ. x. đ.

„ Thoᵐ fił Wiłł ... ... ij. ᵹ.

Smᵃ. xxvij. ᵹ. x. đ. pᵬ.

Holker
[*Holker*]

Đ Johe del Smythy ... ... ij. ᵹ. j. đ.

„ Johe fił Henᷓ ... ... xviij. đ. oᵬ. q .

„ Roᵬto de Waltoñ ... ... xij. đ.

„ Joh Burgeis ... ... ij. ᵹ.

„ Johe fił Simoñ ... ... xv. đ. qᵃ.

„ Wiłło Coco ... ... xij. đ. oᵬ. qᵃ.

„ Adam fił Ellot ... ... xxj. đ. oᵬ.

„ Joh fił Hamound ... ... xviij. đ. oᵬ.

„ Johe de Waltoñ... ... ... xxj. đ.

„ Wiłł fił Stephi ... ... xx. đ.

„ Roᵬto de Coquina ... ... ij. ᵹ. j. đ.

„ Roᵬto Cissore ... ... xij. đ.

„ Wiłł de Reuesone ... ... xx. đ. qᵃ.

„ Simoñ fił Johis... ... ... ij. ᵹ.

„ Rađo Russełł ... ... iij. ᵹ.

„ Wiłło le Lord ... ... xiij. đ.

Smᵃ. xxvj. ᵹ. viij. đ. pᵬ.

Netherkellet
[*Nether Kellet*]

Đ Thoᵐ de Hułm... ... ... ij. ᵹ.

„ Thoᵐ fił Ađ ... ... xij. đ.

D· Roḡo đe Caunsfeld   ...   ...   xij. đ.

„ Laurence fiț Broun   ...   ...   xij. đ.

Smᵃ. v. ŝ. pᵬ.

Bulk cū Aldeclif

[*Bulk with Aldcliffe*]

D· Henꝫ fiț Rađi ...   .   ix. đ.

„ Joħe fiț Laurenc̃   ...   ...   xv. đ.

„ Wilț fiț Huḡ   ...   .   ij. ŝ. iiij. đ.

„ Laurenc̃ fiț Henꝫ   ..   ...   xij. đ.

„ Emna ffraunceys   ...   ...   ij. ŝ. j. đ.

„ Roᵬto Broun   ...   .   xij. đ.

„ Henꝫ fiț Wilți ...   .   ij. ŝ. iiij. đ.

„ Wilți fiț Henꝫ ...   .   x. đ.

„ Joħe de Bare   ...   .   xxj. đ.

Sm. xiij. ŝ. iiij. đ. pᬬ.

Wartoñ

[*Warton*]

D· Wilțo de Nauesby   ...   ...   xviij. đ.

„ Thom̃ Balbayn ...   .   xxd.

„ Wilț de Wiresdale   ...   ...   xvj. đ.

„ Thom̃ de ffarletoñ   ...   ...   xvj. đ.

„ Adam de Holm̃   ...   ...   xij. đ.

„ Nicħo le ffoghler   ...   ...   ij. s. iiij. đ.

„ Joħe fiț Ađ   ...   .   xij. đ.

„ Joħe Chaffare   ...   ...   xviij. đ.

„ Orabelț de Caunsfeld ...   ...   xx. đ.

Smᵃ. xiij. ŝ. iiij. đ.

Caunsfelđ

[*Cantsfield*]

D· Roᵬto fiț Roᵬti...   ...   ...   xix. đ.

„ Adam Bondessoule   ...   ...   x. đ.

„ Adam de Erghū   ...   ...   x. đ.

Smᵃ. iij. ŝ. iiij. đ. pᬬ.

Tunstalł
[*Tunstall*]

Ð Thom̃ de Wartoñ	...	...	xij. đ.
„ Elia de Wratoñ	...	...	xvj. đ.
„ Rico fił Joħ	...	...	xij. đ.

Smᵃ. iij. ß. iiij. đ. pᵬ.

Mellyng cū Wratoñ
[*Melling with Wrayton*]

Ð Joħe Whitling	...	...	ij. ß.
„ Wiłł de Wartoñ	...	...	ij. ß.
„ Adam de Slyne	...	...	xvj. đ.
„ Thom̃ de Burtoñ	...	...	xviij. đ.

Smᵃ. vj. ß. x. đ. pᵬ.

Wraa
[*Wray*]

Ð Wiłł fił Hug̃	...	...	ij. ß. vj. đ.
„ Ric̃ Snaubałł	...	...	xviij. đ.
„ Thom̃ fił Hawiš	...	...	xix. đ.
„ Joħ de Parkesdale	...	...	xv. đ.

Smᵃ. vj. ß. x. đ. pᵬ.

Wenyngtoñ
[*Wennington*]

Ð Thom̃ fił Eleñ	...	...	xxj. đ.
„ Joħe de Caber	...	...	xx. đ.
„ Adam del Wraa	...	...	xvj. đ.

Smᵃ. iiij. ß. ix. đ. pᵬ.

Erghū
[*Arkholme*]

Ð Adam del Mire	...	...	xij. đ.
„ Rico Page	...	...	xij. đ.
„ Henr̃ Tod	...	...	xvj. đ.
„ Joħ fił Henr̃	...	...	xvj. đ.
„ Nicħo del Storches	...	...	xij. đ.
„ Roᵬ del Mire	...	...	ij. ß.
„ Joħ de Eskrige	...	...	xvj. đ.

Smᵃ. ix. ß. pᵬ.

Horneby
[*Hornby*]

Ð Johe fit Raði	...	...	...	xij. đ.
„ Johe fforestař	...	...	...	ij. s.
„ Wilł le Walker	...	...	...	xiiij. đ.
„ Adam fił Reginald	...	...	...	xvj. đ.

Smᵃ. v. s. vj. đ. pƀ.

Hetoñ cū Oxclif
[*Heaton with Oxcliffe*]

Ð Wilł de Hetoñ	...	...	...	xviij. đ.
„ Wilło de Oxclif	...	...	...	xij. đ.
„ Alič de Slene	...	...	...	xviij. đ.
„ Henř de Talker	...	...	...	ij. s. viij. đ.

Smᵃ. vj. s. viij. đ. pƀ.

Boltoñ
[*Bolton le Sands*]

Ð Thom̃ de Boltoñ	...	...	...	v. s.
„ Wilło fił Jacoby	...	...	...	v. s. iiij. đ.
„ Johe ffraunceis	...	...	...	iij. s.
„ Matilł de Rameshou	...	...	...	v. s.
„ Nicho Capło	...	...	...	iiij. s. iiij. đ.
„ Johe fił Jorði	...	...	...	vj. s.

Smᵃ. xxviij. s. viij. đ. pƀ.

Daltoñ cū Hotoñ
[*Dalton with Priest Hutton*]

Ð Raðo fił Wilłi	...	...	...	ij. s. iiij. đ.
„ Patricio fił Wilłi	...	...	...	iij. s.
„ Adam fił Raði	...	...	...	iij. s. viij. đ.
„ Robło de Kellet	...	...	...	xij. đ.
„ Ričo fił Raði	...	...	...	xij. đ.
„ Adam Snartmon	...	...	...	xij. đ.

Smᵃ. xij. s. pƀ.

Oûltoñ
[*Overton*]

Ð Joħe Grayne	...	...	...	iij. ꝝ. iiij. đ. oꝸ.	
„ Roᵹo ſit Wilti	...	...	...	xviij. đ.	
„ Joħ ſit Riĉi	...	...	...	ij. ꝝ. ij. đ. oꝸ.	
„ Rañ de Oûltoñ	...	...	...	xij. đ.	
„ Roꝸto ſit Wilti	...	...	...	xij. đ.	
„ Thoñ de Hesham	...	...	...	xij. đ.	

Smᵃ. x. ꝝ. pꝸ.

Yelonđ
[*Yealand Conyers*]

Ð Thoñ ſit Riĉi	...	..	...	iiij. ꝝ.	
„ Adam de Heſt	...	...	...	iiij. ꝝ.	
„ Huᵹ ffraunceis	...	...	...	iij. ꝝ.	

Smᵃ. xj. ꝝ. pꝸ.

Gersinghᵃm
[*Gressingham*]

Ð Wilt de Gersingham	...	...	...	ij. ꝝ.	
„ Joħe de Twyselton	...	...	...	xij. đ.	
„ Roꝸto de Hetoñ	...	...	...	ij. ꝝ.	
„ Thoñ ſit Riĉi	...	...	...	ij. ꝝ.	
„ Beñ de Gersingham	...	...	...	ij. ꝝ.	

Smᵃ. ix. ꝝ. pꝸ.

Esshtoñ
[*Ashton*]

Ð Cristañ de Gynes	...	...	...	ij. ꝝ. viij. đ.	
„ Joħe Laurenĉ	...	...	...	ij. ꝝ. viij. đ.	
„ Wilto de ffalrigge	...	...	...	xvj. đ.	
„ Joħe de Stodagħ	...	...	...	xviij. đ.	
„ Joħ ſit Wilti	...	...	..	xij. đ.	
„ Joħe de Grisehed	...	...	...	xvj. đ.	
„ Wilto ſit Geruaꝝ	...	...	...	xviij. đ.	

Smᵃ. xij. ꝝ. pꝸ.

H 2

Thirnom
[*Thurnham*]

Đ Thoᷤ fił Rañ	...	...	...	xvij. đ.
„ Thoᷤ fił Roƀti ...	...	..	xvij. đ.
„ Wilł fił Alañ	...	..	...	xiiij. ſ.

Smᵃ. iiij. ſ. pƀ.

ffarletoñ
[*Farleton*]

Đ Joħ le Stedemon	...	...	xij. đ.
„ Joħ Broun	...	...	...	xij. đ.
„ Joħ del North ...	...	...	xvj. đ.

Smᵃ. iij. ſ. iiij. đ.

Daltoñ in fournais
[*Dalton in Furness*]

Đ Joħ de Vrsewik	...	...	vij. ſ.
„ Riᷓo le Coke ...	...	...	v. ſ. iiij. đ.
„ Roƀto de Burscogh	...	...	iij. ſ.
„ Wilło de Vrsewyk	...	...	iij. ſ. viij. đ.
„ Aleᷓ le Taillour	...	...	vj. ſ. iiij. đ.
„ Walᷓo Cokayn ...	...	...	iij. ſ. viij. đ.
„ Roƀto de Hyndeneys ...	...	v. ſ. viij. đ.
„ Thoᷤ le Seriaunt	...	...	v. ſ. viij. đ.
„ Wilł Todde	...	...	...	iij. ſ. iiij. đ.

Smᵃ. xliij. ſ. viij. đ. pƀ.

Heshᵃm
[*Heysham*]

Đ Aleᷓ de Waylegħ	...	...	iij. ſ. viij. đ. qᵃ.
„ Thoᷤ Travers ...	...	...	ij. ſ.
„ Nicħo de Hesham	...	...	iiij. ſ. x. đ. oƀ. qᵃ.
„ Roƀto fił Roƀti ...	...	...	xij. đ.
„ Wił fił Thoᷤ	...	...	...	xij. đ.
„ Adam fił Cłici ...	...	...	iij. ſ. vj. đ.

Smᵃ. xvj. ſ. j. đ. pƀ.

Alyutwait
[*Allithwaite*]

Ð Wilło le Walker	... ...	xij. đ.
„ Joħ fił Joħis ...	... ...	xvij. đ.
„ Wilło fił Roǧi ...	... ...	xij. đ.
„ Rađo Bercař ...	... ...	xviij. đ.
„ Adam de Kendale	.. ...	ij. ꝛ. oƀ.
„ Roƀto del Hulł	... ...	ij. ꝛ. oƀ. qᵃ.
„ Ričo de Kellet ...	... ...	xij. đ. qᵃ.
„ Roƀto del Gate	... ...	xvj. đ.
„ Wiłl de Seele ...	... ...	xvj. d. oƀ.
„ Wiłl fił Berař ...	... ...	xij. d.
„ Thoħ fił Elie ...	... ...	xv. d.

Smᵃ. xv. ꝛ. pƀ.

Ouerkellet
[*Over Kellet*]

Ð Adam del Grene	... ...	xx. đ. qᵃ.
„ Joħe de Hołm ...	... ...	ij. ꝛ. ij. đ. oƀ.
„ Rađo Cissoř ...	... ...	xviij. đ. oƀ.
„ Huǧ le Richemon	... ...	xxj. đ. qᵃ.
„ Huǧ de Bare ...	... ...	xxj. đ. oƀ.
„ Henř del Hulł ...	... ...	viij. đ. qᵃ.
„ Ričo fił Ade	.. ..	xij. đ.
„ Wilł del Kraǧ ...	... ...	xij. đ. qᵃ.
„ Wilło del grene	... ..	xij. đ. qᵃ.
„ Gilƀto fił Alañ	... ...	xij. đ. qᵃ.

Smᵃ. xiij. ꝛ, iiij. đ. pƀ.

Cokerhᵃm
[*Cockerham*]

Ð Ričo le Bar[ke]r [?]	... ...	iiij. ꝛ. iiij. đ.
„ Roǧ Marescall ...	... ...	ij. ꝛ.
„ Joħe Nore ...	... ...	iiij. ꝛ. iiij. đ.
„ Thoħ le Waynmon	... ...	ij. ꝛ. viij. đ.
„ Adam de Erghū	... ..	xvj. đ.
„ Wiłl fił Idoñ ...	... ...	ij. ꝛ. viij. đ.
„ Roǧ de Wynmerlegh ...	...	xx. đ.

Smᵃ. xx. ꝛ. pƀ.

Broghtoñ
[*East Broughton*]

Đ Wilł Waleys	...	...	...	iiij. ꝫ.
„ Joħe de Hopershagħe	...		...	ij. ꝫ.
„ Norchino le Redman	...		...	iij. ꝫ. j. đ.
„ Roᵹ Waleys	...	...	...	iij. ꝫ.
„ Petro fił Hugōis		...	...	ij. ꝫ.
„ Thoɱ del Thorñ		...	...	iij. ꝫ. v. đ.
„ Henř de Jonescoles		...	...	xvj. đ.
„ Adam de Hertbergħ	...		...	iij. ꝫ. xj. đ.
„ Wilło le Wogher		...	...	iij. ꝫ. xj. đ.

Smᵃ. xxvj. ꝫ. viij. đ. pᵬ.

Smᵃ. Wapenĩ xxxvj. łi. x. ꝫ. vij. đ. oᵬ qᵃ. Et. lxiij. ꝫ. iiij. đ.
de xⁿ. Burgi Lancestř.

Smᵃ. xvᵉ.—cciiij×ˣ. vij. łi. xiij. ꝫ. viij. đ.

Smᵃ. xᵉ.—xj. łi. iij. ꝫ. viij. đ.

Smᵃ. toˡ. xvᵉ. t̃. xᵉ.—cciiij×ˣ. xviij. łi. xvij. ꝫ. iiij. đ.

Tax oꝛłantʳ in fine comp̃ de xl. ꝫ. { Taxacio bonoꝝ mobiliũ Taxatoꝝ ꝑdc̃oꝝ ſc̃a ꝑ Theꝫ t̃ Baroñ de Sc̃cio xvi. die Julii anno septimo Reᵹ. E. ꝑcii post conquestũ videłt. { Roᵬti de Shirbourn ad. xx. ꝫ. Joħis de Radeclyue ad. xx. s. Smᵃ. xl. ꝫ.

Hos rotulos recipit Maᵹr Roᵬs de Aylestoñ Theꝫ xiiij die Julii anno vijᵐᵒ. Reᵹ E. ꝑcii post conquestũ ꝑ manus Roᵬti de Shirburñ t̃ Joħis de Rađeclyue Taxatoꝝ t̃ Colł-toꝝ xvᵐᵉ t̃. xᵐᵉ ꝑđc̃aꝝ in Coɱ Lancastř.

Appendix A.

A LIST OF THE TOWNSHIPS COMPRISED IN THE
EXCHEQUER LAY SUBSIDY ROLL, LANCASHIRE, 1327.
[$\frac{130}{5}$].

Exchequer Lay Subsidy, Lancashire.

[I. EDW. III., A.D. 1327.]

Lancastre.

Rotulus Indentatus Riĉi de Hoghton, Gilƀti de Sotheworth. . . . . Taxator₃ ĩ Collector₃ vicesime
đno Regi a laicis concesſ [in Coĩ Lanĉ.] tam de Burgis
qᵃm de aliis villis in eođm Coĩ [de anno] Edwardi Ƚcii
post conquesſ primo.

Wapentach de Derbishir.

Wygan	Dutton
Lyuerpull	Eccleston
Kirkdale	Sutton
. . . . .	Werington
Parĩ	Kirkeby
Astelegh	Orell
Raynford	Kyuƚdelegh
Raynhull	Bolde
Dalton	Ryxton
Lydyate	Halsale

Dounholand

Torbok

Croynton

Ines iuxᵃ Wygan

Bullinge cū Wynstanesleye

Athurton

Mellinge

Hyndelegh

Ines iuxᵃ Crosseby

[Wyn]dhull

Neuton

Goldeburne

Thorneton

Asshton

Parva Crosseby

fforneby

Sefton

Wolston

Hurleton cū Scaresbreke

Dounlitherlond

Eꝰton

Maghall

Pembirton

Lauton cū Kenyan

Hale

Speke

Magna Crosseby

Northmeles cū Crosnes

Gerstan

Derby

Allerton

Sotheworth cū Crofte

Middelton cū Hoghton

Culchith

Westelegh

Knouselegh

Ayntre

Botull cū Lynacre

Lathum cū Burscogh

Skelmaresdale

Bedeford

Pynynton

Haydok

Childewall

Huyton cū Raby

Waꝰtree

Wolueton Magna cū parua

Walton

Hagh

Wynquick cū Hulm̃

Wapentach de Salfordshire.

Aspull

Salford

Mamcestr̃

Withinton

Heton Norrays

Barton

Redich

Asshton

Pennylton

Vrmeston

ffluxton

Harwode

Rouynton

Workeslegh

Hulton

Eggeworth

Middilton

Spotlond

Boulton
Hounersfeld
Westhalghton
Butᵗworth
Prestwich
Clifton
Pennulbury
Chetham
Rumworth cū Lostok
Stretford
Pilkynton
Ruyton

Radeclive
Castelton
Heton cū Haliwall
Bury
Totington
Crompton
Chadreton
Turton
Chorleton
Oldum
Blackerode

Wapentach de Leilondshire.

Hethchernok
Hoghton
Withenhull cū Rotheles-
    worth
Tarleton
Laylond
Vlneswalton
Whelton cū Hepay
Standissh
Walshwhitull
ffarington cū Hoghwyk
Chernoke Richard
Wrightinton cū Parbald
Eukeston
Kerden
Claiton
Burnehull

Rughford
Bekanshowe cū Heskaith
Penworthᵃm
Longeton
Moudeslegh
Hoton
Anderton
Sheuyngton
Croston
Adelinton cū Dokesbury
Cophull cū Worthington
Whithull in bosco
Eccleston
Chorlegh cū Bispehᵃm
Parua Hole
Magna Hole

Wapentach de Blakeburneshire.

Brunley

Ribbelcestr̄

Osebaldeston̄

Coln̄

Bilinton

Merclesden

Padih*m

ffolrigge

Dinkedley cū Wlipshir̄

Lyuesay

Walton

Rysshton

Penulton

Melure cū Eccleshull

Dutton

Huncote

Baldreston

Hapton

Plesington

Parua Harwode

Witton

Chepyn

Thornley cū Whetley

Cliderhou

Worthesthorn

Wisewall

Brereclif cū Extwisell

Mitton cū Henthorn ꝛ Calde-
cotes

Chatteburn

Claiton sup Moras

Blakeburn̄

Reued

Magna Harwode

Chirche

Dounum

Symoundeston

Claiton in The Dale

Worston

Clyuacher

Alneth*m

Samlesbury

Haselingden̄

Oul̄derwent

Twiselton̄

Nethirderwent

Osewaldestwisel

Kyul̄dale

Salebury

Aghton̄

M̄lay magna cū pua

Wapentach de Amunnderneſſe.

Ribbelton

Halghton̄

Westsum cū Middelargh

Grenolf cū Thistelton

Neuton̄ cū Hordern̄

Katerhale

Laton cū Warthebreke
Bispeham cū Northbrek
Lee
Wodeplūpton
M꜀ton Magna
Singelton Magna cū pua
Claghton
Alston cū Hodersale
Outerouthclif
Withe토n cū Prees
Treules
Kirkeh·m
Eccleston Magna
Preston
Etholistoñ
ffrekeltoñ
Pulton
Neusum
Neuton
Stalmyn cū Staynolf
Brynyng cū Kelgrimesargh

Hamelton
Gairstang
Brocholes cū Grimesargh
Whitingh·m
Inskipp
Leirbrek cū pua Eccleston
Gosenargh
Barton
Thorneton
Clifton cū Salewyk
Westeby cū Plumpton
Billesburgh
Riggeby cū le Wraa
Asshton
Broghton
Vprontheclif
Etheleswyk
Preeshowe cū Hakeneshowe
ffisshewik
Lythum
Carleton

Wapentach de Lonesdale.

Lancastr̃
Cokirh·m
Burgh
Leck
Whitington
Vllerston
Erghum
Asshton
Kirkeby Irlith
Penyngton
Berewik
Scotford

Caton cum Claghton
Yeland
Warton
Thirnum
Ellale
Gersingh·m
Kerneford
Bolton
Dalton in ffourneys
Horneby
ffarleton
Wraa

Melling cū Wraton	Dalton cū Hoton
Hesham	Wenyngton
Aldecliue cū Bulk	Slyne cū Heste
Oūkellett	Ouerton
Caunsfeld	Skerton
Pultoñ cū Torisholm̃ ʔ Bare	Alithwait
Aldingh•m	Holker
Lees	Tunstall
Vrsewyk	Hetoñ cum Oxcliff
Tatham	Middelton
Halton	Netherkellett

Appendix B.

LIST OF PERSONS WHO PROMISED TO SUBSCRIBE TO
THE STIPEND OF THE PRIEST OF THE ALTAR OF OUR
LADY AT ORMSKIRK, A.D. 1366.

In festo Sc̃i Thom̃ Apli. ꝛ. pt⁹ Annū́ł [*sic*] xlix. ꝫ. v. đ.
. . . . [illegible] . . . . iij. ꝫ. iij. đ.

Isti pmiserūt ad Salariū Capełti Beate Marie de Ormes-
kirk ad ffestū Sc̃i Michis Archangłi Anno Dñi Miłłmo
CCCᵐᵒ lxvjᵗᵒ.

Burg' de Ormeskirk.

[TOWN OF ORMSKIRK.]

Rołs de Blythe	..	...	...	ijᵈ
Rołs de Wakefeld	...	...	...	ijᵈ
Sym̃ del Wodes				
Ric̃s de Ellerbek				
Alic' de Oltoñ				
+ Henʳ de Copphułt	...	...	...	ijᵈ
Ric̃s Byld	...	...	...	iiijᵈ
Henr' le Sporier				
+ vjᵈ Joħes le Taillour	...	...	...	xijᵈ
+ Wiłłs de Huyton	...	...	...	iiijᵈ
Ric̃s le Fletcher	...	...	...	ijᵈ
Ric̃s le Couper				
Agñ filia Boold				
+ Roꝑus ffaber				

	Thom͡s de Suttoñ					
iiijᵈ	Riĉs Robynson	...	...	...	...	vjᵈ
+	Roƀs le Ledebeter	...	...	...	...	ijᵈ
	Agñ de Boold					
+	Magoͬ del Helmes		...	...	...	ijᵈ
iiijᵈ	Joħes del Vale	...	...	...	...	viᵈ
+	Syñ del Helmes	...	...	...	...	iiijᵈ
	Henͬ del Wolfaŧ					
	Ceciŧ de Kendale					
	Riĉs Halyfax	...	...	•...	...	ijᵈ
	Henͬ le Ledebeter					
+ iiijᵈ	Joħes le Kyng	...	...	...	...	xijᵈ
	Gilƀs fil Roƀti					
+	Syñ Blanchard	...	...	...	...	ijᵈ
	Wiŧs de Wynmarlegħ					
–	Riĉs Shakerewet	...	...	...	..	iiijᵈ
+	Uͬx. Joħis Todd	...	...	...	...	ijᵈ
–	Joħes le Fletcher	...	...	...	...	viᵈ
	Rog̉ Pacok					
	Wiŧs le Spicer					
+	Riĉs Shakelauedy	...	...	...	...	iiijᵈ
	Joħs de Bykerstath					
iiijᵈ	Syñ le Couper					
	Ađ del Brokefeld					
	Roƀs fil Hankok					
+	Wiŧs del Celer	...	...	...	...	ijᵈ
+ ijᵈ	Rog̉ de Morcroft	...	...	...	...	iiijᵈ
+	Alan⁹ Todd	...	...	...	...	iiijᵈ
	Ađ de Tildeslegh					
	Riĉs Lenne					
	Roƀs Nykson					
+	Riĉs fiŧ Joħis Becokson	...	...	...	iiijᵈ
+	Rog̉ le Fletcher	...	...	...	...	vjᵈ
+	Matilđ de Eggeacͬ	...	...	...	vᵈ
+	Joħes le Smyth	...	...	...	...	vjᵈ
	Roƀs Staynes					
–	Ađ Childesfadre	...	...	...	...	iiijᵈ
	Magoͬ de Holbrok					

Margaret ...
... de ...
— J... de ...
— ... de ...
... de ...
... de ...
— ... de ...
... de ...
ⁱ Henꝛ de ...
Thomꝭ de ...
ⁱ ... le ...
ⁱᵈ Mabel le ...
— Nec... de ...
Cecil ... Rich le Sporiố ...
iij^d Aꝺ del Grene ... ...
j^d Aꝺ Pygyn
Willꝭ de Hamelton
+ xij Willꝭ le Sporiố ... ... ꟷ
ii^d Mꝗret de Hurlton

Scaresbrek ꝛū Hurlton.

[SCARISBRICK WITH HURLTON.]

	Thom̄s de Aspynwalt				
—	Rog de Aspynwalt	...	...	...	ij^d
+	Ric̄s le ffrenshe	...	...	...	...	iiij^d
ij^d	Johes de Aspynwalt				
	Willꝭ de Greceby				
	Willꝭ Ryuelyng	...	...	...	...	ij^d
+	Rog del Greues	...	...	...	..	ij^d
ij^d	Ric̄s de Barton				
	Marion Horbert				
ij^d	Willꝭ Dykounson	...	...	...	...	iij^d
	Ric̄s Owitheued	...	...	...	...	ij^d
	Aꝺ Dauy				
	Henꝛ Olyf				

	Ad de Teulond				
	Joħes le Salter				
+	Henr̃ de Wyresdale	...	...	...	ijᵈ
	Rič̃s Thomasmon				
	Magoꝛ de Owattoñ				
+ iijᵈ	Giꝉbs de Gosfordsicħ	...	...	...	iijᵈ
+	Jak Dykounson	...	...	...	ij
jᵈ	Joħs de Owatton	...	...	...	iiijᵈ
+	Ad le Strenger	...	...	...	iiijᵈ
	Henr̃ Ryout				
—	Giꝉbs de Depdale	...	...	...	iiijᵈ
+	Wiꝉꝉo de Shirwallacrs	...	...	...	ijᵈ
+	Ricūs ffaber	...	...	...	ijᵈ
jᵈ	Giꝉbs le Hunt	...	...	...	jᵈ
+	R.[1] Sym̃ Doggeson	...	...	...	iiijᵈ
+	Gilbt [sic] Agñ le Scuster		...	...	ijᵈ
+	Queniꝉd ux. Alani le Dewicar		...	...	ijᵈ
+	Joħes Pety	...	...	...	ijᵈ
+	Robs le Spencer	...	...	...	iiijᵈ
+	Rič̃s Robynson	...	...	...	iiijᵈ
ijᵈ	Robs del Abbay				
jᵈ	Robs fiꝉ Henr̃	...	...	...	iiijᵈ
+	Joħs le Swoon	...	...	...	ijᵈ
	Robs le Bagger				
+	Joħna Pykhare	...	...	...	iiijᵈ
+	Henr̃ del Syche	...	...	...	iiijᵈ
	Alič̃ de Owynbrek				
+	Robs de Bronburgh	...	...	...	ijᵈ
+	Ad Gray	...	...	...	ijᵈ
	Kaꝶina filia Nutricis				
+	Em̃a [?] R. le Sergeant	...	...	...	iiijᵈ
	Elena del Shagħ				
+ ij	Hug̃ del Shagħ	...	...	...	ijᵈ
+ j	Joħs de Bartoñ	...	...	...	iiijᵈ
+	Emmot de Haskeen	...	...	...	iiijᵈ

---

[1] The meaning of the letter R here, and in conjunction with several other names in this Roll, appears to be *Relicta*.

+ Roḡ del Shagħ ... ... iiij^d
+ Joħ del Okenheued ... ... iiij^d
+ Ađ Tewe ... ... iiij^d
+ Eđa de Blythe ... ... ij^d
+ j^d Wilłs de Longetoñ ... ... j^d
  Marḡia del Marhalgħ
  Wilłs de Morcroft
+ Joħs de Morcroft ... ... ij^d
  Emmot Hopcrone
  Riĉ Messenger
  Joħ Dauy
  Joħs Horbert
  Wilłs de Oldome ... ... ij^d
  Magot de Morcroft
ij^d Beatřx de Morcroft
+ Alan⁹ del Brodheued ... ... iiij^d
+ j^d Riĉs de Morcroft ... ... iiij^d
  Riĉ Pye
− Jankyn Broñ ... ... ij^d
+ Wilł de Morcroft ... ... ij^d
j^d Ric de Ekirgarth
  Alan⁹ Benycod
  Ric⁹ le ffletcher
ij^d Ađ del Brodeheued
  Henř le Blawer
+ Thom̃s Beyson ... ... ij^d
+ Jankyn le Walker ... ... vj^d
ij^d Wilł Blethyn
  Henř le Milner ... ... iiij^d
+ Wilłs del Platt ... ... ij^d
  Joħs Spynk ... ... iiij^d
  Joħa fił Tewe
+ Henř de Depdale ... ... ij^d
+ Joħs fił Maryot ... ... ij^d
  Joħs fil Wilłi ... ... ij^d
j^d Joħ le Long ... ... j^d

I

Bykerstath.

[BICKERSTAFFE.]

xij^d	Radulph⁹ de Bekyrstat				
	Riĉ del Marhalgĥ				
+ ij^d	Witts del Helmes	...	...	...	... ij^d
+	Joĥs Cadyk	...	...	...	... iij^d
−	Wyld [*sic*] ...	...	...	...	.. iij^d
	Elena del Hyles	...	...	...	... iij^d
	Joĥs Jakkeson	...	...	...	... ij^d
	Riĉ le Ward	...	...	...	... ij^d
	Joĥs del Hyles	...	...	...	... iij^d
	Witts fil Thoɱ				
j^d	Thoɱ fil Carpenť				
	Joĥna del Lone				
+	Joĥs de Mellyng				
	Riĉ de Mosok	...	...	...	... iiij^d
ij^d	Syɱ fil Joĥis	...	...	...	... iij^d
	Joĥs del Marhalgĥ				
ij^d	Roḡ Wynmenske	...	...	...	... vj^d
+	Joĥ Wynmensk	...	...	...	... vj^d
	Thoɱ del Westheued				
	Henɍ del Halle	...	...	...	... iij^d
+	Joĥ Madok	...	...	...	... iiij^d
	Alan⁹ le Barker				
+	Roḡ del Mosse	...	...	...	... iij^d
	Ađa le Halleknaue				
+	Joĥs del Hulŧ	...	...	...	... iij^d
	Thoɱ de Ruynacre				
+	Elena le Walsh	...	...	...	... ij^d
+	Joĥ del Barwe	...	...	...	... ij^d
+	Joĥ fil Robi	...	...	...	... ij^d
	Syɱ de Bykerstat				
+	Roḡ del Grene	...	...	...	... ij^d
	Ađ Steeŧ				
+	Joĥ le Herdemon	...	...	...	... j^d

ij^d Rič del Barwe ...	...	...	...	ij^d
Roǵ fit Taillo^r				
+ Thoᵐ le Herdemon ...	...	...	....	iiij^d
Joħ de Kirkeby				
Roḃs le Swoon				
+ Ričs de Raynford ...	...	...	...	iiij^d
+ Hawoꝛ del Hult ...	...	...	...	ij^d
Thoᵐ Stotfoldshagħ				
Roǵ del Mourehyles				
+ Joħs le Bakster ...	...	...	...	j^d
Roǵ le Porter ...	...	...	...	iiij^d
Thoᵐ del Hult				
Eᵐa de le Derharme				
— Joħ del Hull sen :...	...	...	...	ij^d
Rič de Rypoñ				
Heñr garc⁹ Thoᵐ				
Roǵ de Mellyng ...	...	...	...	j^d
Witt del Toū ...	...	...	...	iiij^d
j^d Witt del Outsich [?]				
iv^d Johanna del Hull ...	...	...	...	ij^d
Uꭓ. Huǵ Depdale ...	...	...	...	ij^d

𝕭𝖚𝖗𝖘𝖈𝖔𝖌𝖍 c̄u 𝕸ᵗ)ton.

[BURSCOUGH WITH MARTON.]

+ Roḃs Paweson ...	...	...	...	iiij^d
Witt de Depdale ...	...	...	...	ij^d
+ j^d Rič del Bakhous ...	...	...	...	ij^d
Waltᵖ⁹ de Longebak ...	...	...	ij^d
Sȳm Lagard ...	...	...	...	ij^d
Rič Dobbeson				
Alič Benyood				
Margaret le Carꝶ				
Rič Drake				
Joħ de Aghton				

Henr̄ Ryout
Gilƀt⁹ fił Nicholł
Joħ de Eggeacr̄)
— Gilƀt⁹ Benycod ... ... iiij^d
Joħ fflennynge
Ađ de Par ... ... iiij^d
Emma le Warner
Joħ Yemon
— Wiłłs de ffourokshagh ... ... iiij^d
+ Ric̄ Spurwyn ... ... iiij^d
Quenylđ del Toū
Jaƙ Broñ
R. Ric̄ de Moscar
Matilđ ffox
+ Gilƀ fil Joħis ... ... ij^d
Roƀs Pety ... ... ij^d
— Rog̉ de Orełł ... ... ij^d
Joħ del Mor
+ Ric̄ de Berwyk ... ... ij^d
Roƀs del Syche ... ... iiij^d
Rog̉ de Moudeslegh
Alic̄ Milde
Joħ le Turnour
Wiłłs Tabart
+ Ric̄ de Hyllome ... ... ij^d
Joħ fil le Seriant
+ Henr̄ le Turnour ... ... ij^d
+ Alan⁹ Dobbeson ... ... ij^d
+ Joħ le Porter ... ... ij^d
+ Syñ del Quitstones ... ... ij^d
Wiłł le Prestesmon ... ... ij^d
Henr̄ Penyale
Joħ Henr̄son
Alyna fil Walt⁹i
— Rađ Bere
+ Ric̄ de Burscogh ... ... j
Wiłł del Warinawro
Joħ de Blythe

Riĉ de Penwyth·m
Joħ de Moudeslegh
Joħ Willison
Dyot Cay
ijᵈ Riĉ Cay
Joħ le Gardener
Thoñ le Taillour
Riĉ del Walt
Cisse filia Pawe
Ammory R. Joħis
Magot de Raynhull
Roǧ Bryd
Roɓs le Taillo^r ... ... iijᵈ
Alyna Lenne
Margar̃ de Sourby
Roɓ ffaber
Joħa R. le Barker
+ Roǧ le Clerk ... ... ijᵈ
Riĉ ffarwys ... ... ijᵈ
Magot Toppyng
Beton Parlement
Riĉ de Eggeacr̃
Joħ . . . . . .
Gilɓ)t⁹ fil Joħ Gilleson [?] ... ... ijᵈ
Emma le . . . . . .
Matild̃ de Grecby
Gilbt⁹ del Brokefild ... ... ijᵈ
+ Riĉ Carpenℓ
+ Joħ le Hunt ... ... ijᵈ
Rog, de Beulond [?]
Witt le Carter
Roɓs fil ei⁹
[A name illegible]... ... ... ijᵈ
Ad̃ [?] del Rydyng
Joħ Wodeloft
Agñ . . . . . .

Le Westheued et Lathum.

[WESTHEAD AND LATHOM.]

	Thom̃ Jakson	...	...	...	... iiijᵈ
	Henr̃ le Gardener				
	Alic̃ Gresse				
	Hugh del Westheued				
j	Rob del Westheued				
+	Witt de				
+	Ric̃ de				
	[Four names illegible]				
	Alic̃ de Bronylegh				
	Witt de Melt				
	Witts del Crosse	...	...	...	... ijᵈ
+ jᵈ	Alic̃ del Crosse	...	...	...	... xᵈ
ijᵈ	Ysold del Crosse				
	Ad le Carter				
	Ad del Wodes	...	...	...	... ijᵈ
	Thom̃ Kemp̃				
	Maykyn [sic]				
	Witt le Tynkeler				
	Joh de Greseby				
	Joh le Fletcher				
	Ric̃ fil Thom̃	...	...	...	... iijᵈ
	Godith de Smalshagh				
j	Ric̃ Carles ...	...	...	...	... iijᵈ
+	Joh de Burscogh	...	...	...	... iiijᵈ
	Johna Cay				
	Johna				
	Margia fit Henr̃				
+	Joh del Brodfeld [?]	...	...	...	... vjᵈ
	Henr̃ fil Witt	...	...	...	... iiijᵈ
+	Rob Dykeson	...	...	...	... ijᵈ
	Henr̃ de Moudeslegh	...	...	...	... iijᵈ
	Joh de Ellerbᵉ	...	...	...	... iijᵈ
	Ric̃ fil Hankok				

+ Eua R. Inñs ... ...
+ Joħ del Car .. ..
ij Riĉ de Horscar
Roɓ Herblod
Henř le Mercer ... ...
Roɓ Canns
Agñ de Bretherton [?] ... ...
Roɓ de Mosbury
+ Aman del Marbaigh ... ...
Riĉs le . . . .
Gilɓs . . . . . .
[A name illegible]
Hugh del . . . .
[A name illegible]
Joħ del Heth ... ... iiijᵈ
Roᵍ del Shagh
Joħ le Coke
Thoñ de Irby
Riĉ fil Aleĩ
Riĉ fil Pawe
Joħ fil Aleĩ
Roᵍ Paweson
Wiɫɫs de M'rtoñ
Joħ Elot
Joħ Barett
Hugh le Salter
Riĉ de Ellerbec [?]
Joħ Tysing
Syñ Waryng
Roᵍ le Kekker
Riĉ Daweson
Godith le Coudrey
Joħna Page
Emma de M'rtoñ
Wiɫɫs de Prestecotte
Agñ del Goldicar
Roᵍ del Goldicar
Joħ Stykk

Ad de Balshagh
Emma del . . . . . .
Joh del Westheued
Radulphus Fouler [?]
Margar del Scoles
Joh de Balshagh
Robs le Taillour
Emma Page
Nichs de Leylond
Rob le Hunt
Johna filia Dobbe
Joh le Spencer
Joh Hawot
Janyn le Breton
Malkyn fil Henr
Joh fil Robi
Thom O . . . . . .
Will le Carter
Will le Reder
Ric le Parker
Ric fil Elyn
Will fil Hankok
Will le Bower
Will de Asshurst
Ric del Shagh

Skelmaresdale.

[SKELMERSDALE.]

Ric del Wolfall
Thom de Asshurst
Malkyn Waryng
Hugh [?] . . . . . .
Henr fil Beco
Rob Waryng
Rob Walker

Riĉ de Holand
Joħ le . . . mard
Ad de Oldene
Margař le Hunt
Roƀ del Mosse
Joħ de Huytoñ
Roğ Wyldeblod
Roƀ . . . cok
Riĉ le Tasker
Will le Cropper
Riĉ Dobbeson
Relict. Adĉ Osmarshagh
Roğ del Bakhous
Hekok de Par
Joħ del Yate
Henř del Toū
Riĉ fil ffabri
Roğ Coly
Roƀ de Adburgaiñ
— Will del Yate . . . . ;ᵛ
Will Mabbeson
Will [?] le Webster . . . . ⁺
Joħ Coly
Mater e[?]
Joħ del Yate junior
— Ad de Haylegh . . . . ;ᶜ
— Henř fil fabri . . . . ;ᶜ
Aɡħ del Lagħ

INDEX OF PLACES.

INDEX OF NAMES

K

L

WYMAN AND SONS, LIMITED, PRINTERS, GREAT QUEEN STREET, W.C.

LaVergne, TN USA
28 December 2010
210370LV00003B/205/P